# Rectors of Glasgow University

## 1820-2000

*My plans assume that I shall return to England alive; when I see the pro-*
*gramme of the Glasgow week, it seems doubtful. Nothing can be more*
*inhuman; and if there were a society to protect public men, as there is to*
*protect donkeys, some interference would undoubtedly take place*
—Benjamin Disraeli, elected 1871

GLASGOW : UNIVERSITY OF GLASGOW

MMI

ISBN : 0 85261 732 1

# About This Book

This book is about some of the unique traditions of Glasgow University. I have tried also to explain the social and historical background of the elections. The period covered is from 1820 to the present. For most of the eighteenth century and until 1820 the Rectors were almost always local lairds or Edinburgh lawyers. But from 1820 they were politicians or colourful characters.

One small volume cannot cover every rectorship in detail. Moreover, not all elections and Rectors were of equal interest. This means that some Rectors have been given a small amount of space and some a lot. I have, however, covered every name from 1820 to 2000—a total of 63.

No longer does the choice go to statesmen and other great men. The nature of fame or celebrity has changed. Television, radio, the tabloid press, and the "dumbed down" broadsheet press have enhanced the status of broadcasters, sportsmen and sportswomen, pop singers, and film actors. That change is reflected in the choice of candidates to be Rector.

Some splendid traditions and customs have been lost. For example, few students have been turning out in recent years to hear the rectorial Address, an institution that has been established for nearly two centuries. The Bute Hall, the main meeting hall of the university, where the Addresses are nowadays given, is sometimes not even full.

It was at one time unthinkable for candidates to take an active part in the campaigns; that would have been considered undignified. Candidates now do not shrink from taking part and in doing so have destroyed some mystique. The rectorial "fight" is fought no longer, having been swept away not by the followers of peaceful ways but by prim committees.

Losses of tradition have happened outside the rectorial elections. Students no longer sing the great anthem *Ygorra*; that is one reason why its words and music are given here. The Union and the Queen Margaret Union (the Union was for men and the Queen Margaret Union** for

---

* Margaret (c 1046-1093), canonised in 1251. Her father was the English prince Edward the Atheling. When the Normans conquered England she fled to Scotland. The Scottish King, Malcolm III

women) each used to have stronger individual characteristics than now. Single-sex unions came to be thought inappropriate. Both became open to both sexes. Even the traditional rivalry—indeed, antipathy—between the Union and the Students' Representative Council has been lessened.

---

Canmore, married her. Malcolm was the son of the King Duncan murdered by Macbeth. It is through Margaret that later monarchs have traced their descent from the pre-Conquest royal house of England.

Queen Margaret was young, lovely, learned and pious; she refined and anglicised the court. Queen Margaret College, for women at Glasgow University, was named after her; and thus also was the women's union.

# Acknowledgements

My great debt is to Emeritus Professor J. Forbes Munro, who has suggested countless improvements, has restrained me from many follies, and has saved me from several serious blunders. I owe him my warm thanks and apologise for the mistakes and misjudgements I have slipped in when his back was turned.

Professor Malcolm McLeod, Vice Principal, Glasgow University warmly encouraged the project; he also produced references to Disraeli's rectorial Address and Albert Einstein's proposed candidacy. Dr Stephen Rawles carried out splendidly the tricky technical work on the text and suggested valuable improvements. Professor Andrew Skinner looked through the manuscript.

Members of the staff of Glashow University Archives and Business Records department have been helpful beyond the call of duty: Mrs Lesley Richmond (deputy archivist), Helen Briscoe, Lyn Morgan, Moira Rankin, Archie Leitch, Manz Stefan, and others. I also have received help from Michael Bolik, senior archives assistant, archives and records management, Dundee University; Peter D. Freshwater, deputy librarian, Edinburgh University; Michelle Gait, curatorial assistant, Aberdeen University Library; Dr Norman Reid, Keeper of Manuscripts and Muniments, St Andrews University Library; staff at the British Library and the British Library newspaper division; London Library; Mitchell Library (Glasgow City Council); and the National Library of Scotland. Mr Simon Blundell, librarian of the Reform Club, has provided books from the club's splendid collection. The librarian of the *Daily Record* has tolerantly acceded to my repeated requests. Material from the *Daily Record* is reprinted with the *Daily Record*'s permission. The National Portrait Gallery and the Scottish National Portrait Gallery have helped with obtaining many of the illustrations.

The magazine for graduates and friends of Glasgow University, *Avenue*, carried articles about my need for material on rectorial elections. Readers responded with fascinating material. Menzies Campbell MP has kept a significant archive from the Luthuli campaign (of 1962) and Kenneth Dallas a remarkable document from the Tom Johnston campaign (of 1947). Neil MacCormick MEP gave much information about his father John M. MacCormick. Dr Roy Archibald put me on the track of the extraordinary events of 1938. Douglas B. Taylor loaned me an archive of documents from the campaign of 1950. William Rankin loaned documents from Attlee's campaign in 1956. Meta Ramsay (Baroness Ramsay of Cartvale) and the Rev Douglas N. Alexander threw a flood of light on why the Installation of R. A. Butler was so calamitous. Mr Alexander also was a splendid source of information about the Rev George MacLeod. Several former Rectors generously and most interestingly recalled their times; these people included the Rev John Bell and Dr Michael Kelly. A veteran of the student scene, Dr Gavin Henry, dug out documents that spanned a long time.

Miss M. S. Banks has provided me with eyes and ears, scanning the newspapers for news about the Scottish universities.

Alison Brown prepared the index with exemplary skill, and spotted not a few typographical errors.

I am grateful for additional help from: William Gordon Craig, the late Donald Dewar, A. N. Dowie, Charles Dundas, Duncan Ferguson, Neil Gillies, Derek Gibbons, J. Ross Harper, Douglas Harrison, David Holmes, Dan Hood, W. D. Jardine, Noreen Jennings, Huon Mallalieu, Donald Miller, Gavin Morrison, James G. Nisbet, R. H. Proudfoot, James R. Rae, Eileen Reynolds, James Simpson, Hugh O'Dwyer, Gavin H. R. Vernon, and Nelson Wallace.

Many of the owners of copyright pictures waived their fees, for which I am most grateful.

# The Scottish Rectorial System and the Special Ways it has Evolved in Glasgow

The older Scottish universities are St Andrews (founded in 1411), Glasgow (1451), Aberdeen (1495), Edinburgh (1583), and Dundee (founded as University College, Dundee, in 1881 and given university status in 1967). They have a unique distinction among British universities. The student body elects, every three years, a senior officer, the Rector.

The list of former Rectors of these universities in past 200 years is like a roll-call of fame: Prime Ministers, scientists, writers, and winners of Nobel Prizes. And also actors, comedians, a professional footballer, and a television cook. Glasgow has had, from 1451 to 2000, a total of 182 holders of this distinguished office, starting with William Elphinstoun, Licentiate in Decrees and Official General of Glasgow.

The Rector is, by law, entitled to chair the University Court, the supreme governing body in each of the older Scottish institutions. He or she is expected to represent the interests of his "constituents" there. (There are two exceptions. At Edinburgh, the professors also have the vote; and at Dundee the Rector does not chair the Court.)

Elections in modern times have been traditionally lively, with supporters of each candidate holding public meetings, issuing pamphlets, and carrying out "stunts" to gain publicity. The pamphlets have been notable for scurrilousness.

The Rector, traditionally, is formally installed in a ceremony and gives a speech or Address to his or her constituents. The Addresses have sometimes reached heights of oratory and sometimes have been marked by lively behaviour in the audience. That tradition of liveliness, even rumbustiousness, goes back for at least a century and a half.

The title "Lord Rector" was common in the nineteenth century and until the mid-twentieth century but the word "Lord" has since then been generally dropped.

The rectorial system is, in all, a highly colourful aspect of life in these universities.

## Rectorship down the Centuries

The Rector of Glasgow was originally the head of the University. The office was held by senior priests until the Reformation: the University was established by a Bishop of Glasgow, William Turnbull, and was closely linked with the Cathedral. From the Reformation until the late seventeenth century the holders of the office were ministers of Glasgow and the Glasgow region. During most of the eighteenth century and the early nineteenth the holders were usually local lairds or Scottish notables or legal figures in Edinburgh.

During that time, too, the powers and responsibilities of the Rector changed. The Reformation and the Glorious Revolution of 1689 resulted in the Principal becoming the effective head of the University. The Rector was transformed into a "Visitor", an external figure to hold in check possible abuses of internal governance. However the character changed. From 1820 to 1974 politicians were almost invariably chosen, including 11 former, current, or future Prime Ministers. The Universities of Scotland Act, 1858, laid down the Rector's modern role and decreed that he or she was to be the chairperson of the University Court. The political tradition ended in 1974 when a television sports commentator was elected. He was followed by, among others, a newscaster, a pop musician, a presenter of children's television programmes, and an actor who played a leading part in a "soap".

## Two Great Men of the Eighteenth Century

Only two people were chosen during the eighteenth century whose names are familiar to us now. They were Adam Smith (1723-1790), one of the University's and Scotland's greatest sons, and Edmund Burke (1729-1797), brilliant orator and political philosopher and author of *Reflections on the Revolution in France,* which was read all over Europe.

Adam Smith published in 1776 the *Wealth of Nations,* a profoundly influential work. The book examined the consequences of economic freedom and the function of markets. Smith said that the division of labour was the main source of economic growth, rather than land or money.

He went to Glasgow University at the age of 15 and then to Oxford University, but Oxford was not at all to his liking: the place was full of factions, Jacobitism was strong, the people tended to be dissolute, and the Scots were disliked.

Smith was appointed Professor of Logic at Glasgow University in 1751 and was Professor of Moral Philosophy from 1752 to 1764. While he was professor he took a full part in the administration. He stood for the Rectorship in 1768. This was a result of academic politicking of which the details are now obscure. Sir Adam Fergusson of Kilkerran was the only other person put forward. Smith was backed by some dissident elements and was heavily defeated. He was given the honour in 1787; this time, no other person was put forward.

Adam Smith (Hunterian Museum)

Smith said, in a letter to the Principal:

> No preferment could have given me so much real satisfaction. No man can own greater obligations to a Society than I do to the University of Glasgow. They educated me, they sent me to Oxford, soon after my return to Scotland they elected me one of their members ... The period of thirteen years which I spent as a member of that Society, I remember as by far the most useful and therefore by far the happiest and most honourable period of my life.

Edmund Burke, elected in 1783, was a dominant figure in the Whig Party; his most fruitful years were from 1770 to 1782 when the Tory Lord North was Prime Minister—a time of corruption and incompetence. The University chose him when he was a leading member of the Government. The choice of a non-Scot was, as far as we know, unprecedented. Lord

Rectors were usually distinguished local persons. They were expected to use their influence to help the University. But as soon as Burke was elected the Government fell, the Tories came back into power, and Burke became a mere Opposition MP. In 1784 the Principal of the University, William Leechman, was seeking a favour; he wrote not only to Burke but also to two members of the Government, Henry Dundas and the Marquis of Graham.

Edmund Burke (Hunterian Art Gallery)

Burke's installation:

... drew a large concourse of spectators, including all distinguished for rank and eminence in the surrounding country, anxious to see a man of whom they had heard so much.

He took the oath of fidelity, rose,

... expressed his thanks for the honour done him—his regard for the learning and talent assembled within the walls in which they were—his esteem for the national character, by which, he confessed, he had been favourably impressed.

Burke described the election as "by much the greatest honour I have ever received."

A historian records:

After this great orator had spoken about five minutes, he became suddenly confused, in consequence of the novel situation in which he was placed, and concluding that he was unable to proceed, as he had never before addressed so learned an assembly.

He said to his friend William Windham:

> They [the Scots] are a people acute and proud, of much pretension, and no incon-
> siderable performance, and notwithstanding undue egotism and excessive nationality,
> on the whole very estimable.

Burke wanted Windham to succeed him—Windham had been a student
at the University. But John Millar, Professor of Law, wrote to Burke that
this was impractical because:

> ... there are individuals who have a claim to be gratified with respect to their private
> connexions, in return for their having indulged their colleagues on former occasions.

This means, in plain language, that Burke's friends in the University
when he was chosen had done some horse-trading. They had gained support for him by promising their support at a later time for someone else's
man. The students had the vote but the professors did too, and the professors had much influence on the way the voting went.

## All Sorts of Fun and Games—and Hooliganism

The rectorship, in the public mind, is associated with stunts, eccentric or
colourful candidates, and—very much in the past—with rowdiness or even
hooliganism at installations. The first colourful candidate of all was Alastair
Sim at Edinburgh in 1948. The first eccentric candidate at Glasgow was
perhaps Rosamund John, film starlet, who took 14 votes in 1950. Albert
Pickard, a property owner who had a knack for stunts and self-publicity,
stood in 1953. (He once advertised land for sale at so much a square yard,
"cheaper than linoleum". He named a patch of land "Pickardilly".)
Someone in 1993 claimed to be the candidate from the Scottish Monster
Raving Loony Alliance.

The other old Scottish Universities have experienced much the same in
the years since the end of the Second World War. St Andrews has elected
John Cleese, comedian, Alan Coren, humorous writer, Frank Muir, radio
and television personality, Tim Brooke-Taylor, entertainer and broadcaster,
and Nicholas Parsons, radio and television personality. Aberdeen has had
Jimmy Edwards, comedian, Sandy Gall, television newscaster, Colin Bell,
broadcaster, and Clarissa Dickson Wright, television cook.

Edinburgh has had Alastair Sim and James Robertson Justice, actors,
Archie MacPherson, sports journalist, Donnie Munro, leader of the Gaelic
band Runrig, and John Colquhoun, professional footballer.

Dundee has had Peter Ustinov, actor and entertainer, and Stephen Fry,
writer and actor.

Lively behaviour when the Rector is installed and gives his Address was a long tradition. The authorities issued a poster in 1866, saying:

---

# TO THE STUDENTS

The Principal and Professors of the University take this opportunity to express the earnest hope that, on the occasion of the approaching Installation of the Lord Rector, the conduct of their Students, in the presence of so large and distinguished an Assembly, will be such as to maintain their own character as Gentlemen, and, at the same time, the honour of the University. They cannot too strongly reprobate the most unseemly and childish practice of throwing about peas and other missiles, by which the meetings of the University have, on several occasions, been interrupted. They are resolved that this and all such practices, being injurious to the character and subversive of the discipline of the University, shall cease.

But they are, at the same time, extremely adverse to have recourse, for this purpose, to the exercise of academical authority. They much more willingly appeal (as they now do) to the sense of propriety and dignity by which all the members of an Academical Body ought to be inspired. It will give them the highest gratification to find that this appeal has not been made in vain, and that the unseemly conduct alluded to has ceased, not in consequence of the imposition of authority, but by the voluntary and united resolution of the Students themselves.

---

Dried peas were, for many generations, a favoured missile.

A passage in Byron's *Childe Harold's Pilgrimage* tells of a dying gladiator "butchered to make a Roman holiday." A professor in the nineteenth century said that a Rector had been "butchered to make a bejant's holiday." A bejant was a first-year student.

The nadir was reached at the installation and Address of R. A. Butler in 1957. The behaviour of some of the students was utterly disgraceful. Since that outrage, the installation and Address have been held within the University's precincts, where the audience is subject to the University's rules and where behaviour has been impeccable.

## *The Rectorial Fight: a Tradition Abandoned*

The custom was for a battle to take place at the start of polling. Two small armies were formed near the polling station in the main building. Students from the political group whose man was leaving office tried to stop any students from voting. Neil Gillies has recalled the time when he took part in the rectorial fight. He has written:

> I went to the University from Ardrishaig at the beginning of October 1947 where I took up residence at Maclay Hall. Well over 100 students lived there. About half our number were ex-service. Others, like myself, were straight from school.
>
> We had no shortage of seasoned commanders. On the Friday evening [the day before the election] the decree was issued that no porridge was to be eaten at breakfast the following morning. The porridge was poured into empty dustbins and mixed with other horrors that were available, such as fish skeletons and heads.
>
> Earlier in the week one of our number had ingratiated himself with the owner of a fish and chip shop in Woodlands Road and in due course relieved the latter of a substantial pile of chip bags at no cost to us. The bags were filled with the putrid mixture, covered with soot, and thoroughly doused with water so that they would burst on impact.
>
> Another lot turned up who seemed to have arrived on the scene with no weapons or ammunition. They decided to lift the covers of the road drains and dredge up the sludge to launch at their adversaries.

A different kind of fight was seen in 1938. The previous Rector was a pacifist campaigner, Canon Dick Sheppard, who started the Peace Pledge Union. The pacifists in the University refused to take part in the fight—it was against all they stood for. Members of the Distributist Club—which had nominated of one of the candidates—were supposed to act instead, as the defenders, but did not turn up. Members of the army that had assembled were stumped. They decided to fight the spectators. The spectators ran away. So the democratic front picked sides and the sides fought each other.

University authorities did not like rectorial fights at all. The mess had to be cleared up and people sometimes got hurt. Newspapers and newsreels (shown in cinemas) loved to cover students' events and that sometimes harmed the University's image.

The elections were held on a Saturday. Very many students lived at home and were disinclined to make the special journey to vote. The Students' Representative Council wanted a bigger turnout and sought to have the polling changed to a weekday. The Senate agreed—provided there was no fight. The last rectorial fight was in 1953. It was fairly free of mess and injuries. The tradition was lost, perhaps needlessly. Official thinking had won that fight.

## Glasgow's Love of Politics

Glasgow has had a long line of politicians as Rector since 1820. They include 11 Prime Ministers but the tradition of political figures came to an end in 1974. The other Scottish universities had politicians, but not as many as Glasgow did. Expression of popular opinion was difficult in the eighteenth and nineteenth centuries. Representation of the people in the way we know it was impossible because fully democratic institutions did not exist. The General Assembly of the Church of Scotland could not deal with political matters.

Political parties were therefore keenly interested in rectorial elections as a way of testing feelings and achieving a success in what we would call public relations and publicity. The elections have also been sarcastically described as "tapping the barometer of public opinion". The students' political clubs were the driving force in this process and were backed by outside sympathisers. Some groups of students from time to time put forward candidates of literary or scientific fame, but the political tradition was too strong. Moreover, the political clubs were able to raise money without much difficulty; while backers of other kinds of candidates could not.

The Campbell Club was formed to mark the re-election of Thomas Campbell, a Whig, in 1828. From it came the Liberal Club, sometimes called the Liberal Association. The Peel Club was formed after the election of Sir Robert Peel, Conservative former Prime Minister and future Prime Minister, in 1836. From it came the Conservative Club. The original aim of the Peel Club was to commemorate his election, to testify to the members':

> ... admiration for his character as a scholar and a statesman, and also to adherence to those great Constitutional principles on which national happiness so much depends.

The club produced a magazine, mainly of general interest, called the *Peel Papers*.

Some merchants, bankers, manufacturers, and other people of Glasgow petitioned Parliament in 1840 about the clubs:

> Your petitioners have beheld, with deep regret, the great evil to the educational and other interests of the University of Glasgow, caused by the organised Association of the Students thereof into two political clubs arrayed against each other ... May it therefore please your Honourable House to adopt such measures as to you in your wisdom may seem meet, for the purpose of abolishing both of the said Political Clubs within the University. And you petitioners will ever pray.

The Peel Club accused its rival the Liberal Association of being behind the petition, the aim of the Liberals being to destroy the Peel Club, and said with heavy sarcasm:

Devout worshippers at the shrine of wisdom, sacred be your tears! hallowed be the sighs which the recreant conduct of the rising generation draws from the lowest depths of an oppressed bosom!

Election campaigning was developed early on. In 1820, when the students forcefully asserted their rights by choosing Francis Jeffrey, the backers of each party put up placards, held meetings, and went around canvassing. It was not long before leaflets were printed and became a vital part of the scene. From the speeches made by students to other students, advocating one candidate or another, arose the tradition of public speaking that has endured ever since at Glasgow University.

In the old College buildings, abandoned in 1870, the Conservative committee met in the back room of the janitor's house. The Liberal committee met in a room called the Coal Hole; it was not really a coal hole but was the room for the bell ringer. The Independents, backing non-political candidates, used another place, the Blackstone Room.

Elections were annual until 1858, but the convention was that re-election for a second year was automatic. Challenges were made after one year if the Rector turned out to be unsatisfactory (Lord John Russell, for instance) or if the political club which lost the previous election wanted to recover its position. Regular meetings were therefore held to decide if a candidate was to be put up the next academic year. This meant that electioneering in some form was almost continuous. Elections were made triennial in 1858 and the politicking lessened.

James Bridie wrote in his autobiography about the elections of the early 1900s.*

> The election itself used to be a memorable affair. The political associations of Glasgow and the West of Scotland took us very seriously and would subscribe large sums of money to the funds of the Conservative and Liberal Clubs. The bulk of this money was spent in renting and fortifying two large shops in Gibson Street, a steep thoroughfare leading up to the University. These shops were liable to attack by members of the opposing clubs. They were gutted and furnished with tables, benches, and pianos and were used as meeting houses and committee rooms. The attacks to which they were liable were of two kinds: they might be burgled in the small hours of the morning by desperate bands who disfigured them with paint and took any records or party literature they could find and threw them in the [river] Kelvin. They could be attacked *en masse* by the full forces of the enemy. The big assaults were usually prearranged.
>
> The defending party crammed as many of its supporters as the shop would hold inside with store of ammunition. Permitted ammunition was eggs, pease-meal in paper bags, soot, and the offal of animals. A hose-pipe was also used. The plate glass was removed from the windows and stout storm boarding substituted. Barricades were built inside the shop. For all this the politicians of Glasgow cheerfully paid.

The records show that many gifts of money for campaigning were fairly small—perhaps a few guineas, coming from quite ordinary firms. The

---

* *One Way of Living*, published in 1939.

owners or managers of these firms were supporters of one party or another and their names and addresses were either passed down from one generation of students to another or were handed over by the political parties. What the records do not reveal is the amount of money given by the political parties from central funds or at least West of Scotland funds. Those amounts are likely to have been large.

Many attempts were made to break the hold of the political clubs before the political tradition died out in the 1970s. During the nineteenth and twentieth centuries the literary or scientific figures put forward without success included Scott, Wordsworth, Dickens, Tennyson, Ruskin, Sir John Herschel, Lord Kelvin, H. G. Wells, Chesterton, and Hemingway.

Even larger numbers of distinguished people have declined to be nominated. Their names are hard or impossible to trace because the written record is scanty. It is known, however, that no less a person than Albert Einstein was approached in 1947. He replied:

> It is quite impossible for me to become a candidate for such an important position in the British intellectual sphere. I thank you for the kindness and the good intentions involved in your proposition and I trust that you will find more effective and realistic means to further the cause of World Government.

The Scottish Nationalists wanted Sir James Barrie to stand in 1928 but had to be content with R. B. Cunninghame Graham, who was both a writer and a politician. At the other extreme, Marilyn Monroe was invited to stand in 1956 and declined. The students who approached her managed to get the *Scottish Daily Express* to give them some money in return for the exclusive story about their plan. The payment was disguised as a contribution to their expenses.

One success in achieving a non-political Rector was through a pact between the political clubs in 1914 to let the President of France, Raymond Poincaré, go ahead unopposed. It was a gesture of solidarity with Britain's ally in the War.

Glasgow's 11 Prime Ministers are a distinguished roll call. Other leading politicians who were Rector might have reached the Prime Ministership: for example Joseph Chamberlain, Lord Curzon, Austen Chamberlain, R. A. Butler, and Lord Hailsham, but here the students were backing runners that turned out not to have staying power. Some politicians were rejected at the polls: George Canning, David Lloyd George, Winston Churchill, and Edward Heath, future Prime Ministers, for example. Some great men had several shots at election: William Ewart Gladstone lost in 1865 but won in 1877; Lord Rosebery lost in 1887 but won in 1899.

## *The Parties and the Rectorship*

### Whigs and Liberals

The Liberals were dominant in Scottish politics for most of the Victorian period, although the party was prone to factionalism. It was the lack of a strong Conservative opposition that made factionalism possible as an indulgence. The student body was of course not representative of society as a whole, any more than the Members of Parliament were representative —the vote for everyone over 21 was not to be achieved until 1928. But the students regularly chose Whigs or Liberals, starting with Francis Jeffrey in 1820. The Whigs and Liberals during the Victorian period included Lord John Russell, Macaulay, Gladstone, and Bright. The Liberal Party was weakened in the country at large after 1886, when it was divided over Home Rule for Ireland and later over the Boer War. A grave economic crisis in 1907-1908 was the last straw for many Liberal loyalties. The *Times* reported in 1908 that about 16,000 people in Govan, Glasgow, were on the verge of starvation.

No Liberal was chosen Rector after the First World War except Sir Archibald Sinclair, later Lord Thurso, in 1938. He won partly because he opposed Britain's policy of appeasing Hitler. Sinclair was also a Scot and the other candidates were only minor figures. What influence the Liberal Club had after that was in nominating or backing distinguished figures such as Albert Luthuli (1962).

### Conservatives

The Conservatives included Peel, Disraeli, and Balfour. Towards the end of the Victorian era the middle classes in Scotland and indeed Britain shifted towards a party that had previously been associated with landowners. More Conservatives took the office in the early part of the twentieth century: Curzon (1908), Bonar Law (1919), Birkenhead (1922), and Baldwin (1928).

Conservative politicians were elected in the 1950s also: Butler (1956) and Hailsham (1959). These two had something else in common: both failed, in spite of strong hopes, to become leader of the Conservative Party and Prime Minister. The Unionists (Conservatives) in general elections between 1950 and 1964 averaged no less than 46 per cent of the vote in Scotland; Labour had 47 per cent. At the same time the students had a higher proportion of middle-class people than the population at large. These facts partly explain why Butler and Hailsham won the rectorship.

The last Tory grandee of this period to be a candidate was Iain Macleod, one of the cleverest men in Parliament, who stood in 1965. He was defeated by Lord Reith, a very strong candidate. Reith took all the "nations" (the nations were the "constituencies" in which the students voted, see below) but that concealed his main rival's support. Reith's votes were 1,857 against Macleod's 1,239. In the following election the Tory was Lady Elliot of Harwood, widow of Walter Elliot. She came fourth in a field of five: she was defeated even by Daniel Cohn-Bendit the revolutionary French student.

(The Conservative Party in Scotland was called the Scottish Unionist Party between 1912 and 1965. I have, for this book, called it the Conservative Party for that period. The union in question was the union with Ireland: the Conservatives were exploiting the working class's fears of Roman Catholicism and of the economic threat posed by Irish immigration.)

## Labour

Growth of the Independent Labour Party and the Labour Party in Scotland was inhibited at the beginning by the strength of Liberalism—indeed, Scottish left-wing leaders such as Keir Hardie throve better in England than they did in Scotland. In the Glasgow rectorials, Keir Hardie was nominated in 1908, Sidney Webb in 1925, E. Rosslyn Mitchell MP in 1928, Tom Johnston in 1931 and 1947, and Lord Attlee in 1956. None of them succeeded. In fact, no left-wing politician did succeed until Jimmy Reid in 1971. He was far from being a routine political figure with a seat in Parliament; he was a Communist shop steward who fought to save shipbuilding on the Clyde. He defeated an ordinary Labour politician, Margaret Herbison.

The University still awaits a straightforward Labour statesman as Rector.

## Scottish Nationalists

A great triumph was achieved by the Scottish Nationalists when R. B. Cunninghame Graham, writer, politician, and colourful figure, came within a whisker of defeating Stanley Baldwin, the Conservative Prime Minister, in 1928. Compton Mackenzie, the writer and nationalist candidate, won in 1931. John MacCormick, an outstanding leader of the movement, won in 1950. The Scottish Nationalist Club also influenced the election of other candidates who did not have its specific party label, such as Lord Reith (1965).

## Distributists

The Distributist club is an extraordinary survival from Distributism, a political movement of the 1920s and 1930s which was led by Hilaire Belloc and G. K. Chesterton. Members of the club are traditionally Roman Catholics. The Distributist club and its beliefs are outlined in Appendix A.

## The Tradition of Debating and Campaigning

Politics were only one element in the elections. Other elements were the calibre of the candidates, the amount of money for campaigning, and the personalities and skills of the people running the campaigns. The *Gilmorehill Citizen,* a campaign newspaper for George MacLeod in 1968, said:

> For the Corporate-Lifers the Rectorial is simply another opportunity for getting the masses organised. They polish their pedestals and oil their voices and present themselves as sponsors of ill-fated candidates. They emerge from board rooms and coffee rooms, welcoming a heaven-sent chance to see themselves in the public eye once more ... It's just as well to remember them—and ignore them, for they are concerned only with their own welfare.

Debates at the Dialectic Society (a debating club which claimed to have been founded before the University), the University Union, and the Queen Margaret Union (the University has two Unions) were at the heart of student life—the "corporate life." Debates at the Union went on from morning to midnight. These debates often reached a very high standard. The Union's teams won the Observer trophy for British university debating no fewer than eight times from the mid-1950s to the early 1980s and the World Universities Debating Championships five times.

The Union debating halls in the twentieth century were training grounds for future Members of Parliament such as Walter Elliot, J. Dickson Mabon, Sir Teddy Taylor, John Smith, Menzies Campbell, Charles Kennedy, and Donald Dewar.

## The "Working Rector"

There has been for more than a century a feeling that the Rector ought to be active in promoting the interests of the students. A reforming Act of Parliament in 1858 set up the University Court, the highest governing body, and made the Rector its chairperson. If he or she is absent, someone else takes the chair; and if present often yields the chair to someone more experienced in the day-to-day business, such as the Principal. A recurrent theme in many elections has been the "working rectorship." The working Rector would, especially, attend and perhaps chair the meetings of the Court.

It has been claimed that the local lairds who filled the office for much of the eighteenth century were "working Rectors", and indeed they may have helped the students from time to time. But they did not conform to the later idea of what the post meant: active work for the students.

Each generation seems to re-discover for itself the idea of a working Rector. One of the earliest references to the issue is from 1842. The Rector was the Marquess of Breadalbane, who was an esteemed public figure, a Whig, and a wealthy landowner. Lord Breadalbane gave some advice to the students in his Address about the sort of person they should choose as his successor. Politics should not enter the matter, he said. Someone from north of the Tweed should be preferred. And they should look for "those qualifications which will lead him [the Rector] to take an interest in their affairs and be of some use to the University."

Yet it was not until 1931 that a candidate was successful on a "working Rector" ticket. That was Compton Mackenzie, but he was promoted mainly as the Scottish Nationalist candidate and was a famous author. He did attend some meetings of the University Court for a year but then dropped out.

Some people grumbled about the absence of eminent writers, artists, and scientists from the roll of Rectors, an issue sometimes linked with the issue of the "working Rector". A letter dated March 22 1893, in the *Glasgow Herald,* signed by the presidents of the Conservative and Liberal Unionist clubs, said:

> On our present methods there is some hope of electing men distinguished in literary and artistic spheres, but it would be a somewhat deluded expectation to look for such if there should once be attached to our rectorial office the condition of presiding at the meetings of the University Court.

People elected on a "working Rector" ticket did not always fulfil their promises to attend the University Court. On the other hand, "non-working" Rectors did do their bit to help the students, by appearing at notable events such as fund-raising bazaars; Birkenhead and Austen Chamberlain are examples.

An honourable course was taken by George MacLeod (Lord MacLeod of Fuinary), who held office from 1968 to 1971. He and his Rector's Assessor (that is, the Rector's associate on the University Court) held weekly "surgeries" during term. Students did come with their problems, although not in great numbers. It was worthwhile not only in practical terms but also as a symbol that the Rector and his Assessor were "there" for the students. Surgeries were held by some later Rectors such as Michael Kelly and John Bell.

Working Rectors have, by and large, a good record of attendance at meetings of the University Court. Lord Reith missed only one meeting for the first two years of his term but then he had a heart attack and was unable to attend. John Bell attended 25 meeting out of 31; Johnny Ball 20 out of 27; Pat Kane 20 out of 33; Richard Wilson 19 out of 21.

## *The Nations and the Rules about the Election*

The Rector was originally the executive head of the University. All members had a vote, both teachers and students. Elections were held each year, but often in the early centuries the same names re-appear over a period; and in the eighteenth century and in the nineteenth until reforms of 1858 re-election for a second year was usual. Voting for more than 500 years was by "nations." Each voter belonged to a constituency, his or her nation, according to where he or she was born. The person who won a majority of the nations won the election. When the nations were equally divided, the outgoing Rector or the Vice-Rector (until 1858) or the Chancellor of the University (after 1858) had the casting vote. That was a crude system and brought about injustice. For example, at the election of 1865 the candidates were John Inglis and William Ewart Gladstone. The nations were equally divided; Gladstone had six votes more than Inglis. The Chancellor gave his casting vote to Inglis. The same sort of thing happened in 1887. Names of the nations were changed from time to time and their boundaries were slightly adjusted but for the period covered in this book were:

*Glottiana:* The county of Lanark, which included Glasgow. This was therefore by far the biggest nation.

*Loudoniana:* The counties of West Lothian, Midlothian, East Lothian, Dumfries, Peebles, Selkirk, Roxburgh, Berwick, Wigtown, Kirkcudbright; and places outside Scotland.

*Rothseiana:* The counties of Bute, Renfrew, and Ayr.

*Transforthana:* The counties of Orkney, Zetland, Caithness, Sutherland, Inverness, Ross and Cromarty, Moray, Nairn, Banff, Aberdeen, Perth, Angus, Kincardine, Clackmannan, Fife, Kinross, Argyll, Stirling, and Dunbarton.

A basis for the electorate was needed when the University was set up. The nations were fixed to coincide more or less with the pre-Reformation Sees of Glasgow, Galloway, Lismore, and the Isles. The pre-Reformation scheme survived through many changes in the country as a whole until it gave way to business-like, efficient ways of thinking.

Voting by nations was abolished for the election of 1977 and all later ones. Voters were put in one "constituency." Out went Glottiana, Loudoniana, Rothseiana, and Transforthana.

In came the system of a "single transferable vote." The old system had thrown up some strange anomalies. One could say, in the phrase about Cavaliers and Roundheads, that the old system was wrong but romantic and the new was right but repulsive.

The ancient system of nations was in existence for 526 years. Impetus for reform came in 1974 when local government in Scotland was reorganised. Counties, such as Clackmannanshire, Banff, and Kirkcudbrightshire, became history in the sense that they had no electoral or administrative existence. In their place came Strathclyde, Tayside, and such less romantically-named entities.

Everything depended, for the Scottish-born students, on where the student was born. In the old days the student at least knew the county—but what could one do if the counties were no longer on the map? It is of course possible from each student's place of birth to work out the old county and therefore his or her nation. But the administrative burden would have been large; one would need in many cases an old map or an old gazetteer. One thing remains, however. Students do not any longer vote by nation but each still does have a nation.

The election was from 1727 held on November 15 or the nearest suitable date. Under the Universities of Scotland Act 1858, the date was changed to October or November and not later than the second Saturday in November. The University Court was however given the power to alter that.

Since 1984, the election has been held in March. The reason given in the minutes of the Court are that the previous date disrupted the arrangements for matriculation, which is the enrolment of all the students at the beginning of each academic year. The change of date also gives a longer period for campaigning and allows freshers to adjust themselves to university life before voting.

The Universities of Scotland Act 1858 carried out radical reforms in many areas. It also took away the vote from the professors. The watchful David Murray, historian of the University, growled:

> It is to be regretted that this ancient institution has been radically altered with no object and merely from the itch for change.

On the other hand, the professors were given strong representation on the newly-created body the University Court.

Students were asked verbally and publicly for whom they wanted to vote and the vote was registered accordingly. In 1874 the Liberals and the Independents complained that the professors in charge of polling in the nations of Transforthana and Rothseiana had tried to bring undue influence to bear. The complaint went to the Senate and the Court but nothing was done about it. The open vote lasted well into the twentieth century.

Edinburgh University chose a student in 1971 and again in 1972—the second time it was Gordon Brown, who was to achieve great eminence in the Labour Party and government. Both these rectors were in fact enrolled as post-graduates, but its was a break with tradition to have a student in the post. Brown not only insisted on chairing the Court—he also presumed to influence its decisions. Glasgow chose a student, John Bell, in 1977, again a sharp break with tradition. Bell was a graduate, was in the faculty of Divinity, and had been a very active President of the Student's Representative Council.

These events in Edinburgh seem to have given the authorities at Glasgow some anxiety; and students were banned in 1981 from standing. The University's Ordinance No 186 states comprehensively:

> No matriculated student at the University, nor any part-time student or individual matriculated for examination or graduation purposes only, shall be eligible to be nominated for election as rector.

On the other hand, students are well represented on the Court. From 1971, the President of the Students' Representative Council has been a member *ex officio*. The Rector, under the reforms of the nineteenth century, used to appoint an Assessor (his or her assistant and co-member of the Court.) That official is now called the SRC Assessor and is elected by the Students' Representative Council.

With so many representatives on the Court, perhaps the students do not need a working Rector. And with so many representatives on the Court, perhaps the students believe they can afford to elect colourful candidates.

A lack of serious candidates and a proliferation of colourful ones are perhaps reasons for the low turnout at recent polls. Turnout was 17.69 per cent in 1987, 16.56 per cent in 1990, 19 per cent in 1993, and 17.6 per cent in 1996.

## Religion, Sectarianism, and Prejudice

The Scots have always been keen on theological discussion; and a bad aspect of that is religious intolerance. Both of these are found in the history of the rectorship. At St Andrews University, the first Rector was Lawrence of Lindores, who was Inquisitor of Heretical Pravity in Scotland (he was also Dean of the Faculty of Arts, Bursar, and Head of the Colleges.)

William Leechman became Professor of Divinity at Glasgow in 1734. He was soon in trouble over alleged heresy. He wrote to a friend:

> I don't believe it is possible for one in your Situation to imagine to what hight bigottry and nonsense in Religion prevails in this Country, especially in this part of it ... you may easily perceive, how difficult a task it must be to teach pure and genuine Christianity, and at the same [time] not to expose myself to the fury of Bigots: There is the utmost care taken to watch every word pronounced by me. The Zealots always have some Secret Spies among the Students ...

Anti-semitic feelings came into the propaganda against Disraeli's candidature in 1871. Anti-Catholic feelings came into the propaganda against the Marquis of Bute's candidature in 1883. Compton Mackenzie, a Roman Catholic, was chosen in 1931; his religious beliefs were important in the reaction to his campaign and his victory.

Roman Catholic students have since the 1920s formed the bulk of the membership of the Distributist Club. The "Distribs" have taken a big part in Union debates as a political club and they have intervened from time to time in rectorial elections by giving support to a candidate: for example, Paderewski in 1934.

In the mid-1950s a report was current in the University Union that a remarkable notice had gone up in Turnbull Hall, the chaplaincy for Roman Catholic students. The notice was allegedly about the forthcoming elections to the Union board of management, and was supposed to have given lists of candidates under the headings:

> The following are Catholic ... the following are non-Catholic ... the following are anti-Catholic.

Whether or not the notice existed, and there is no reason to doubt its existence, the report itself is evidence of the feelings that existed then.

Racial prejudice does not appear to have been prevalent. Indeed the students have chosen two South African campaigners against apartheid: Albert Luthuli in 1962 and Winnie Mandela in 1987.

## Pressure to Reduce the Rights of the Students

The students were deprived of their right to vote between 1691 and 1717. The excuse at first was that holding an assembly of students might be dangerous. The country had not settled down after the Revolution of 1688. But later it was an arrangement between John Stirling, the Principal from 1701 to 1728, and Sir John Maxwell of Pollok, the Rector from 1691 to 1717, who was a local magnate. Maxwell stayed Rector because he and Stirling allowed no proper elections.

A friend of Stirling said he was "an excellent gospel preacher" and was "singularly sweet in prayer, and very much taken up in ejaculatory prayer, even to his being mocked for it by his enemies." Stirling may have been an eloquent clergyman but he was domineering and manipulative and he antagonised many of the professors. Professors and students joined hands to defy the Principal, and the issue was the status of the rectorship. Among the students were Irish Presbyterians, older than the others, who were accustomed to the struggles of Dissenters in their homeland for civil and religious liberties. Some students took the matter to the Court of Session. Disorders took place constantly. Some students lit a bonfire opposite the college gate in 1722 to celebrate the general election. A senior member of the staff wanted to have the bonfire put out and was assaulted by John Smith, an Irish student of Divinity.

Students attacked in 1725 the house of Sir Hugh Montgomerie of Hartfield, the Rector, who had been manoeuvred into office by Stirling.

> The Colledge of Glasgou is very thin this session

wrote the librarian, Robert Wodrow, in 1725:

> and the Masters may blame themselves; their divisions and breaches have lessened the reputation of society, and multitudes nou go to Edinburgh.

Two Royal Commissions were held. In the end the Principal had to give way. A properly-conducted election was held in 1726, although Wodrow recorded that the staff had "had their oun difficultys to keep the boyes from tumultating, and factions." And when the rights of the students were restored Wodrow was unhappy about so much power being put in the hands of young people: some were as young as 12. He wrote about the "boyes" having "sensless pretended priviledge."

The election of 1727 was perhaps the most extraordinary ever to be held. There were two candidates, George, Master of Ross, afterwards the thirteenth Lord Ross of Hawkhead, and James Hamilton of Aikenhead, who won. Wodrow wrote:

> Mr [Alexander] Dunlop [Professor of Greek] and his side used their utmost interest with the boyes, and dunned them for many days to have the Master of Ross chosen. Mr [William] Anderson [Professor of Ecclesiastical History] and the other side were for Aikenhead. The tounsmen and merchants of Glasgou struck in with Aikenhead, invited the boyes to taverns; in short, for some weeks before, there was nothing but clubbing, and the poor boyes taught to be party men. The Masters fell foul upon one another, and gave [each] other hard names in their classes to the students. Mr Dunlop's side brought in young surgeons and prentices to be made *cives* [students] in the University, in order to votes [*sic*], and the other side folloued ther example, in bringing young merchants and others ... there was nothing but hurry, and the utmost confusion.

The backers of Ross went to a judge in Edinburgh, without telling their opponents what they were doing. They told the judge that Aikenhead did not have a majority of either voters or nations and that there was:

> ... plain and palpable Packing by Matriculating as Students great Numbers of Apprentices and shop-keepers.

The judge issued an order. The Master of Ross appeared at a meeting of the University with the document and declared himself to be Rector. The dispute was not settled when the time for another election came round again; this time the Master of Ross was chosen.

The right of the students to take part in the election, restored at this period, were not seriously challenged for another hundred years. Attempts to put the choice in the hands of the professors alone were next made in the early nineteenth century. Two senior professors, William Richardson of

Humanity (i.e. Latin) and John Young of Greek, wanted in May 1813 to ask Parliament to pass an Act giving the University Senate the power of election. The University adopted in 1819 a petition to the House of Commons, asking for a change in the electoral system. But the matter was dropped the next year. These proposals angered students and they in 1820 ousted the current Rector in protest and picked another to their liking: Francis Jeffrey (see page 2.)

The senior members of the University—that is, the professors and the administrators—have not always liked the rectorship as it exists in modern times. The status of the Rector became an issue at St Andrews in the 1950s. The relationship between St Andrews University and University College, Dundee, needed to be clarified and reformed. The University of St Andrews Bill, as originally drafted, had a provision that the Principal, rather than the Rector, was to chair the Court. A meeting of the Principals of the Scottish Universities agreed that the other three universities would make representations supporting the clause. But the clause was amended or withdrawn before the Bill was passed into law.

It is notable that the rectorship is absent from all the universities founded since Dundee—for example, Strathclyde, Stirling, Heriot-Watt, and Paisley.

In 1988 the authorities at St Andrews, Glasgow, and Aberdeen sought to have the Rector stripped of the power to chair the Court, but Edinburgh hung back. A united front was needed and the idea was dropped. But it arose again. The National Inquiry into Higher Education was set up under Sir Ron Dearing and reported in 1997. Its Scottish sub-committee was chaired by Sir Ron Garrick, an industrialist.

The Garrick report said:

> We have ... noted that all university Courts now have permanent student representation. We consider the Rector is a valuable asset to Court, and therefore should be retained, to act, as originally envisaged, as a spokesperson for students. However, we believe that the office of Rector should no longer be linked automatically to the chairmanship of the University Court. We believe that the chairman of Court should more properly be elected by all members, and we agree with the National Committee that this should be for a period no longer than three years, renewable for three years. If satisfying the criteria for eligibility, the Rector could, of course, stand for election to the position of chairman.

The Garrick report said:

> We recommend ... that the appropriate legislation should be enacted to support this change in institutional governance.

Brian Wilson, Minister for Scottish Higher Education, rejected the idea.

The General Council of the University (to which all graduates belong) might have campaigned with vigour against the tradition being abolished. Many members of the House of Lords and the House of Commons at that time were former student leaders or graduates of the Scottish universities. And some of them would have vigorously opposed any attempt to change the status of the rectorship.

# The Silver

The office of Rector in the University of Glasgow has associated with it certain ceremonial objects of silver.

The Rector's Mace (Glasgow University Photographic Service)

## The Mace

The most significant object is a mace, which is carried on academic occasions when the Rector is present. It is three feet long. The shaft is of black wood. All the silver parts are gilded.

The top end has six "blades" like the mace as a weapon. There are three knops or ornamental features, one at the base and two spaced out in the middle. The one at the base has, in low relief, the symbols of the four nations—symbols which, carved in stone, are at the entrances to the Union and to the McIntyre building (formerly the Queen Margaret Union and before that the Union.)

The knops on the shaft have—again in low relief—thistles and saltires and portraits of four persons who were important to the establishment of the university:

Saint Mungo, patron of Glasgow and of the Cathedral where the University began. His image is based on likenesses of Sir Hector Hetherington, who was Principal from 1936 to 1961 and was one of the greatest Principals.

James II of Scots, in whose reign the University was founded. Scotland did not at this time have portrait painters and this is an imaginary likeness from a later era. The original is in the National Portrait Gallery, Edinburgh, but for the mace the king has been given a crown.

Pope Nicholas V, the great Renaissance prince, patron of the arts and letters, and collector, who issued the document of foundation. His portrait is taken from a contemporary medal.

Bishop William Turnbull, the prime mover in the establishment of the University. Again, no contemporary portrait of him is known to exist. His image is from photographs of the designer, maker, and donor of the mace, Donald Wintersgill.

### Rector's Cup

The Rector's Cup is in a tradition of "standing cups" for colleges, livery companies in the City of London, and private persons. They are to emphasise status. This cup is ornamented with three large amethysts and four large garnets. Amethysts are supposed to be a defence against drunkenness—perhaps a reason why episcopal rings are of amethysts. Garnets are supposed to change colour in the presence of poison. The Cup has a cover or lid and is gilded inside.

### The Badge of Office.

The Badge of Office is gilded. has amethysts and garnets, is inscribed RECTOR OF GLASGOW UNIVERSITY and has a representation in relief of the Rector's Mace.

# Reassertion of the Students' Rights

Kirkman Finlay (Scottish National Portrait Gallery)

*Kirkman Finlay (1772-1842), enlightened and dynamic businessman and MP.*

*Elected 1819*

Kirkman Finlay was a Lord Provost of Glasgow and Member of Parliament, for Glasgow, Dumbarton, Renfrew and Rutherglen (1812-1818) and for Malmesbury (1818-1820). The city had been Europe's market-place for tobacco until the rebellion of the American colonies: the trade collapsed in the 1780s. Finlay helped to put the city's commerce on a wider basis.

He also in 1793 took a prominent part in leading the opposition to the East India Company's monopoly of the Oriental trade. Parliament refused to renew the monopoly. Finlay immediately sent a Clyde ship to Bombay (now Mumbai). That was the beginning of much trade with the Far East, in cotton, indigo, tea, and jute. The family firm, James Finlay and Co., has a long and honourable record in Scottish business.

It was in Finlay's time, in 1840, that the decision was made to build an artificial dock, Kingston Dock, in Glasgow—and from that arose more trade and more prosperity.

Napoleon, with the Berlin Decrees, put an embargo on Britain's trade with Europe: the aim was to destroy the British economy. Finlay was one of those who organised, with skill and daring, a flow of "contraband".

Finlay's election by the students in 1819 would normally have been followed by re-election the next year. But some of the students believed that he had been in favour of taking away from the students their right to vote in rectorial elections (see page XXVI). This belief was in fact wrong but a group of students nominated Francis Jeffrey, overcame the strenuous and united efforts of the professors, and returned Jeffrey.

This seems to have been an outbreak of what might have been called, in a later generation, student power. The Senate, which had voted for Finlay unanimously, was dismayed. It recorded its high esteem for Finlay and gave him thanks for his work in the interest of the University and education generally. He had been, as an MP, a useful ally and contact.

On the day of the election the students formed a procession to the house of the departing Rector and held some kind of demonstration. The professors, angered at their candidate losing, were severe on some of the students who had taken part in the disturbance, making them read out an apology in their own name and as representing the others.

Jeffrey in his speech at his installation tried to smooth the ruffled feelings and to persuade the students that their suspicions arose partly or wholly from misunderstandings. Finlay showed no resentment that he had been displaced by Jeffrey and attended Jeffrey's installation.

# Students take Power
# into their own Hands

Francis Jeffrey (Hunterian Art Gallery)

*Francis Jeffrey, later Lord Jeffrey, Whig,*
*lawyer, editor, and critic (1773-1850)*

## Elected 1820

This election was one of the most important of all. His predecessor Kirk-man Finlay would have been reappointed in the normal course of events but the students rejected Finlay. It was the first time the students took control of what was going on and sidelined the professors. It was the first election that was political and it began a political tradition that was to last for nearly 140 years. And Jeffrey began the tradition of Addresses which has continued almost unbroken.

Jeffrey was for nearly 30 years the editor of the *Edinburgh Review*, a most influential journal. He was educated at the High School in Edinburgh and at Glasgow University. He had his first taste of rectorial elections when he was a student aged 14. He challenged the candidacy of Adam

Smith for the post of Rector, saying that Smith was the choice of the professors while the students had rights too. A contemporary account tells of Jeffrey haranguing a mob of boys on Glasgow Green and trying to rouse them to their manifold duty of organising opposition to the professors' nominee. Jeffrey was:

> ... a little, black, quick-motioned creature with a rapid utterance and a prematurely-developed moustache, on which his audience teased him mercilessly.

He went on to Oxford University but was there for less than a year: he disliked it and found his companions dissolute and uncongenial. When he was there he got rid of his Scottish accent and acquired an unpleasing English one. He was described as having "a high-keyed accent and a sharp pronunciation" and to have "extreme rapidity of utterance." These oddities were softened over the years.

Jeffrey's early years as a lawyer were years of struggle. But he and some friends launched the influential *Edinburgh Review* in 1802. It became the leading magazine of public opinion and its critical judgements on works of literature were the most feared. He was its editor until 1829 and was outstandingly good at the job. Among his most notable colleagues on the *Edinburgh Review* were the wit Sydney Smith and the lawyer and politician Henry Brougham. In social company and in family life he was charming and warm.

During his political and literary career he supported reform, for example Catholic emancipation and the Scots legislation that paralleled the English Reform Act.

Jeffrey was savage in his book reviews. He was politically a Whig but in literary taste was conservative. He was unsympathetic to the Lake Poets such as Wordsworth and Coleridge but encouraged Keats. Jeffrey wins the applause and gratitude of many for his review of Wordsworth's poem *The Excursion*: he says in his opening words: "This will never do."

His savage literary criticism occasioned a savage reply. This was Byron's poem 'English Bards and Scotch Reviewers', which includes the lines:

> ...the mingled howl
> Of northern wolves, that still in darkness prowl;
> A coward brood, which mangle as they prey,
> By hellish instinct, all that cross their way;
> Aged or young, the living or the dead,
> No mercy find—these harpies must be fed...
> Hail to immortal Jeffrey! once, in name,
> England could boast a judge almost the same...

Byron later added, in a footnote:

My northern friends have accused me, with justice, of personality towards their great literary anthropophagus,* Jeffrey; but what else was to be done with him and his dirty pack, who feed by 'lying and slandering', and slake their thirst by 'evil speaking'?

Jeffrey also built up his legal practice until he was a dominating figure at the Scottish Bar.

A historian of the University, John Barras Hay, produced in 1839 a book called *Inaugural Addresses of Lord Rectors of the University of Glasgow*. The preface says:

The office of Lord Rector of the University of Glasgow, has at all times been filled by men of eminent learning, illustrious rank, or high public station. But Francis Jeffrey, in his Installation of 1820, imparted new interest to that Academic distinction. Instead of accepting the Rectorship in the formal and almost silent manner of his predecessors, that celebrated Critic regaled with an eloquent address the audience that thronged to witness his return to "the early Nurse of his studies". The example which he set has been followed by the distinguished individuals who have succeeded him, and the Lord Rectors' Addresses now form a valuable addition to the stores of our national eloquence.

Jeffrey's friend Henry Cockburn, later Lord Cockburn, a fellow lawyer and fellow Whig, writes in his memoirs:

Jeffrey surprised us this year, almost as much as he surprised himself, by his elevation to the Lord Rectorship of the College of Glasgow. It was the first official honour he had received. And its proceeding from the students was a fact that concurred with many others in shewing the ebbing of the old shallow tide.† The reign of the professors and the adjoining lairds had plainly received a shock. Since 1787, when Adam Smith was elected, no person had been appointed solely from literary or scientific merit. The collegians, ashamed of the habitual abasement, took the decision into their own hands, and have kept it, and justified the use of their power, ever since.

Cockburn also said:

He was elected as a homage to his personal literature, and to the great work with which his name was associated, and to his public principles and conduct.

Cockburn recounts that he and many of his friends turned up for the installation. Most of the professors, he said, were horrified at the sight of such a crew of Whigs.

It seemed delightful however to the students, to whom the rector made a beautiful speech. His ceremonious banquet with the college authorities was succeeded by a night-long supper at the hotel with his friends. The honor [sic] done to Jeffrey, the triumph of the students, and the change of times, inspired the party into the best joyous conviviality it has ever been my good fortune to partake of.

Jeffrey said in his Address:

It was here that, now more than thirty years ago, I received the earliest, and by far the most valuable, part of my academical education; and first imbibed that relish and ven-

---

* Cannibal.
† I.e. reform of the old corrupt system.

eration for letters, which has cheered and directed the course of my whole after life; and to which, amidst all the distractions of rather too busy an existence, I have never failed to return with fresh and unabated enjoyment....

Though I have been able, I fear, to do little to honour this early nurse of my studies, since I was first separated from her bosom, yet I presume to say, that I have been, through all that interval, an affectionate and not inattentive son

His career took a different turn between 1829 and 1834. In those years he became Dean of the Faculty of Advocates (he then gave up the editorship), Lord Advocate, and a not very successful Member of Parliament; and he was, finally, appointed as a judge of the Court of Session.

# A Great Scotsman is Denied the Post

Sir James Mackintosh (courtesy of the National Portrait Gallery)

*Sir James Mackintosh, Whig; Member of Parliament, lawyer, and philosopher (1765-1832).*

*Elected 1822*

Mackintosh has been described as "an able and faithful defender of liberal principles." He was much loved and admired by his contemporaries. But Mackintosh suffered from ill health, from too much love of society and talk, and from comparative poverty. He found it difficult to devote himself fully to his plans and projects.

He was the son of an army officer who inherited a small estate. He was born and brought up near Inverness and attended King's College, Aberdeen; studied medicine at Edinburgh; went to London; and became a writer and a barrister. When he appeared in court he could be remarkably eloquent, even reducing his hearers to tears. He delivered a brilliant series of lectures in 1799 on the law of nature and the law of nations.

Mackintosh took a post as a judge in India, for the sake of a pension and the leisure to write. He stayed there for seven years and read a great deal but produced nothing. He returned for the sake of his health and became an MP without great success. He wrote historical works and a defence of the Whig view of the French Revolution, but later abominated the Revolution. His most important work was *A Dissertation on the Progress of Ethical Philosophy*. He became a member of a glittering circle of Whig politicians and intellectuals. His writings made him one of the founders of the Whig interpretation of history which was to dominate British intellectual life for the next 150 years.

The diarist Charles Greville wrote of a meeting with Mackintosh:

> I was never in Macintosh's [*sic*] company for so long before, and never was more filled with admiration. His prodigious memory and the variety and extent of his information remind me of all that I have heard and read of Burke and Johnson, but his amiable, modest, and unassuming character makes him far more agreeable than they could either of them (particularly Johnson) have been, while he is probably equally instructive and amusing. ... I could not help reflecting what an extraordinary thing success is in this world, when a man so gifted as Macintosh has failed completely in public life ... he has not the art of pushing or of making himself feared.

The great Macaulay adored him and wrote, when reviewing Mackintosh's last historical work:

> We have in vain tried to separate the book from the writer, and to judge of it as if it bore some unknown name. But it is no purpose. All the lines of that venerable countenance are before us. All the little peculiar cadences of that voice from which scholars and statesmen loved to receive the lessons of a serene and benevolent wisdom are in our ears. We will attempt to preserve strict impartiality. But we are not ashamed to own that we approach this relic of a virtuous and most accomplished man with feelings of respect and gratitude which may possibly pervert our judgment.

In the rectorial election he was opposed by Sir Walter Scott. This time, the nations were equally divided. The casting vote was with Jeffrey as the retiring holder of the office. It has been said that his heart told him he should honour Scott but his head told him he should honour Mackintosh.

He voted for Mackintosh on the grounds that Mackintosh had a better academic background and had more votes. On the other hand, Scott was a Tory and Jeffrey and Mackintosh were Whigs. Jeffrey's decision was partly political and the excuse was thin. Scott in fact lived 40 miles away; Mackintosh 400. Scott's name is imperishable. Mackintosh's was not.

Mackintosh's Address contained the usual bow to the audience but was not very flattering.

> I hold in my hand an old edition of Ptolemy, printed in 1530, in which is given a character to the various nations of the world. The character assigned to the Scots is, that they are, first, prompt to revenge; second, full of the pride of birth so that they boast of royal descent, though in a state of beggary; and third, that they are much addicted to moral and metaphysical subtleties.

He touched on another old theme.

There is now, Gentlemen, none of that spirit of hostility to our countrymen of other persuasions, that formerly was said to distinguish the people of this country. This spirit of intolerance is fast wearing away from every country. Catholic chapels are now erected at Amsterdam and Geneva; I have seen a Catholic bishop at Boston; and even in Glasgow I have been delighted to see erected, within these few years, a Catholic chapel, probably the most beautiful in the Island.* [The editor of the text notes that here disapprobation was manifested by a part of the audience]

Those of you who have manifested symptoms of disapprobation, would probably have withheld doing so, if you had waited for the following sentence. Far be it from me ever to assert any sentiment inconsistent with my original convictions of the doctrines of a sincere Protestant, or with the most determined opposition to the arbitrary doctrines, and dominant and intolerant spirit of the Church of Rome. On the contrary, the reason I rejoice in the existence of such a Catholic edifice is, that it proves that the stain of intolerance has been wiped away from the Protestant Church.

In a brief passage he accuses the Roman Catholic Church of arbitrary doctrines and of intolerance, acquits the Protestant Church of those offences, and congratulates himself on his broadmindedness.

---

* The "Catholic edifice" is St Andrew's Chapel, which became St Andrew's Cathedral in 1889. It is in Clyde Street. It was designed by James Gillespie; the silhouette is in the Perpendicular Gothic style and the details are in the Decorated style. Many of the furnishings were designed later by Pugin and Pugin.

# Lawyer who defended Queen accused of Adultery

Lord Brougham (Hunterian Art Gallery)

*Henry Brougham, Whig statesman, lawyer, reformer, anti-slavery campaigner, orator, and polemical writer. Later Lord Brougham (1778-1868).*

*Elected 1824*

For his whole career he upheld humanity and freedom. Brougham was a figure of importance in British politics for two decades. He was at one time in effect the leader of the Opposition. He was tall, thin, and commanding, according to one acquaintance, and gaunt and ungainly, according to another. His face was ugly but expressive. His voice was powerful and even pleasant to listen to, although he sometimes talked far too much. For the most part he was full of life, wit, and gaiety. Brougham could also be bitter and jealous.

He went to Edinburgh University at the age of 14—a usual age—and in his mid-twenties was one of the founders of the *Edinburgh Review*, which for much of the early nineteenth century was so important in literary and political matters. He went to London because he thought that his radical views would have more scope there, was called to the English Bar in 1808, and entered Parliament in 1810.

One of his greatest triumphs was the successful defence of Queen Caroline, wife of George IV, in 1820. The King had married her in 1795 when he was Prince Regent—he was obliged to marry: that was the only way his father and the Government would clear his huge debts. Princess Caroline of Brunswick was an appalling choice. She was coarse, tactless, and eccentric and she was rumoured to have had affairs.

The Prince was shocked when she came to Britain and they met for the first time. He said to one of his aides: "I am not well. Pray fetch me a glass of brandy." Almost as soon as the marriage took place, the Prince and she separated. She lived mostly in Italy from 1814, where she led an apparently dissolute life and seemingly had lovers. When the Prince succeeded to the throne in 1820 she returned to Britain.

She received a rapturous welcome from the populace. Public sympathy was for Queen Caroline regardless of her character and behaviour. The King was regarded by ordinary people as a libertine, a glutton, a drunk, a spendthrift, and a cruel husband. He had also married Mrs Maria Anne Fitzherbert, a Roman Catholic widow, in 1785. The King, George III, had not given his consent, which meant that the ceremony was illegal under the Royal Marriage Act of 1772. The Prince afterwards denied that there had been a marriage.

The Government started proceedings against Queen Caroline in the House of Lords for adultery. The case was sensational. Brougham was one of the lawyers representing the Queen. The Government dropped the case, partly because of his forensic brilliance, partly for other considerations. This success made him a popular hero from 1820 to 1830 and taverns were named the Brougham's Head.

Brougham took up Queen Caroline's case not for her sake but to further his career and to attack the King and the King's Tory friends.

Brougham sought to reform the law of libel and for decades campaigned against slavery. He was keen to promote education, for example through the Mechanics' Institutes and the Society for the Diffusion of Useful Knowledge, which brought out inexpensive editions of books. He was one of the founders of London University. This was his record at the time he was chosen as Rector.

This election was remarkable. Sir Walter Scott (Tory) was another candidate. Scott had for years been denying that he was the author of the Waverley novels but in 1825 he admitted the truth—which in fact everyone really knew. A third candidate was Henry Mackenzie, yet another writer and lawyer. For more than half a century he was "one of the most illustrious names connected with polite literature in Edinburgh." He wrote a sentimental novel, *The Man of Feeling*, in 1771. But the voters seem to have decided he was too old, at 79, to take on the job.

The contest was politicised. Brougham won two nations and Scott two; Mackenzie did poorly. A casting vote had to be given. A bitter academic dispute took place: could the retiring rector, Mackintosh, give the vote in writing or did he have to be present? Other pedantic issues were raised. The professors seem to have been bent on trouble-making. In the end Mackintosh turned up and gave his vote to Brougham.

The installation and Address took place speedily. The Address was, predictably, on the spread of knowledge and the excellence of Greek studies. He also spoke about the great orators. The proper employment of eloquence was in the cause of liberty.

A great dinner was held in his honour in Edinburgh, soon after his installation. He wrote in his memoirs about the speech he made:

> I seized the opportunity to declare my decided approbation of the Scotch system of education, as contrasted with the English ... That was the system so invaluable in a free State—a system which cultivated and cherished higher objects than mere learning, which inculcated a nobler ambition than the mere acquisition of prosody and the dead languages. My English friends will cry aloud against this doctrine, which they will designate as rank heresy.

He went on to become Lord Chancellor in 1830 and to push for reform of the legal system. He helped with the passage of the Reform Bill in 1832 and was active in other reforms—for example, he established the Central Criminal Court and the judicial committee of the Privy Council.

But after he lost the Lord Chancellorship in 1834 he went into political decline, showing signs of poor judgement. Towards the end of his life he became more boastful and apt to fantasise about his achievements.

Brougham was capable of extraordinary acts. He once gave a great speech in the House of Commons and at the end, in a theatrical gesture, fell on his knees, prayed, and did not get up. He had been fortifying himself with mulled port and his friends thought he had drunk too much to get up, so helped him. In fact he was all right.

In 1839 he put it about that he had been killed in an accident to his carriage. He scrutinised the newspaper obituaries to see who were his enemies and who his friends.

He is one of the rare people who have given their names to the language, such as Charles Mackintosh who invented the first waterproof cloth and John Loudon Macadam who revolutionised the construction of roads. A one-horse, four-wheeled carriage called a brougham was designed for him. It was light and handy, mostly used for informal occasions, rather like a cab but more comfortable and with better visibility. The brougham dates from the late 1830s and survived until the development of cars.

A prolific contributor to the *Edinburgh Review*, he did most of the political articles and Francis Jeffrey the literary criticism. It has been said of the *Edinburgh* that:

... the editors seemed to value themselves principally on their severity and they have reviewed some works seemingly with no other object than to show what their powers in this particular line of criticism are.

Brougham was responsible for writing a paragraph in a damning review of Byron's *Hours of Idleness*—not a poem that was or is much esteemed. Byron had just finished reading the review when a visitor came in, saw his face, and at once asked: "Have you received a challenge, Byron?" He had—from the *Edinburgh Review*.

Byron, who did not know then that the author was Brougham, was full of thoughts of "rage, resistance, and redress," drank three bottles of claret and felt better. He wrote twenty lines of poetry and felt "considerably better." He spent a year writing a new poem—'English Bards and Scotch Reviewers'—which made his name. (See page 4.)

A story is recorded about the election of Brougham's successor—a story that does him no credit. A potential candidate was Thomas Campbell the poet. Brougham told him that he had no chance because he would be opposed by Sir James Moncrieff, who was a great lawyer (he was to become a Lord of Session). Moncrieff happened to be Brougham's friend. The intention was to put off Campbell.

Campbell announced he was not going to stand. But Campbell's friends found that almost no canvassing had been done for Moncrieff and what canvassing had been done had been by Brougham. The attempt to "nobble" Campbell was exposed and Campbell's candidacy went ahead. He won.

Campbell was still talking about the trickery nearly a year later. A diarist, John Hobhouse, recorded:

The other day Thomas Campbell, the poet, called on me, big with complaints about Brougham, and told me several traits of his character which I would fain think unfairly drawn.

A biographer of Brougham, Chester W. New, has written:

No one who knew Brougham would believe that he did that out of spite for Campbell, but a good many would believe that Brougham could act in that manner to wangle an office for a friend or arrange an appointment that was for some reason desirable.

The two men were in the end reconciled.

# Rector at Odds with the Principal

Thomas Campbell (Hunterian Art Gallery)

*Thomas Campbell, poet, critic, and journalist*
*(1777-1844)*
*His sympathies were Whig*

*Elected 1826*

The students again asserted their rights. They rejected the man the professors wanted to be chosen—George Canning, the Foreign Secretary, a Tory. Canning was to become Prime Minister the next year. The professors who were foiled by Campbell's election were full of resentment. Most of them at this time wanted the rector to be chosen by the teaching staff alone.

Campbell's reputation was great in his lifetime. His first volume of poetry, *The Pleasures of Hope*, was published when he was aged 20 and ran through four editions in a year. He was buried in Westminster Abbey and a statue of him was put up in George Square, Glasgow.

He was born and brought up in Glasgow, the eleventh child of a tobacco merchant who went bankrupt because the trade was disrupted by the

American War of Independence. He entered Glasgow University at the age of 13 on a bursary (won in competition with a much older boy) and carried off many prizes. Campbell began to study law in Edinburgh but his real calling was poetry. He travelled on the Continent, settled in London in 1803, and took up writing and journalism.

His best-known poems nowadays are perhaps "The Battle of Hohenlinden" (he visited the site soon after the battle had taken place—Napoleon's forces crushed the Austrians), "Ye Mariners of England," and "The Battle of the Baltic". No fewer than 12 of his poems are in the anthology of poetry Palgrave's *Golden Treasury*, which has gone through innumerable editions since it was first published in 1861.

The other candidates in the rectorial election were Canning and Sir Thomas Brisbane. Canning, who became Foreign Secretary in 1822, was also a fine orator and a minor poet. Brisbane, born in Largs, Ayrshire, and educated at Edinburgh University, became a soldier and distinguished himself in Flanders, the West Indies, Spain, and North America. He had been an outstanding Governor of New South Wales. The capital of Queensland is named after him. He was also a notable astronomer.

All the professors except perhaps two had agreed to support Canning and used their influence for him. The students resoundingly rejected the professors' man. The voting was Campbell 283, Brisbane 196, Canning 79. One of the students, when asked at the poll for whom he wanted to vote, struck a theatrical attitude and at the top of his voice thundered "Campbell!" (There was no secret ballot—indeed the secret ballot was not introduced until the 1960s. Students at the poll as recently as the 1950s were asked: "For whom do you wish to vote?" and were then handed an appropriate slip to sign and return.)

At the time of the election Campbell had been editing for six years *The New Monthly Magazine* in London. It was a precarious living. He was short of money for the trip and for extra expenses such as smart new clothes. One of his sisters offered to help. He wrote to her:

> I have been disappointed a good deal in my accounts with my bookseller [i.e. publisher]. The motive that prompts me to decline your proffered gift, still holds good with me ... I would as soon think of taking the pillow from your head, as of appropriating to myself any of the spare money which you ought, for your tranquillity, to be sure of having about you at a time when you require every possible comfort. But if you can give me the loan of the sum you mentioned, only till Midsummer, I can promise you its return with certainty ... You would not, I know, like to see your brother perform the only high part, as to station, which he has ever played in life, in a so-so manner.

When he went to Glasgow to deliver his inaugural address, and reached the college buildings, it had been snowing and a snowball fight was going on. One of his biographers wrote:

That he was just going to deliver a solemn address to the same youth never for a moment crossed his mind. Such an absence of mind, on an occasions of similar importance, so incongruous, pompous doctors or stiff ceremonialists would have it, was not to be palliated, but it was strictly in character. The feeling of his youth came upon him, the spirit of past years animated him. He rushed into the melee, and joined in the frolic in his fiftieth year, as if he had been but fifteen. He flung about his snowballs with no inconsiderable dexterity as well as rapidity. Then when the moment for delivering the address was come, the students being summoned, and he proceeding in the van, they entered the hall together. It was impossible to say who was most delighted in the scene, Campbell who had thus recalled a scene of perished years, or the youth, at the vivacity of their new lord rector, whose celebrity and office would seem to inspire formality and the gravest carriage.

His address was received most warmly. An anonymous writer said much later:

> We have had the most distinguished men of the day successively elected to the office of Rector ... I have heard all their addresses; but none of them came up to that of Thomas Campbell. Perhaps we were disposed to be enthusiastic, knowing that he was an old gownsman of our own; but, whatever the pre-disposition might have been, the streams of eloquence issued from him and carried us onward in admiration and applause until poetry itself poured on us like a whelming flood; a flood that carried the soul captive in its resistless power. To say we applauded, is to say nothing. We evinced every symptom of respect and admiration from the loftiest tribute, even our tears—drawn forth by his eloquent recollections of olden times—down to escorting him with boisterous noise along the public streets.

Another person who was present said:

> I had the exquisite gratification, yesterday, of witnessing the rapturous reception which Mr Campbell met with in the College Hall—crowded to excess. His address was elegant, and poetical in a high degree, and delivered with great ease and dignity. At one part of it, however, he seemed to be rather beating about, and searched his pockets for some memoranda, which he did not find. This was unfortunate for his audience, as his speech was very original; and taken altogether, he did, in my apprehension, great honour to his situation.

The Rector did admit that all had not been well during the speech. He wrote:

> It was spoken from notes, and not previously written out or got by heart ... I left my notes at home; and when I found out my mistake, I was ready to drop down with apprehension. But, strange to tell, at that alarming moment, a look and a nod from the Rev Dr MacG [Stevenson MacGill, professor of Divinity] on the bench beside me—the very man who had most violently opposed my election—recalled by some accidental association, the idea which should next follow! I got back the clue of association, and went through famously.

The pressure of the crowd at the installation was so great that a student's leg was broken and his health badly affected. The university authorities gave him £10 in compensation.

A round of dinners and other celebrations was held. One of his friends recorded that he dined with the *Senatus Academicus*. It was only the second time he had been in that particular room. The first time, he had appeared as a culprit before the Principal, for being one of a group of students who had broken the windows of the college church with stones.

The Rector and the Dean of Faculty were the "Visitors" who were the only people entitled to supervise and check what went on in the university. Campbell and the Dean, Sir John Connel, spent hours at their duties. They looked into finances. They heard reports from the professors and interviewed them. Campbell went round the buildings, listening to the lectures.

> They [the professors] even expressed their thanks to me [Campbell said] for not running away, like most of the Rectors, leaving their duties unfulfilled, and the Professors to be calumniated by the suspicions of the students.

He was far more active than most rectors of the nineteenth century.

The custom at that time was for the office to be filled for one year and for the holder to be re-appointed unopposed for the next year. No law said that the limit was two years, but for a long time that had been the practice. Campbell was re-elected unanimously in 1827 and was proposed for a third term in 1828. His opponent was Sir Walter Scott, a Tory. Two nations voted for each. The casting vote was in the hands of the vice-rector, Gavin Gibb, Professor of Hebrew and Semitic Languages who also managed at the same time to hold on to his post as minister of St Andrew's Church, Glasgow.

Gibb gave his casting vote for Sir Walter who was declared elected. A fine old academic row broke out. Several students said that the Vice-Rector's vote was not according to the statutes, took legal action, and sent word to the candidates about what was happening.

Sir Walter refused to take office. Feelings ran high among both the professors and the students. Campbell rushed from London to Glasgow to rally his men. Another election was held: Campbell versus Sir Michael Shaw Stewart, who had Tory sympathies. This time Campbell won three nations.

It was significant for several reasons. The Whigs had triumphed, and politics was confirmed as important in the rectorial system. The students had again defied the professors. And the students' representative, the Rector, had come strongly to their aid, not only in this matter but also in others. Campbell again made a conciliatory speech.

Campbell's third election triggered off a series of hostile actions by the Principal, some professors, and others. The Principal and others said the election was invalid because nobody had ever before held the post for three years. (In fact Sir John Maxwell of Pollok had held the post from 1691 to 1717).

Campbell replied that what had happened was not invalid. He said it was not contrary to the constitution and practice of the University, and the statutes contained nothing that forbade such a thing. Some students had protested to him but he said that the protests themselves were invalid. The

Principal and five professors said that Campbell did not live in Scotland and so could not carry out his duties. Campbell again rejected the arguments.

More was to come. One student, acting for a group opposed to Campbell, claimed that the third election was "in breach of a statute passed during the civil wars in Scotland," that many who voted were ineligible, and—again—that the election was not according to custom and thus invalid.

Another reason for the friction may be that the Scottish universities were at this time being investigated by a Royal Commission. The students were worried that their status and rights might be at risk, as they had been a few years before. Campbell was active in their defence. He said:

> At this crisis, it is of great moment, that, as the friend and advocate of the students, I should conciliate the Commissioners. After all, I fear my poor boys will get scant justice from the royal visitors. My consolation is, that I have done my best.

The system remained unchanged until an Act of Parliament of 1858.

# First English Politician elected by the Students

Lord Lansdowne (courtesy of the National Portrait Gallery)

*Marquis of Lansdowne, Whig statesman (1780-1863)*

*Elected 1829*

Lansdowne is significant. He was the first English political figure to be elected by the student body: Edmund Burke in 1783 was a different case because at that time the professors dominated the choice. Lansdowne has been described as "a true liberal in his love of tolerance." He was prominent in his party for more than 50 years. He was educated at Edinburgh and Cambridge Universities. At Edinburgh he was in the same classes as Palmerston, Cockburn, Brougham, and Jeffrey (all to be Rectors of Glasgow) and the wit Sydney Smith. He went into the House of Commons when he was 22 and became Chancellor of the Exchequer when he was 25. He inherited the peerage when he was 29. Lansdowne had a chance to become Prime Minister in 1852 and 1855 but declined. Lord John Russell said of him:

While honest as the purest virgin, Lansdowne was too yielding, too mild, and most unfit to deal with men in important political transactions.

His opponents for the rectorship were Lord Hope (Charles Hope), Lord President of the Court of Session since 1811, a strong Tory, and Lord Moncrieff (James Moncrieff), a judge of the Court of Session and a lay religious leader. Moncrieff opposed the appointment of ministers of the Kirk by wealthy patrons—the issue that eventually split the Kirk in 1843. One of the professors, a supporter of Hope, objected to the choice of Lansdowne because Lansdowne lived far from Glasgow and could not carry out the duties of his office.

Lansdowne went on to support the Reform Bill, public subsidy for education, relief for victims of the Irish famine, and free trade. He had such a long career and had so much experience that towards the end of his life he was consulted on many questions of State.

# Rector takes Office again
# by his own Vote

Lord Cockburn (Scottish National Portrait Gallery)

*Henry Cockburn, Whig statesman, reformer, advocate,
judge of the Court of Session, and talented author,
later Lord Cockburn. (1779-1854)*

## Elected 1831

Cockburn's tenure was marked by some curious goings-on. He voted
himself into another year of office. He intervened when the University
overspent on two professors' houses. He prevented a professor who
wanted to retire from naming his own successor.

Cockburn was a zealous reformer and became a leading figure in the
legal profession in Edinburgh along with Francis Jeffrey. He was one of
the Scottish Whigs who wrote for the *Edinburgh Review*. He kept his
Scottish accent and the common touch, which helped him a great deal
when arguing a case before a jury. When he was elected he had been
named Solicitor-General for Scotland in 1830 and took a large part in the

drafting of the Scottish Reform Bill. He was of less than average height and had a handsome and intellectual face.

He met Francis Jeffrey and Henry Brougham through a debating club when they were students at Edinburgh University. Their friendships were to be significant in Scottish and British affairs. He was called to the Scottish Bar in 1800; his career was advanced by his all-powerful uncle, Lord Melville (Henry Dundas), who held many high offices of state. Dundas was for decades the Government's "ruler" of Scotland through bribes, patronage, and influence. The Dundas family were Tory but Cockburn showed independence of mind and was dismissed from his offices in 1810. His Whiggism prevented his political advancement.

The Whigs nominated Cockburn, the Tories nominated John Gibson Lockhart who was an alumnus of the University, and the Independents nominated Joseph Hume. (The Independent Clubs were formed at some elections to nominate a candidate who was not from one of the main political parties but was a figure notable in the arts or literature. The Independent Clubs did not have a continuous existence.)

John Gibson Lockhart is remembered mainly for his biography of Sir Walter Scott, his father-in-law, but he wrote other biographies and was a novelist and critic. He was editor of *Blackwood's Magazine* and the *Quarterly Magazine*, rivals to the mighty *Edinburgh Review*. He savaged the Whigs.

Joseph Hume went to Glasgow University at the age of 11 and to Oxford University at 13, took a job in India as a surgeon with the East India Company and made a fortune there. On his return he became an MP (he sat in Parliament for about 38 years, speaking often and lengthily.) He was in favour of free trade, Catholic emancipation, economy in public spending, the abolition of flogging in the Army, and many other causes.

Cockburn captured two nations and the others one nation each. The votes were Cockburn 203, Hume 170, and Lockhart 150. Cockburn was re-elected unopposed for a second one-year term in 1832, as was the custom. He was nominated again in 1833 but ran into trouble.

He had an opponent in 1833: Sir Daniel Sandford, the Professor of Greek. The result was awkward. Cockburn with 175 votes won Loudoniana and Transforthana but Sandford with 153 votes also won two nations, Glottiana and Rothseiana.

The Vice-Rector, Robert Buchanan, Professor of Logic, refused to give a casting vote. The casting vote devolved upon Cockburn, as the preceding Rector, and he voted for himself. He declared that he would have voted his opponent into the office but said that Sir Daniel, being a professor, was ineligible. The Principal, six professors, and some students protested. The number of students protesting was notably small—21.

Cockburn intervened in the University's internal affairs, as he was entitled to do, but not many rectors had done that since the early eighteenth century. The professors at the time of Cockburn's tenure did pretty much as they liked. For example, it was not uncommon to hold a teaching post and at the same time be minister of one of the churches in the city. One job or the other was not going to be done properly. The professors gave themselves pay rises in 1803 and 1817, shortened the teaching session in 1811, put up the students' fees in 1818, paid their local property taxes out of the University's funds, had the power to keep their posts and their pay until they were very old while the work was done by assistants, and sometimes did not shrink from giving employment to their sons.

Certain of the professors were able to spend much of the University's income without supervision from outside; the only supervision from inside was by the "Visitors", who were the Rector and the Dean of Faculty. And the Dean of Faculty was given his job by the same people who controlled much of the spending. It was all ripe for abuse, even if the abuse was not grave.

When Cockburn was in office the Professor of Moral Philosophy, James Mylne, wanted to retire but said that he should be succeeded by Dr William Fleming, the Professor of Oriental Languages. Cockburn hotly opposed this unusual arrangement and Mylne stayed in place. Fleming did in the end get the job, but not until much later, when Mylne died in 1839.

Another curious arrangement was devised among the professors. Improvements were carried out to the houses of Robert Davidson, Professor of Law, and of Sandford. The faculty approved the spending of £287 on Davidson's house and £380 on Sandford's. The figures were exceeded. A total of £524 was spent on Davidson's and £827 on Sandford's. The Visitors wanted the two professors to make good the difference—£237 in Davidson's case and £447 in Sandford's. These were substantial amounts. A compromise was reached. Davidson paid £70 and Sandford £100.

Cockburn became a Lord of Session in 1834. He wrote a *Life of Jeffrey* (1832), *Memorials of His Time* (1856), and *Journal 1831-1844* (1874); these works include masterly pen-portraits of literary and legal figures.

# Aristocrat who Loved the Turf

*Lord Stanley, statesman, later 14th Earl of Derby (1799-1869).*
*He was Prime Minister several times in the 1850s and 1860s*

### Elected 1834

Stanley was, when the students chose him, a Whig, and he followed a line of Whigs. The Conservatives did not capture the post until the next election, in 1836, with Peel. But he was a Conservative when he was Prime Minister. The students may have been surprised at what happened to their former Rector but the man changed his political line quite often.

Stanley came from a family of great Lancashire magnates. He was charming and handsome, yet was a strange mixture of personalities. He could be grave, authoritative, impressive, and statesmanlike. He was an excellent Latin scholar and when he was Chancellor of Oxford University gave speeches in Latin that were the envy of many professional scholars. He wrote English in a clear and lively way.

In his leisure he was different. He loved racing. A commentator wrote that at leisure he:

> ... had no thoughts but for the turf, full of the horses, interest in the lottery, eager, blunt, noisy, good-humoured ... at night equally devoted to the play, as if his fortune depended on it.

In the betting room at Newmarket,

> ... he was in the midst of blacklegs,[*] betting men, and loose characters of every description, in uproarious spirits, chaffing, rowing, and shouting with laughter and joking. His amusement was to lay Lord Glasgow a wager that he did not sneeze in a given time, for which purpose [Glasgow] took pinch after pinch of snuff, while Stanley jeered him and quizzed him with such noise that he drew the whole mob around him to partake of the coarse merriment he excited.

But the author of this, the diarist Charles Greville, never liked nor trusted Derby.

Stanley entered Parliament as a Whig in his late twenties in 1828 and was promoted: to chief secretary for Ireland in 1830. He was instrumental in passing the Irish Education Act of 1833 which reformed the schools. He became colonial secretary in 1833 and carried through an Act to give more rights to slaves in British possessions in the West Indies and to help them towards freedom. He left the Whigs in 1834 over secularisation of the Church of Ireland's property. Firstly he sat as a independent and then as a Conservative. On his resignation he described the Whigs as "thimble-riggers at a country fair."

His opponent in the rectorial election was the first Earl of Durham, who came from an ancient family. Durham led a radical faction of the Whigs and wanted to be leader of the party. His colleagues found him hard to work with for he was ambitious and vain.

Stanley succeeded his father as Earl of Derby in 1851 and was Prime Minister in 1852, from 1858 to 1859, and from 1866 to 1868. It was during his last premiership that the Reform Bill of 1867 was passed. He was said, with wild exaggeration but some truth, to have abolished slavery, educated Ireland, and reformed parliament.

The writer Bulwer-Lytton described him as:

> The brilliant chief, irregularly great,
> Frank, haughty, rash—the Rupert of debate.

---

[*] Crooks who were in racing.

# City and University Honour
# a Great Man

Sir Robert Peel (Glasgow University Archives)

*Sir Robert Peel, Conservative statesman (1788-1850).*
*Prime Minister 1834-1835 and 1841-1846*

*Elected 1836*

Of Peel it has been said: "The promotion of the welfare of his countrymen was the absorbing passion of his life." He was one of the greatest Prime Ministers and held strong views but was not dogmatic in his opinions and was prepared to yield. Peel was unusually tall and had an aloof air but among friends was warm and amusing. He collected Old Master and British paintings and drawings. Many of them are now in the National Gallery, London.

He inherited a large fortune from a calico printing business founded by his grandfather and expanded by his father. He also inherited a baronetcy. He entered Parliament when he was 21. From 1812 to 1818 he was

Secretary for Ireland and showed strong anti-Catholic feeling: he was named "Orange" Peel.

He was Home Secretary almost continuously from 1822 to 1830 and has been called the greatest reforming Home Secretary ever. Peel instituted the London police force, called after him "Peelers" or "Bobbies," reformed prisons, abolished the death penalty for many offences, and carried through the Catholic Emancipation Act of 1828 in spite of his former stance.

He was Prime Minister from November 1834 to April 1835 but was replaced by a Whig, Lord Melbourne.

He was not told that he had been nominated for the office of Rector. His opponent was Sir John Campbell, the Attorney-General in the Whig Government of the day. Campbell was a Scot, self-made, and a son of the manse. Peel made an elegant tribute to the students for choosing an Englishman. Sir John Campbell was to become Lord Chief Justice and Lord Chancellor. Lord Brougham described him as one of the two greatest bores in London; the other was Thomas Babington Macaulay (Rector 1848-1850).

Glottiana, Loudoniana, and Rothseiana were for Sir Robert and Transforthana was for Sir John. The voting was: Sir Robert, 321; Sir John, 221.

Peel's election was an especial honour since Scotland tended to be Whiggish. To come for his installation and Address meant a journey of 400 miles in the depths of winter and on the eve of a parliamentary session. But he did not hesitate and indeed wrote to a friend:

> I feel that I have no alternative, that would be inconsistent with the advice I have given to others and my own feelings as to the state of public affairs, and the necessity of unremitting exertions on the behalf of all who wish to preserve a National Church, and the Constitution of their Country, if I were to damp the ardour of the academic youth of Scotland by a cold refusal of this distinction.

He refers to the preservation of the "National Church" because of the huge controversy that was to culminate in the Disruption of the Kirk in 1843.

His friend Sir James Graham, a politician who began as a Whig but who was to become Home Secretary under Peel, primed him about the subtleties of Scottish politics and sensibilities. Graham later wrote to Lord Stanley:

> Tho' this performance in Glasgow will be of the tight-rope description, yet our Bob may keep his legs there.

He had two speaking engagements in Glasgow: his Address to the University and at a grand dinner for the city's notables and others. It was the academic one that gave him most worry. He did not know much about students (he had left Oxford University a quarter of a century before, and he knew nothing about the red-gowned Scottish species).

Peel's installation was in the Common Hall of the University which was crowded "to excess." The rector took an oath that he would faithfully perform his duties. His Address followed and lasted an hour and ten minutes. He "appeared under the influence of a very strong emotion". And this speech was tricky because to be memorable was difficult and to be original was impossible.

Peel said in his Address to the students that

> ... the scheme of academical education in the universities of Scotland, modified as it has progressively been, by changes in the state of society, and by new demands for knowledge, is admirably adapted to meet the great end of all instruction.
>
> A boundless field of exertion lies before you—whatever be your pursuit—the avenues of distinction are wide open to you, or, at least, obstructed by no barrier of which you may not command the removal. (Great applause.) I say, that if any one of you will determine to be eminent, in whatever profession you may choose, and will act with untiring assiduity in the pursuit of that determination, if health and strength be given, you will be successful. (Loud cheering.)
>
> It is by tolerating habits of indolence and procrastination in matters that are apparently of little moment, of which the world takes no notice, that bad habits are acquired in matters of much weight.

A sumptuous dinner was given that night at the University, attended by the great and the good but not by any representative of the students. A banquet was held in his honour by Glasgow's civic leaders. The banquet was held in a specially constructed temporary hall of timber and tarpaulin because no public building was big enough: 3,430 people attended. No fewer than 37 toasts were scheduled to be given, although time ran out and not all were in fact given. (The event began at 5.05 pm and ended at 1.30 am.)

The toast to the students (who, said the person proposing it, had "done themselves honour by electing Sir Robert Peel") was replied to by Norman McLeod, a student of divinity who was to become a notable figure in the Kirk. He said that:

> ... he hoped the students would continue to heap additional honours upon themselves, by returning Conservative Lord Rectors. (Cheers.)

The guest of honour spoke for two hours, encouraged by cheers and other applause.

People at the top tables had turtle soup, venison, "and other delicacies of the season, French wines, etc." Other diners had cold dishes: "roasted and boiled beef, veal and mutton, turkeys, chickens, pigeon pies, hams, tongues, lobster, pastries, jellies etc."

"Everyone was pleased with the quality of the viands", wrote an observer, "and the quantity was abundant." The gentlemen who occupied the seats in the Gallery (no women were present) had sandwiches, fruit, and biscuits. Port and sherry were served to everyone, without limitation.

It is remarkable [wrote the same observer] that in such a large assembly of persons, there were not more than two or three individuals who could be said to have been injured by wine, and these left the meeting without the least disturbance.

Each ticket cost 25 shillings, equivalent to perhaps £75 now. The dinner made a profit of £451 11s 9d (about £22,600 now) which went to charity. Sir Robert added 200 guineas (£10,500 now).

The supporters of Peel at the university set up the Peel Club in 1836 to:

... testify their admiration of his character as a scholar and a statesman, and also their adherence to those great Constitutional principles on which national happiness so much depends.

The Peel Club became the Conservative Club. Peel gave the Peel Club a silver mace.

A speech at the inaugural meeting of the Club revealed that party feeling ran high and that the tenure of Thomas Campbell the poet and Whig from 1826 to 1829 was still rankling:

The election of Sir Robert Peel to the Rectorate was a death blow to the Whigs. (Cheers.) For many years they enjoyed the exclusive privilege of electing to this distinguished office, creatures of their own ... I would decidedly protest against their making, not scholarship, but Whiggism, the standard of all excellence ... They saw no beauty in the literature that emanated from other than Whig pens; there was neither philosophy, nor eloquence, nor poetry in the works that were not gilded by the pageantry of Whig principles.

The Peel Club dominated the election of the rectors for a few years but was hit by internal jealousies and by a shift in political opinion.

Peel was again to be Prime Minister, this time from 1841 to 1846. The general election of 1841 was really a contest over free trade and protection. The Whigs wanted a fixed but moderate tax on imported corn and the Tories wanted to keep the old system of tax. Were the landowners to receive high prices for their corn when the poorest did not have enough to eat? Protection won.

Peel's Government, however, brought in a series of Acts to allow greater freedom of trade. The Irish potato crop was devastated by a fungal disease in 1845 and Ireland began to suffer from famine. Peel put through legislation to reduce import taxes on corn. Repeal of the Corn Laws split the Conservative Party and Peel's Government fell soon afterwards. It had swept away a large number of indirect taxes and it had brought in a free market economy which transformed the finances of the country.

He said in his last speech as Prime Minister:

I shall leave a name execrated by every monopolist who ... clamours for protection because it accrues to his individual benefit; but it may be that I shall leave a name sometimes remembered with expressions of goodwill in the abodes of those whose lot it is to labour, and to earn their daily bread by the sweat of their brow, when they shall recruit their exhausted strength with abundant and untaxed food, the sweeter because it is no longer leavened by a sense of injustice.

He did not take office again but stayed an MP and spoke on important issues such as Ireland. The Peelites remained a force in politics.

Peel was riding on Constitution Hill, London, which runs from Hyde Park Corner along the side of Green Park, on 29 June 1850 when his horse became restive. He fell and was badly hurt. Lord Palmerston, one of the leaders of the Liberals, wrote:

> He was a very bad and awkward rider, and his horse might have been sat by any other equestrian; but he seems, somehow or other, to have been entangled in the bridle, and to have forced the horse to step or kneel upon him ... that which killed him was a broken rib, forced with great violence into the lungs.

The people went in thousands to show their love and respect for him. He died three days later in great pain. It was said he was prematurely cut off:

> ... before his strength had begun to fail or his mind to decline—a mighty soul lost to the world.

The French historian, diplomat, and politician Francois Guizot, who was for a time Ambassador to Britain, described him as:

> ... the most liberal of conservatives, the most conservative of liberals, and the most capable man of all in both parties.

He had built up the shattered Tories and had created a new party: the Conservative party.

# The Rector upsets his Audience during the Address

Sir James Graham (courtesy of the National Portrait Gallery)

*Sir James Graham, Whig statesman who drew close to the Conservatives (1792-1861)*

*Elected 1838*

In his public career between 1818 and 1861 Graham was one of the ablest members of three different Ministries. But an old college friend whom he later snubbed (as being beneath him) wrote: "I take vanity and self-sufficiency to be the prominent features of his character." His aloofness was a handicap to his career and led to political blunders. He was one of the people who were inflexible and insensitive during the events that led up to the Disruption of 1843, when the Church of Scotland split. The Disruption was a calamity that might have been avoided. Graham's Address to the students took an inflexible line on Church affairs that offended people present and he had a rough reception.

Graham, who was from Cumbria although his name looks Scottish, entered Parliament as a Whig, became First Lord of the Admiralty (when in that post he reformed the navy), and helped to draft the great Reform Bill of 1832. He resigned from his Government post in 1834 over reforms to the Irish Church, an issue that absorbed much parliamentary and general debate. He lost his parliamentary seat in Cumbria in 1837, which was a severe personal blow because local loyalties mattered a great deal there. He found another seat in 1838 but when he returned to Parliament he was an embittered man. By the time he was chosen by the students he had retreated from his position as an advanced reformer and indeed had drawn close to the Tories.

In 1843 the Church of Scotland went through the cataclysmic Disruption—it lost almost half of its ministers and members; they formed the Free Church of Scotland. The key issue was the right of some landowners to appoint ministers to parishes, whatever the wishes of the congregations. The dissidents believed that the landowners should not have that right.

Another grave matter was the right of the General Assembly of the Church of Scotland to erect new parish churches. That sometimes conflicted with the interests of the patrons. Evangelicals in the Church, who were gaining influence, said that the rights of patrons were interfering with the Church's obligation to meet the spiritual needs of the people.

The Government owned the rights to nominate the ministers in about a third of the parishes and these rights were valuable. For 10 years the debate went on, but few Englishmen understood the history of the Kirk and the feelings of the Scots.

The Conservative Prime Minister, Sir Robert Peel, and Graham, his Home Secretary, were at a vital period inflexible towards the efforts of the General Assembly to change the system. Graham opposed any concession which offended "the principles which ought to govern the Established Church." He said that the Conservatives would not allow patronage to be transferred to "a variable and irresponsible multitude." The Free Church's adherents took revenge on the Conservatives: for decades afterwards the burghs were Liberal strongholds.

Graham's rival for the rectorship was Augustus Frederick, Duke of Sussex, a son of George III, an eccentric, and a person who loved literature and scientific institutions. His political views were liberal. That estranged him from his father and for that reason he could not obtain well-paid jobs like his brothers. He was in favour of removing the civil disabilities of Roman Catholics, Jews and dissenters, abolishing the corn laws, reforming Parliament, and banning the slave trade. He collected books and had more than 1,000 editions of the Bible.

The future Poet Laureate, Wordsworth, was asked to stand. He felt unable to take the post, but wrote to his co-sponsors about:

... the satisfaction which I have derived from this occurence as an evidence of the sense entertained among the Students in your University of the importance of imaginative Literature. A right undersanding upon the subject, and a just feeling is at all times momentous, but especially so in the present state of society, and the opinions now so prevalent respecting the relative values of intellectual pursuits.

The result of the election—Graham 275 votes, Sussex 209—pleased Graham immensely. He wrote to a friend:

I defeated the Duke of Sussex by a considerable majority ... If this can be taken as an index of the feeling of the middle classes in Scotland, it is very consolatory. At all events it is a proof that the rising youth entertains sound and decided principles; and when they prefer a country gentleman to the Queen's favoured uncle, they rescue their countrymen from the charge of time-serving sycophancy and of interested calculation.

Trouble was to emerge when Graham delivered his Address in December 1838. He had told his supporters in the University his views about the relations between Church and State. He was warned not to touch on the matter in his Address but went ahead anyway. He spoke at first on classical and scientific education and on the merits of students spending their time prudently.

A sceptical observer wrote:

His address, which was prepared with punctilious care, and which was not wanting in skilful adaptation to the tastes and feelings of the audience, hardly realized perhaps their expectations, and was in no way calculated to raise his character for didactic composition. In the main it kept the well-worn track, which so many of his distinguished predecessors had trodden, in eulogy of classic and scientific pursuits, and in admonition to economize youthful time. But these things could not be said better than they had been said before; and a lay sermon on collegiate virtue is at best hard to listen to with any outward semblance of enthusiasm.

Sentence after sentence rolled musically along, tingling with exquisite quotation, and seeming to challenge from the most fastidious critic the discovery of a fault. But few attempts were made to raise a cheer, and none could be said to be successful ... Trained as he had been in the school of rhetoric, where interjaculation by the hearers forms a constant and necessary part of the performance, he had grown more dependent upon it than he was perhaps himself aware; and when it failed, he failed also.

He then spoke of the benefit of an indissoluble connection between Church and State.

Whereupon, to his no small astonishment, an uproar arose, in which vehement applause was mingled with equally vehement groans; and discordant cries of disapprobation were but partially drowned by Kentish fire.[*]

Not much of the Address remained to be given but in any case Graham cut short what he had to say.

---

[*] Kentish fire is "a prolonged and ordered salvo or volley of applause, or demonstration of impatience or dissent, said to have originated in reference to meetings held in Kent in 1828-1829, in opposition to the Catholic Relief Bill."

It is notable that he preserved letters of congratulation from his friends and allies. It seems that his friends, after his rough reception during the Address, felt they had to rally round him.

Graham had other appearances in Glasgow at this time—he was for example awarded the freedom of the city. Sir Robert Peel, his predecessor as Rector, wrote:

> I watched your progress in Glasgow, and rejoiced in your complete success, with a double interest and satisfaction, both from my recent connection with the University, and from the sincere pleasure which any event redounding to your honour and reputation must give me as an attached friend. Nothing could be more judicious than the course you pursued, more able than the addresses, literary and political, you were called upon to deliver, more cordial and gratifying than your reception.

Graham wrote afterwards:

> None but Scotch Reporters were present, and it was clear that they did not yet understand English, when spoken without the drone of a bagpipe.

The custom was for a second one-year term to be a formality. But in this case, discontent with the Rector was shown. Graham was opposed, by Sir John Herschel, one of the leading astronomers of the nineteenth century and a pioneer of photography. Graham won again.

Graham became Home Secretary under the Tory Government in 1841. He was later to become one of the schismatic Peelites and supported the removal of tax on imported corn. He became leader of the Peelites when Peel died in 1850 and was again First Lord of the Admiralty from 1852 to 1855.

Queen Victoria was supposed to have hated Graham but Graham said that he and other ministers got on very well with her. He said they treated her with profound respect and the greatest attention. He made it a rule to address her as a sensible man, laying all matter before her, with the reasons for the advice he tendered, and he thought this was the most legitimate as well as judicious flattery that could be offered to her, and the more because there was no appearance of flattery in it, and nothing but what was fit and proper.

# Free Church Supporter

Marquess of Beadalbane (Glasgow University Library)

*Marquess of Breadalbane, wealthy landowner
and Liberal MP (1796-1862)*

*Elected 1840*

He was the ablest lay person to support those who were to form the Free
Church of Scotland in 1843. He was also a munificent donor to the Free
Church. Indeed, the photograph of which a detail is reproduced above also
features a number of notables concerned in the Disruption. Queen Victoria
visited him at his mansion, Taymouth Castle, in 1840. She held a review of
Scottish volunteer soldiers in 1860 and Breadalbane was there at the head
of 500 of his clansmen.

# Ex-Spendthrift and another Free Church Supporter

Fox Maule (courtesy of the National Portrait Gallery)

*Fox Maule, later Lord Panmure and still later Earl of Dalhousie (1801-1874)*

*Elected 1842*

Defeating Lord Bute in 1842, Fox-Maule was re-elected in 1843, defeating Lord Eglinton. Maule was a spendthrift in his youth. He was in the army for 12 years and was a Liberal MP from 1837 until he inherited a peerage in 1842. He supported the Free Church when it was formed in 1843, one of the few Scottish noblemen to do so. He was Secretary for War (1846-52, and 1855) and held other offices of state.

His given name may be from Charles James Fox, the eighteenth-century Whig leader who was a close friend of his father.

# Scottish University Reformer

Lord Rutherfurd (Scottish National Portrait Gallery)

*Andrew Rutherfurd, later Lord Rutherfurd,*
*Whig, lawyer and judge (1791-1854)*

*Elected 1844*

Rutherfurd's legal talents were highly thought of by his colleagues and contemporaries. He became an MP in 1839 and served as Lord Advocate. He played a part in the great debate before the Disruption of 1843, calling for reform. Rutherfurd sponsored important legislation to reform Scots law and to amend outmoded rules in the Scottish universities.

His opponent for Rector was Lord Eglinton (see page 48). Rutherfurd won three nations. He:

... made a judicious and pleasant Address, in his style of pure and elevated thoughts and finished expression.

After his election he went on to carry through more legislation to reform Scots law and became a judge of the Court of Session in 1851.

In private life he was a delightful companion, but in public life he incurred unpopularity owing to his unconciliatory and somewhat haughty demeanour.

# A Great Man is Chosen
# but is too Grand to Turn Up

Lord John Russell (Hunterian Art Gallery)

*Lord John Russell, Liberal statesman and reformer*
*(1792-1878). He was Prime Minister from 1846 to 1852 and*
*from 1865 to 1866. He became Earl Russell in 1861*

*Elected 1846*

This was one of the least satisfactory elections. The winner was ungracious to his constituents. The loser was a great literary figure.

Russell was a son of the Duke of Bedford and studied at Edinburgh University. He entered Parliament in his early twenties. His strenuous efforts for reform won the Whigs many seats in the general election of 1830. Wellington, the Prime Minister, was driven from office. Earl Grey became Prime Minister and gave Russell and three others the task of framing the first Reform Bill, which was a step towards a democratic system of parliamentary elections. He held important offices between 1835 and 1846.

His rival for rectorship was William Wordsworth, who had been Poet Laureate since 1843 but had long passed the peak of his powers. Wordsworth was one of many distinguished writers and scientists who were rejected by the student electorate in favour of politicians. He was nominated by the Peel Club as the Conservative candidate. He was at first reluctant—he had refused to stand in 1838—and wrote to the secretary of the Wordsworth Committee:

> Whether I consider the distinguished place which the University of Glasgow has always had in general estimation, or recal to mind the number of eminent Persons who have filled the Office of Lord Rector, I must needs regards the proposal made to me of allowing myself to be named as a Candidate for the forthcoming Election as a high Honor; and one which would have been received with unmingled pleasure had circumstances permitted me ...
>
> Allow me to conclude with the expression of a hope, that my inability to comply with the request of your Committee will in no way obstruct or interfere with the salutary or benign influence my humble endeavours in literature may have upon the understandings and affections of the Students who have thought of me at this time as worthy to be placed in so conspicuous a Station.

His nomination went ahead anyway.

Russell wrote during the contest that he "should be very sorry to be the cause of preventing the election of Mr Wordworth" and "I think this would be a good opportunity to make the distinction purely literary. It is a great honour to be thought of for the honour, but I should greatly prefer seeing it conferred on Mr Wordsworth, whose genius has performed so much in which men of all political parties find delight". Russell was perhaps being less than candid: his subsequent behaviour seems to suggest that he simply did not want the rectorship.

Two nations, including the biggest, Glottiana, voted for Wordsworth and the other two for Russell. The casting vote was with the vice-rector, John Nichol, professor of astronomy. Wordsworth was relieved, and wrote to a friend:

> I should have much disliked being compelled to go to Glasgow,[*] and above all being obliged to make an exhibition of myself, and to stumble through a speech, a work in which I have no experience whatever.

Russell was invited to be installed and give his Address in October or in November the next year, but said he was too busy to appear. The Irish were disaffected, the Chartists were stirring unrest, and revolutions in Europe were brewing.

He was not warm to his acquaintances. His own father told him that he gave great offence to his followers in the House of Commons:

> ... by not being courteous to them, by treating them superciliously, and de haut en bas, by not listening with sufficient patience to their solicitations or remonstrances.

---

[*] He was 76 years old

Russell's refusal to appear at the University gave offence to the Conservative students, who at the next election—in the November of 1847—put up William Mure of Caldwell, a local figure. The Liberal students put up Lord John again, but they were lukewarm in supporting their own man. Russell lost.

The system of annual elections may appear cumbersome, and indeed it was abandoned in 1859, but at least it gave a chance for an unsatisfactory Rector like Russell to be got rid of.

The students tended at this period to be more "liberal" or Whiggish than the professors; but sometimes, having demonstrated their preference for one party, they tended to swing in the opposite direction. Sir Robert Peel was a Conservative; after Peel it was perhaps appropriate that the honour fell on Russell the Whig.

Russell was Prime Minister from 1846 to 1852 and in 1865. He held other high offices at various times in his career: Colonial Secretary, Leader of the House of Commons, and Foreign Secretary. He became unpopular over an inopportune Reform Bill in 1854, the alleged mismanagement of the Crimean War, and other issues..

He was the last person before Tony Blair to sire a child when Prime Minister.

# Stop Gap Rector following in Father's Footsteps

William Mure (Glasgow University Archives)

*William Mure of Caldwell, landowner, was a classical scholar,
and colonel of the Renfrewshire militia (1799-1860)*

## Elected 1847

Mure was a stop-gap Rector elected to replace the unsatisfactory Lord
John Russell. Mure was a Member of Parliament from 1846 to 1855, for
the Conservatives, but spoke in the House very little. He wrote on ancient
Egypt, Spanish literature, and—especially—the language and literature of
ancient Greece. He was described as of "commanding presence, winning
manners, and kindly disposition." Mure's father had been Rector in 1793-
1794.

# Great Man's Terror
# about his Address to Students

Lord Macaulay (Hunterian Art Gallery)

*Thomas Babington Macaulay, historian, writer of verse, literary critic, Whig politician, lawyer, and civil servant; later Lord Macaulay (1800-1859)*

*Elected 1848*

Macaulay wrote for the *Edinburgh Review* for 20 years, was the author of such favourite poems as "How Horatius Kept the Bridge", and produced the resoundingly popular *History of England from the Accession of James II*. His writing is magnificent: magisterial, powerful, sonorous, yet lively and gripping. He takes a theme and plays variations on it. His sentences, when long, are constructed with a sure and elegant touch.

But his public speaking was not very good and his social manners were awkward. He was short and fat and with a round, plump face.

Not a ray of intellect beams from his countenance; a lump of more ordinary clay never enclosed a powerful mind and lively imagination.

He could pour forth immense quantities of knowledge on the most important or the most obscure subjects yet he did not allow for the interests of his listeners. The wit Sydney Smith once called him a book in breeches. Macaulay was at a dinner party when the talk came round to Sir Thomas Munro, a soldier who became governor of Madras and was one of the architects of British power in India. Macaulay spoke at length on the subject. The beautiful and autocratic Lady Holland, whose *salon* was attended by the greatest wits and statesmen, interrupted him and said she was tired of Sir Thomas Munro.

Macaulay later in the dinner party spoke about a sermon of St Chrysostom until Lady Holland told him she was tired of that subject too. She tried to stump him and mock him by saying: "Pray, Macaulay, what is the origin of a *doll?* When were dolls first mentioned in history?" Whereupon he started on a learned disquisition on dolls in Roman times. Again, he was cut short.

He had by heart all of Milton, Demosthenes and the New Testament in Greek, and much of the Bible in English. He had the gift of recalling at will passages from books he had read. Lord Melbourne (Prime Minister 1835-1841) said: "I wish I was as cocksure of anything as Tom Macaulay is of everything."

He was ready to demolish received ideas. Highland dress, tartans, and the bagpipes became fashionable during the late eighteenth century and the early nineteenth. George IV visited Edinburgh in 1822 and was dressed for public appearances in kilt, plaid, bonnet, and tartan coat. Macaulay said it was incredible that the monarch should show respect for the Scottish nation by:

... disguising himself in what, before the Union [of the Parliaments] was considered by nine Scotchmen out of ten as the dress of a thief.

His nephew and biographer Sir George Otto Trevelyan wrote that Macaulay dreaded the ceremony of his installation:

... one of those occasions which are the special terror of an orator, when much is expected, and everything has been well said many times before.

His year of office fortunately chanced to be the fourth centenary of the body over which he had been chosen to preside; and he contrived to give point and novelty to his inaugural Address by framing it into a retrospect of the history and condition of the University.

Macaulay wrote in his diary:

It is strange, even to myself, to find how the horror of public exhibitions grows on me. Having made my way in the world by haranguing, I am now as unwilling to make a speech as any timid stammerer in Great Britain.

His Address began with a translation into formal language for this occasion the thoughts he put in ordinary language for his diary.

I do not think it strange that when that great master of eloquence, Edmund Burke, stood where I now stand, he faltered and remained mute. Doubtless the multitude of thoughts which rushed into his mind was such as even he could not easily arrange or express. In truth there few spectacles more striking or affecting than that which a great historical place of education presents on a solemn public day. There is something strangely interesting in the contrast between the venerable antiquity of the body and the fresh and ardent youth of the great majority of the members.

He went on to his historical survey.

Perhaps it may be doubted whether, since the Christian era, there has been any point of time more important to the highest interest of mankind than that at which the existence of your University commenced. It was at the moment of a great destruction and of a great creation.

He spoke of the fall of the Byzantine Empire in 1453—the University, he said:

came into existence just in time to see the last traces of the Roman empire disappear, and to see the earliest printed book.

At this juncture, a juncture of unrivalled interest in the history of letters, a man, never to be mentioned without reverence by every lover of letters, held the highest place in Europe. ... the founder of the University of Glasgow, the greatest of the restorers of learning, Pope Nicholas the Fifth.

Nicholas

... gave his sanction to the plan of establishing a University of Glasgow, and bestowed on the new seat of learning all the privileges which belonged to the University of Bologna. I can conceive that a pitying smile passed over his face as he named Bologna and Glasgow together. At Bologna he had long studied. No spot in the world had been more favoured by nature or by art. The surrounding country was a fruitful and sunny country, a country of corn fields and vineyards ...

Glasgow he just knew to be a poor, a small, a rude town, as he would have thought, not likely ever to be great and opulent; for the soil, compared with the rich country at the foot of the Apennines, was barren, and the climate was such that an Italian shuddered at the thought of it.

But it is not on the fertility of the soil, it is not on the mildness of the atmosphere, that the prosperity of nations chiefly depends. Slavery and superstition can make Campagna a land of beggars ... Nor is it beyond the power of human intelligence and energy, developed by civil and spiritual freedom, to turn sterile rocks and pestilential marshes into cities and gardens.

He ended by saying:

I assure that, while I live, I shall never cease to take a deep interest in the welfare and fame of the body with which, by your kindness, I have this day become connected.

He recorded: "The acclamation was prodigious."

He still had to face the ordeal of being presented with the freedom of the city. He wrote in his diary:

I had broken rest, partly from the effect of the bustle which was over, and partly from apprehension of the bustle to come. I turned over a few sentences in my head, but was very ill-satisfied with them ... I felt like a man going to be hanged; and, as such a man generally does, plucked up enough courage to behave with decency. We went to the City Hall, which is a fine room, and was crowded as full as it could hold. Nothing but huzzaing and clapping of hands. The Provost presented me with a handsome box, silver gilt, containing the freedom of the City, and made a very fair speech on the occasion. I returned thanks with sincere emotion, and, I hope, with propriety. What I said was very well received, and I was vehemently applauded at the close.

The University has, most regrettably, very few portraits in oil or marble of its former Rectors. One of the portraits it does have is Macaulay's, in an unusual way. A print-seller and publisher in Princes Street, Edinburgh, called James Keith, persuaded the Principal and professors to ask Macaulay to sit for the portrait; Keith would pay for it and give it to the University, There was a condition—Keith was the keep the portrait for a while, so that an engraving could be made of it. Keith's aim was to market engraved copies as a commercial enterprise. The portrait was done, by Sir John Watson Gordon, who was, after the death of Sir Henry Raeburn, the leading Scottish portrait painter. Macaulay was a proud, independent man. It is unlikely that he would have agreed to sit if he had known all about what was going on.

# Pro-Slavery Historian of Europe

Sir Archibald Alison (courtesy of the National Portrait Gallery)

*Archibald Alison, lawyer and historian (1792-1867)*

*Elected 1850*

Alison's opponent was Lord Palmerston, who had been three times Foreign Secretary and was to be Prime Minister.

This was, as usual, a political election: Alison was of Conservative leanings. He was born in England, the son of a Scottish minister, and was brought up in Edinburgh. He became Sheriff of Lanarkshire at a large salary and settled in Glasgow where he became popular. Alison wrote a History of Europe that sold in huge numbers. He also wrote for political and literary reviews. Alison was against the spread of democracy, opposed the northern States of the United States in the Civil War, and believed that slavery was necessary. Alison's happy marriage:

... detached his mind from dangerous excitements [and] delivered him from the dangers incidental to a disposition which led him in a peculiar manner to prize the society of elegant and superior women.

He became a baronet in 1852. His funeral in Glasgow was attended by between 100,000 and 150,000 people.

# Sportsman, Aristocrat, and Romantic

Lord Eglinton (Hunterian Art Gallery)

## Lord Eglinton, landowner and
## Conservative statesman (1812-1861)

### Elected 1852

Eglinton was immensely popular, especially in Scotland. He was high-minded, frank and genial in his manners, athletic, and cheerful. He was generous—by the time of his death he had gone through great wealth and did not have much left. His horses won the St Leger twice and the Derby once. He was twice Lord Lieutenant of Ireland, and kept court there in princely style.

He was famous for putting on the "Eglinton Tournament", a most extra-ordinary event.

The tournament, which was held in 1839, was a manifestation of a craze for Gothic architecture, the stories of King Arthur, Scott's *Ivanhoe,* the Age of Chivalry, the revival of heraldry, and the Middle Ages in general. Lord Eglinton decreed that a tournament with knights, ladies, and jousting would be held at Eglinton Castle, his neo-Gothic mansion in Ayrshire. A medieval banquet would be held too. The idea caught the imagination of the age. His friends bought costumes, arms, and armour, or had them made. The ladies had dresses specially designed. Family jewels were produced. Grandstands were put up, with cloth of gold and crimson damask.

The public was enthusiastic. Demand for tickets was enormous. Tens of thousands of people made their way to Eglinton Castle, by boat, train, horse, and foot. The transport system collapsed: the 30-mile highway between Glasgow and Ayr was blocked solid. Hotels and inns could not cope and people went hungry and without shelter. And it poured and poured. The event was a washout. Costumes were ruined, the jousting was a farce, everyone was miserable. Spectators in their thousand found that getting away was even harder than getting there. The romantic affair, so eagerly looked forward to, was a disaster. It cost Lord Eglinton, it has been estimated, the enormous sum of £30,000 to £40,000. The event was remembered for a long time but Eglinton kept a stiff upper lip.

Eglinton had stood for the rectorship in 1843 and 1844, being defeated by Fox Maule and Andrew Rutherfurd, both Whigs. This time his opponent was the Duke of Argyll, also a Whig, who was to be returned in 1854.

Eglinton was opposed for his second year of office, although the convention was that a Rector was returned unopposed for a second year. Tennyson, who had been Poet Laureate for two years, was put forward by the Liberal Club. The Liberals were trying to unseat the Conservatives' man. The nations were tied. Eglinton refused to vote for himself (although that had been done in the past) and the Vice-Rector, Professor Harry Rainy of Forensic Medicine, followed his own political beliefs and gave the casting vote for Eglinton.

# Radical Duke

*Duke of Argyll, Liberal statesman, nicknamed the Radical Duke (1823-1900)*

## Elected 1854

Argyll, a good orator, held Ministerial office almost continuously from 1853 to 1874 and again in 1880-1881. Many of his posts were minor ones, but he was Secretary of State for India for six years. He was especially interested in foreign affairs and Ireland. He also wrote on scientific subjects, especially geology and evolution, and on religion and politics. On science and evolution his beliefs were old-fashioned. Argyll's contemporary Gladstone overshadowed him. He also lacked a businesslike drive.

In the rectorial election both the Liberal and the Conservative clubs agreed at first to support the Duke but the Conservatives later nominated Benjamin Disraeli. Some Liberals wanted Thomas Carlyle, the historian, on the grounds that a literary figure should be chosen rather than a politician. The political clubs violently opposed Carlyle and his name was withdrawn the night before the election. The Duke of Argyll won all the nations.

# Literary Figure who is now Forgotten

Sir Edward Bulwer-Lytton (Glasgow University Archives)

*Sir Edward Bulwer-Lytton, novelist, poet, dramatist, historian, essayist, journalist, and M.P. (1803-1873).*
*He became the first Baron Lytton in 1866*

*Elected 1856*

Bulwer-Lytton was in his youth a good boxer, rider, and fencer. His literary output was enormous. An edition of his novels ran to 40 volumes and his poems and plays to five volumes. His works were hugely popular but almost all have been forgotten. The ones that are remembered include the novels *The Last Days of Pompeii* and *Eugene Aram.* A production of his play *Money* was put on at the National Theatre, London, in 1999 with success. He married an Irish beauty, Rosina Wheeler, in 1827 against his mother's wishes. His wife was to suffer from monomania about his treatment of her and indeed he was neglectful and irritable. He inherited Knebworth House, Hertfordshire, from his mother. He was a Liberal MP from 1831 to 1841 and a Conservative MP from 1852.

The Liberal Club nominated Lord Stanley, who was a Conservative but shared many opinions with the moderate Whigs and was to join the Liberal party. Lytton was nominated by the Conservatives as a literary figure although he was also a Conservative MP. The Liberals had fun with this. They pointed out that the Conservatives, in 1853, had opposed the Liberals' man, Tennyson, because he was a literary figure and they were now claiming support for their man as a literary figure.

He was re-elected unopposed in 1857 but was opposed in 1858 by the Earl of Shaftesbury, philanthropist and social reformer, and by Charles Dickens, who was at the height of his fame. Lytton won.

After the installation, one of the professors, John Ferguson of Chemistry, said:

> The rector ... was a striking personage, with a curled moustache, and a pointed beard, dressed in the gold-braided rectorial gown he looked not unlike the mystic or Rosicrucian he affected to be.

His son became the first Earl of Lytton and was also to be Rector.

# A National Hero

Lord Elgin (courtesy of the National Portrait Gallery)

## *Lord Elgin, Liberal statesman and colonial administrator (1811-1863)*

### *Elected 1859*

Elgin was an accomplished diplomat and a vigorous administrator. His father was the "rescuer" of the Elgin Marbles. He began life as an MP but was appointed Governor of Jamaica (1842-1846) and Governor-General of Canada (1847-1854). Elgin did well in both jobs. He was going to be the plenipotentiary or ambassador to China and was on his way there in 1857 when he heard that the Indian Mutiny, or first war of independence, had broken out. Elgin had reached Singapore at that point. He diverted his troops to India and delayed his mission to China. When he did reach China he concluded with the Emperor the Treaty of Tientsin (1858) and also negotiated a treaty with Japan for freer trade with Britain and the freer admission of foreigners.

China made treaties at the same time with France, Russia, and the United States. The Chinese agreed to allow the importation of more foreign goods, including opium. This marked the zenith of Western exploitation of the country. China the next year resisted the terms of the treaties. Several thousand British and French troops occupied Peking (Beijing). They destroyed the gorgeous Summer Palace there (in Chinese, Yuanmingyuan, or Garden of Perfect Brightness). This was in reprisal for the Chinese murdering several British subjects, including the correspondent of the *Times*.

Britain's man on the spot was Elgin. It was extraordinary that Elgin was associated with the tragic loss of the palace while his father was the "rescuer" of the marbles from the Parthenon.

Elgin, when he became Rector, in 1859, was a celebrity. Lord Derby and Lord Grey, from opposite sides of the political divide, sang his praises. The Prime Minister, Palmerston, had appointed him to the Cabinet although in a minor post. One of his biographers, Sydney Checkland, wrote:

> In the popular mind he had saved India and humbled China and Japan, carrying British power to the farthest corners of the world. to confront ancient civilisations ... for many he was a hero enabling Britain to fulfil her destiny.

Lord Elgin was supported in the election by the Liberals and the Independents, who said:

> He is a Burgess of the City of Glasgow, a beloved Scotch noblemen, a lineal descendant of 'The Bruce of Bannockburn,' and one who has ever distinguished himself in the cause of University Reform.

The Conservatives put up Benjamin Disraeli, who at that time was an eminent politician and writer but whose Prime Ministership was in the future. One brilliant student speaker, Radolphus Abercrombie, destroyed Disraeli's cause. It was said of him:

> No report could reproduce the verve and sparkle of Abercrombie's oratory. His face, his gestures, his voice commanded attention. The feelings of the audience were raised to an extraordinary degree, all his hits went home, and the effect had not time to evaporate before the election.

Elgin's margin was 553 votes to 411. His charm, fame and ability do not seem to have been the only important factors. The *Morning Herald* spoke of Elgin as "one of the regular Whig team" and the *Glasgow Herald* said: "doubtless his [Elgin's] political creed stood him in good stead in a community which goes a long way in the Liberal direction." One factor that is hard to quantify was anti-Semitic feeling. The Elgin supporters produced some verses which ran in part:

> Awa wi' your Jewish beerdie (i.e. beard.)

And:

> We'll hae nane o' your Wandering Jews,
> Thou wee bit Jewish lairdie.

The students who ran Elgin's campaign wanted him to pay the expenses they had run up. It is not known if he did or not. His Address was described as interesting and instructive and quietly delivered, but not a flight of oratory.

Elgin was again in China in 1860 to enforce the treaty. His last posting, in 1861, was as Viceroy and Governor-General of India. The Viceroy went travelling round his dominions in 1863. When he was in the Himalayas he had to cross a bridge made of birch branches, much battered by the rainy season. The physical exertion and the high altitude affected his heart and he died at Dharmsala, a hill town, on the way back. Dharmsala is now where the Dalai Lama has his headquarters.

# Eminent Statesman
# turns out to be Unsatisfactory

Lord Palmerston (Glasgow University Archives)

*Lord Palmerston, Whig statesman (1784-1865). He was Prime Minister almost continuously from 1855 to his death*

## Elected 1862

Palmerston was rude to the students. He made an unsatisfactory Address. Under the old system he might have been ousted after one year. Instead, under a new rule he served for three years. But at the next election the man he had defeated was chosen as Rector.

Palmerston's interests were politics, field sports, and women. He was an MP for 58 years, and a Minister for 48 of them. He was Foreign Secretary for nearly 16 years and Prime Minister for nine and a half. He started his parliamentary career as a Tory and was Secretary at War from 1809 to 1828. He joined the Whigs in 1830 and was three times Foreign Secretary between 1830 and 1851. These were the years of Britain's greatness abroad. His foreign policy was frequently xenophobic, which won him huge popular support at home. The Royal Navy ruled the waves. He seemed to hold the world in his hands.

He fought against the slave trade all his life and was a champion of liberal movements in Europe. He prosecuted the later stages of the Crimean War with vigour. Palmerston intervened in the affairs of most European countries and in many corners of the globe, using gunboat diplomacy. Palmerston also passionately desired peace and his more daring actions were to preserve peace. He was a conservative at home and a liberal abroad. In politics he was always a Palmerstonian.

Palmerston's brusque speech, assertive manner, and robust defence of what he saw as British interests abroad brought him the nicknames "Pumicestone" and "Firebrand Palmerston." And his love affairs brought him the nickname "Lord Cupid."

His affairs with women were innumerable, although their extent is not fully known because he and his mistresses destroyed love letters and other evidence. Among his mistresses were Lady Cowper, Princess Lieven, and Lady Jersey, who were dictators of society and promiscuous; Princess Lieven was also a skilful intriguer in politics and diplomacy: she was Russian and was married to the Russian ambassador.

Palmerston was staying at Windsor Castle with the Queen in the late 1830s when he was Foreign Secretary. One of his mistresses was staying there too. He went in search of her late at night and went into the room where she usually slept. She was however elsewhere and another woman was there. Prince Albert later alleged that:

> ... while a guest under her [the Queen's] roof ... he had committed a brutal attack upon one of her ladies in waiting, had at night by stealth, introduced himself into her apartment, barricaded afterwards the door and would have consummated his fiendish scheme by violence had not the miraculous efforts of his victim and assistance attracted by her screams saved her.

This letter was, however, written in 1850, long after the incident, and at a time when the Queen and Palmerston, again Foreign Secretary, were having one of their quarrels.

His opponent at Glasgow was John Inglis, the Lord Justice Clerk, who was of Conservative leanings. Palmerston won three nations. Here the inadequacy of the system is shown again, for the voting showed a quite different pattern: Palmerston 556, Inglis 474.

Palmerston did not behave well in the matter of the rectorial—but he was careless of other people's feelings. He sent a telegraph the day before the poll saying that if he was elected he would not accept office. It was too late to re-arrange the nominations and the election. The voting went ahead. But when he won he sent a letter of thanks, which was reproduced and sent around the students.

When he went to Glasgow for his installation and Address he was cheered by great crowds and sailed down the Clyde on a new steamer. People packed the banks on both sides of the river.

The Address was a failure. One person who was present, and who later became a distinguished historian, wrote that the Address was "perhaps the worst ever delivered on such an occasion". Palmerston was unprepared and had not even taken the trouble to find out the nature of the post or the kind of audience he had.

> He rambled on in the limping style of the House of Commons, each sentence beginning 'Gentlemen,' for fully an hour in the hope that an idea would present itself to him, but none came and when baffled he sat down. I was in the front row, immediately opposite the Duke of Argyll, whose face presented a curious appearance as the inept utterances of his parliamentary colleague fell upon his ears.

This performance was surprising because Palmerston had been a student at Edinburgh University for a year (he later went to Cambridge University) and represented Edinburgh in Parliament for 20 years. But those experiences were long in the past.

A story is told about Rugeley, Staffordshire, which became famous as the home of a notorious poisoner called William Palmer, who was hanged. The citizens of Rugeley hated to be reminded of the connection and wanted to change the name of their town. They asked the Prime Minister for permission. He replied that they could change the name but they would have to call the town after him. Or so the story goes.

Another story goes that Palmerston died on a billiard table when in the arms of a maid at Brocket in Hertfordshire, a mansion which his wife had inherited. His principal biographer gives a completely different account of his death. But it is significant that such stories were linked with him in the popular mind.

# Brilliant Defence in a *Cause célèbre*

Lord Glencorse (Glasgow University Archives)

*Lord Glencorse (John Inglis), lawyer and judge,*
*of Conservative leanings (1810-1891)*

*Elected 1865*

Inglis established his reputation as a lawyer by his brilliant defence in 1857 of Madeleine Smith, accused of poisoning her former lover, Pierre Émile L'Angelier, from Jersey, Channel Islands. She had become engaged to a wealthier man and had bought arsenic three times. Her passionate love letters to L'Angelier were published during the trial. The verdict was "not proven". Inglis was successively Solicitor-General for Scotland, Lord Advocate, Dean of the Faculty of Advocates, Lord Justice-Clerk (1858) and Lord President of the Court of Session (1867). Many of his legal judgements are classics. He was one of the people who helped to draft the reforming Universities of Scotland Act of 1858 and he took a close interest in Scottish university affairs afterwards. He loved golf and was president of the Royal and Ancient; and he wrote on historical subjects.

His rival for the rectorship was W. E. Gladstone. The nations divided equally, but Gladstone had six more votes than Inglis. The casting vote was with the Chancellor, the Duke of Montrose, who gave it to Inglis on party political grounds. Under the old system the vote would have been with the retiring rector, Lord Palmerston, who would have chosen Gladstone on party political grounds.

# Last Rector in the Old College

Lord Stanley (Glasgow University Archives)

## Lord Stanley, statesman (1826-1893)

### Elected 1868

Stanley succeeded to the Earldom of Derby in 1869. He was a keen mountaineer in his youth. He was at first a Conservative but shared many opinions with the moderate Whigs. When he was elected to the Rectorship he had supported social legislation, for example to remove civic and legal disabilities from Jews and to provide the public with free libraries. He had been Colonial Secretary and the first Secretary of State for India.

His opponent for the Rectorship was Robert Lowe, a Liberal politician. (Lowe was to be Chancellor of the Exchequer and Home Secretary. He was raised to the peerage as Lord Sherbrooke in 1880.)

The nations were divided equally. The Chancellor of the University, the Duke of Montrose, gave his casting vote for Stanley. In this case, the voting was for Stanley anyway: he won 539 votes and Lowe 524. Stanley—or Derby—was in office when the University left the old college buildings in the High Street in 1870.

Derby was to be Foreign Secretary from 1874 to 1878 but quit the Conservatives in 1880 and became leader of the Liberals. And he became leader of the Liberal Unionists in 1886.

# Flamboyant Adventurer and Prime Minister

Benjamin Disraeli (Glasgow University Archives)

*Benjamin Disraeli, Conservative statesman, later Earl of Beaconsfield (1804-1881). He was Prime Minister in 1868 and from 1874 to 1880*

*Elected 1871 and—uniquely—re-elected 1874*

Disraeli has been called the most romantic of British statesmen, the most inscrutable, and according to his great rival the most courageous. He has been called a brilliant adventurer, impudent, a poseur, a charlatan, and a gambler of the highest nerve. His speech, appearance, and clothes were sometimes garish. He cultivated on his forehead a curl that was the delight of caricaturists. It was Disraeli who gave the Conservative Party a shape like that of the present Party.

He was Prime Minister in 1868 and resigned in the face of a hostile majority. Disraeli was therefore one of the few to stand for the Rectorship after being Prime Minister and was to be Prime Minister again. On the other hand it has to be said that he had been defeated before he was ever elected—by the Duke of Argyll in 1854 and by Lord Elgin in 1859. His name had been mooted in 1858 but the idea was dropped.

Disraeli was born in the Jewish faith but his father, an author and writer, had him baptised when he was 13. He had a tough start in life, trying the law, publishing, and the commodities market and suffering from a nervous breakdown. He had difficulty in getting into Parliament but managed that in 1837 when he was in his early thirties. His maiden speech was probably the most disastrous ever. It was over-ornate and was drowned in laughter. Among the few words that could be heard were: "Ay, and though I sit down now the time will come when you will hear me."

He wrote political novels in the 1840s. They aimed to promote his ideas of Tory democracy. They are imperfect as novels: he was first a politician. Yet they have lively characterisation and strong insight into the gulf between rich and poor.

Disraeli came to dominate the Conservatives and, when he was Prime Minister, the House of Commons. It was extraordinary for a flamboyant character of Jewish origin to lead the party of English squires and landed gentry.

His opponent in the rectorial election of 1871 was John Ruskin, the most influential writer on art in the nineteenth century. Ruskin had achieved much. He had published *Stones of Venice*, *Modern Painters*, and *Sesame and Lilies*, all seminal works of criticism and art history. Ruskin was the great defender and advocate of Turner's works and was a social reformer, philanthropist, and visionary.

In the rectorial election campaign, the Conservative side said: "With reference to Mr Ruskin's literary merits, we take the following extract from the *Edinburgh Review*."

The *Review* said:

> *Modern Painters* is the worst book of a bad series of books, mischievous to art, mischievous to nature, but mischievous above all to those young and eager minds, animated by the love of art and literature, which may mistake this declamatory trash for substantial or stimulating food. We are the less disposed to acquit Mr Ruskin, because he is not altogether without the faculties which might have made him a useful and elegant writer.
>
> But all these qualities are perverted and destroyed by the entire absence of masculine judgement, by the failure of the logical faculty, and by a strange propensity to mistake the illusions of his own fancy or his own vanity for the laws of reality and the principles of truth.

Glasgow was determined to make a great fuss when Disraeli came for his installation as Rector. Disraeli wrote to a friend a few days before that the expedition was assuming colossal proportions.

My plans assume that I shall return to England alive; when I see the programme of the Glasgow week, it seems doubtful. Nothing can be more inhuman; and if there were a society to protect public men, as there is to protect donkeys, some interference would undoubtedly take place.

Disraeli's Address was delivered in the Kibble Chrystal Art Palace, a huge greenhouse in the Botanic Gardens,* near the University; his speech was considered a fine piece of oratory. He spoke quietly, in "measured and appropriate language" which seemed to arise naturally from his thoughts. He did not have notes. But a reporter there from *The Times* had already been given a text of the speech. Disraeli delivered exactly the prepared text.

One passage in his Address is uncannily like passages from Birkenhead's highly controversial Address of 1923, but has a rather different aim. Disraeli said:

A people who recognise no higher aim than physical enjoyment must become selfish and enervated. Under such circumstances, the supremacy of race, which is the key of history, will assert itself. Some human progeny, distinguished by their bodily vigour or their masculine intelligence, or by both qualities, will assert their superiority, and conquer a world which deserves to be enslaved.

He made the obligatory bow to his audience:

I address a race of men who are proud, and justly proud of their country. I know not that the sentiment of patriotism beats in any breast more strongly than in that of a Scotchman. Neither time not distance I believe enfeebles that passion. It is as vehement on the banks of the Ganges as on the banks of the Clyde, and in the speculative turmoil of Melbourne, as in the bustling energy of Glasgow. Why is a Scotchman proud of his country? Because the remembrance of it awakes a tradition of heroic exploits and inspiring emotions, of sacrifice for its own sake in the field and on the scaffold; of high examples of military skill and civil prudence, of literary and scientific fame; of commanding eloquence and profound philosophy, and of a fascinating poesy and romance—all of which a Scotchman feels ennobles his existence, and all of which, he is conscious, have inevitably sprung from the circumstances of his native land.

Disraeli was applying here his own dictum: "Everyone loves flattery." (He added: "And when you come to royalty you should lay it on with a trowel.")

William Allingham (1824-1889), an Irish poet whose diary is a rich record of literary life, wrote of Disraeli:

His novels worth little or nothing. His address to the young men of Glasgow almost as empty as if "the people's William" [i.e. Gladstone] had made it. Dizzy no humour, no love in his jesting.

---

* The Kibble Palace was first built in 1863-1866 as a conservatory at Coulport House, Loch Long, for John Kibble, and was transported to the Botanic Gardens, Glasgow, in 1873. It was extended and in it was put erotic sculpture that the Victorians excused as art. The Kibble Palace still stands.

Disraeli was complimented with a municipal banquet, the freedom of the city, and the presentation of an address from the local Conservatives—the flattery was returned. He told a friend: "Glasgow, without exception, was the greatest reception ever given to a public man."

His career during his second premiership included the buying of a 40 per cent share in the Suez Canal in 1875. Queen Victoria became the Empress of India in 1876. Disraeli dominated the Congress of Berlin in 1878. That conference settled a crisis in the Balkans—and Britain gained Cyprus: this was a period of imperial expansion. The Suez Canal and Cyprus were of special importance because they lay on the route to India by sea and India fascinated Disraeli.

A great deal of legislation was carried out for the benefit of the poor, in housing, health, labour relations, and pollution. He went to the country in 1880 confident of victory but Gladstone and the Liberals won. Disraeli retired and died the next year.

# Grand Old Man's Speech lasts an Hour and a Half

W.E. Gladstone (Hunterian Art Gallery)

*William Ewart Gladstone (1809-1898), Liberal statesman. Four times Prime Minister*

*Elected 1877*

He was, at the height of his fame, almost a cult figure in Scotland; engravings of his portrait were in many homes. He was of Scottish descent. Scotland was devoted to the Liberal Party because it was seen as the party of progress and the rights of man, compared with the Conservative Party which was seen as reactionary. The people remembered the decades of corruption under the Tories before 1832 and the Tories' long-fought battle to prevent reform.

Gladstone's pre-eminence, wrote Roy Jenkins (Lord Jenkins of Hillhead), was a function of the width of his interests, the force of his energy, and the power of his oratory.

No one else has been Prime Minister four times. No one else would have devoted half his last day in office to translating an ode of Horace. No one else could have held by the sheer physical force of his personality great provincial audiences for an hour and forty minutes of orations way above their heads, infused neither by Disraeli's wit nor by Palmerston's blow-hard chauvinism ... I hesitate to claim that he was the greatest Prime Minister ... but I have no doubt that he was the most remarkable specimen of humanity of all the fifty who, from Walpole to Major ... held the office.

Gladstone was a supreme master of parliamentary debate. The Liberals came to power, with Gladstone as Prime Minister, in 1868. His first Ministry lasted until 1874. He was again Prime Minister from 1880 to 1885, in 1886, and from 1892 to 1894. He disestablished and disendowed the Church of Ireland, reformed English education, and extended the suffrage. He defended the Christians in the Balkans against persecution by the Ottoman Empire. He was always deeply concerned with theological and liturgical battles. He wanted Home Rule for Ireland but the legislation was defeated; the Liberal Party split over the issue.

He engaged many prostitutes in long conversations late at night. Gladstone attempted to "rescue" them from their way of life. Gladstone scourged himself for what he regarded as his faults of impiety and impure thoughts. He put in his diaries on certain days a special symbol resembling a whip.

Gladstone had been a candidate for the Rectorship in 1865 but had been defeated by Lord Glencorse (John Inglis), who was a lawyer and a distinguished judge. His candidature in 1877 was stronger because he had been Prime Minister since his previous attempt. His opponent this time was Sir Stafford Northcote, Conservative, who was Chancellor of the Exchequer, and Gladstone won easily.

His biographer H. C. G. Matthew wrote that the result of the voting in the rectorial election confirmed to some extent:

> ... his own return to popularity among the Scottish university classes—he had been defeated for the Chancellorship of Edinburgh University in 1868.[*]

The Scottish Liberals were encouraged by Gladstone's success at Glasgow University and sought in 1878 to strengthen the Liberal cause in the Forth-Clyde valley.

When he came to Glasgow for his installation and Address, he was put into a carriage drawn by one horse; but ahead of him was a larger carriage drawn by four handsome greys. This four-horse carriage had in it a venerable figure draped in a fur rug. The spectators took that person to be the Rector himself. In fact it was a man called "Old Clough", who dished out buns, tea, coffee, and meat pies at the so-called restaurant at the University.

---

[*] Chancellors at the older Scottish universities are elected by the graduates.

With Old Clough were the leaders of the Conservative Club. They said to him: "Bow, you beggar, bow." The game fellow did his best to masquerade as the greatest living statesman. One account said: "How the unaccountable cheers puzzled the occupants of the simple ... vehicle that followed can only be imagined." A torchlight procession followed, taking the Lord Rector to the house in West George Street where he was to stay. At the destination the torches were piled into a bonfire. It was a scene, said Gladstone, "worthy of Turner". The Lord Rector appeared at a window and dismissed the crowd with "Good night and God bless you".

The Address and installation were held the next day at the Kibble Palace, not far from the University. More than 2,000 students were present, the Liberals to one side of the platform and the Conservatives to the other. Behind the students and round the walls were members of the general public; on the platform were distinguished personages and the Professors. One account says that:

> ... after a brief time for the students to show their enthusiasm once more, the most perfect quiet and attention followed.

Another account says that at the beginning there was a great uproar.

> After the Principal had offered the opening Latin prayer, the uproar broke out again. Gladstone rose and stood impassive, high above the tumult, whilst professor upon professor vainly appealed with uplifted hand for silence. After a long time (one of my friends afterwards told me it was twenty minutes) the G.O.M. made up his mind that sufficient tribute had been paid to him. I recall vividly how he merely raised his hand and said: 'Gentlemen.' Immediately all was still.

The Address lasted one and a half hours. Long speeches were not unusual. Gladstone was known to speak for two and a half hours in a major debate in the House of Commons. His speech to the students—like many others by Lord Rectors—mentioned education a great deal. But some of the passages have an extraordinarily modern resonance.

He spoke of the Scottish universities:

> Of the governing and teaching bodies, as known to you on this side of the border, we can say with truth what we cannot as yet say with universal truth of Oxford and Cambridge, that their members are, every one of them, working bees. Of your modest endowments you may boast, what is to a limited extent open to question in the South, that they are without exception applied, rationally and directly, to the promotion of true academic purposes. You have also a great advantage in this, that among your students there is hardly a sprinkling, or at all events there is a very much thinner sprinkling, of youths, who, unhappily for themselves and for others, arrive at an University without any adequate sense of its mission, or of their own...
>   Such youths contemplate it as a pleasant lounge subject to the drawback of lessons of routine, which it is their chief care to keep down to a minimum: or accept it as a condition of their social standing, or as a promotion from their school-life; or turn it physically to account as a area for corporal exercises without any higher care. The rapid growth of wealth in the country tends to enlarge the numbers of these pseudo-students in the English Universities; but it is the aim of reform, and the constant care

of the authorities, if they cannot be exterminated, to keep them down. Among you, Gentlemen, I trust that these anomalous varieties of the academic sub-kingdom of the human species are scarcely known. May they long be strangers to your precincts...

Oxford and Cambridge have a noble office, and, in its own way, an unrivalled position: but the Scottish Universities have also their own proper and admirable work. To them it is given, far more than elsewhere, to draw freely from that grand and inexhaustible repository, the mass of the people.

Gladstone spoke of:

... the amount of resolute unsparing personal effort and sacrifice, through alone it is that the youth of Scotland come so extensively to the benefits of Academic training.

He added:

These are not the children of wealth and ease, grudging whatever is given to study as stolen from luxury and amusement. They are the hardy offspring of a hardy land, who win by toiling the privilege of further toil, and in thus cumulating effort give a double strength to the fibre of their faculties and will.

He went on to speak of the finances of students. About two thirds, he suggested:

... keep their place in the University, absolutely or almost in every case, by one form or another of private employment added on through the whole, or a portion, of the year, to the burden of their studies.

He quoted a professor as saying:

In the Humanity [Latin] Class this year are included joiners, miners, brass founders, boot-makers, tailors, grocers, engineers, ship-builders, drapers, stewards of steamers, a toll keeper, a pocketbook-maker, a blacksmith, [and others].

On a higher plane, he said:

I submit to you, Gentlemen, that man is the crown of the visible creation, and that studies upon man, studies, in the largest sense of humanity, studies conversant with his nature, his works, his duties, and his destinies, are the highest studies.

Gladstone wrote later: "The blue caps [the Tory students] as well as the red [Liberal] cheered fervently at the close". John Morley, his friend, wrote:

Themes, familiar but never outworn nor extinct, were handled with vigour, energy, and onward flow that made them sound as good as novel, and even where they did not instruct or did not edify, the noble music pleased.

All present were so captivated by the sheer quality of the physical performance that they were sorry, even after ninety minutes, "when the stream of fascinating melody ceased to flow".

That was before the invention of microphones. Orators like Gladstone were able to address huge audiences if their audiences were very quiet and if the halls in which they spoke had good acoustics. And people like Gladstone learned by experience how to project their voices and at what level. Nonetheless, Gladstone took a lozenge before big occasions like this one.

His biographer John Morley wrote that Gladstone in his great speeches was:

> impressing himself upon the kindled throngs by the breadth of his survey of great affairs of life and nations, by the depth of his vision, by the power of his stroke. Physical resources had much to do with the effect; his overflowing vivacity, the fine voice and flashing eye and a whole frame in free, ceaseless, natural, and spontaneous motion. So he bore his hearers through long chains of strenuous period, calling up by the marvellous transformation of his mien a strange succession of images....

On the other hand, Queen Victoria is said to have complained that he spoke to her as if he was addressing a public meeting.

A student who was present at the Address wrote later:

> The address, I think, disappointed most of us. Mr Gladstone had obviously asked for and been supplied with statistics regarding the classes from which the students sprang. It was equally apparent that the information surprised and delighted him. That an actual university education was available to any lad of the people was apparently astonishing and splendid. So he devoted a large part of his address to facts we all knew well, while we had desired that a great man should deal with a great subject. But we were all overawed by the noble dominant figure standing erect before us—the pale intellectual face, glowing eagle eyes, and wonderful voice. A tremendous personality. The Kibble Palace was crammed. There was some sunshine which heated the glass, and the place became unbearably close. My younger brother wisely fell asleep, but had the prescience to wake in time to hear a fine peroration, which ended with these words: "Work onwards and work upwards, and may the blessing of the Most High soothe your cares, clear your vision, and crown your labours with reward."

Gladstone's rosy view of Scottish education is in contrast with the darker view of the rector of Edinburgh High School, James Donaldson, who wrote in 1882: "The Scottish universities are schools with curricula fixed nearly on the old Reformation programme." He argued that "an educational revolution" had taken place in the world at large and with it had come much greater "competition for distinction in science, scholarship, theology, and all the higher intellectual pursuits." But here the Scotsman "has to fight with bow and arrow against men with rifles and cannon. He is the handloom weaver of the intellectual world."

Gladstone had a busy day in Glasgow. After the address the Senate entertained him to lunch with 70 people attending and he gave another speech. The Principal, in proposing the Lord Rector's health, said he hoped Gladstone had not grudged the time given to the serene, if dull, seclusion of academic things. Gladstone replied:

> I only quarrel with your word dull. Let me assure you, gentlemen, nothing is so dull as political agitation.

In the early evening he addressed a political meeting at St Andrew's Hall, attended it is said by 6,000 or more people, for another hour and a half. In the evening he went to the City Hall where he spoke to 2,500. He wrote in his diary that it had been an "overpowering" day.

The Grand Old Man, as he had become known, was to be Prime Minister another three times. His defeat over Home Rule for Ireland and his advancing age led him to resign in 1894. He lived for just over four years more but during that time was half blind and half deaf. Gladstone is buried in Westminster Abbey.

On the great man's death, a bronze statue paid for by public subscription was put up in George Square, Glasgow. The artist was William Hamo Thornycroft RA, who received commissions for many public sculptures. The cost, including the pedestal and the placing in position, was £3,500. He is shown in the robes of Lord Rector and is holding a book. Near him in the square is a bronze statue to another Lord Rector, Thomas Campbell.

# During the Address the Precious Mace is Harmed

John Bright (Hunterian Art Gallery)

*John Bright, orator and Liberal statesman (1811-1889)*

## Elected 1880

Bright's opponent was John Ruskin, art critic and social reformer. Ruskin, who had stood before, was backed by the Independent Club, an *ad hoc* group of people who wanted a non-political election. Tennyson was at one point mooted as a candidate. This kind of conflict was present from 1820 onwards: should the choice fall upon a politician or on a person distinguished in another field, such as science, literature, or art?

Tennyson, who had been Poet Laureate since 1850, was approached in May 1880 by two students and agreed to be nominated, but did not realise that the two were the president and secretary of the Conservative Club. When he realised that he would be a political candidate, opposed by a Liberal, he withdrew. The Conservatives urged him to go ahead. His brother-in-law, Edmund Lushington, former professor of Greek at the University, joined in the pleas. (Lushington was to become Rector in 1884). The Liberals pressed Tennyson not to stand. In the end, after much to-and-froing, he did not.

Bright was called "the great Tribune of the People" and was one of the most eloquent speakers of his time. He was active in the Anti-Corn Law League from its beginning in 1839 and campaigned with Richard Cobden, economist and radical politician, for free trade.

Bright was born in Rochdale, Lancashire; his father was a Quaker and owner of a cotton-spinning business. The young Bright loved swimming; in later years he became good at billiards and fly-fishing. He was a teetotaller from his late twenties and never had a decanter or wine glasses in his house.

He entered Parliament in 1843. He criticised the East India Company for maladministration. He wanted Irish unrest to be tackled at its causes, for example by reforming land law. He opposed the Crimean war, opposition which brought accusations that he was lacking patriotism. Bright was closely associated with the Reform Act of 1867: seats were redistributed and a million town labourers were added to the electorate. He was deeply concerned with education: he was largely self-taught and in his rectorial Address he spoke of his regret at not having been to university.

The Liberal Club declared that its man Bright was one of the foremost statesmen of the age:

> ... one who has bravely and successfully striven for right and justice.
>
> To no other Statesman is so much praise due for the accomplishment of Reforms—which Conservatives and Liberals alike praise ... By many he is declared to be the first Orator in Great Britain ... Mr Bright's speeches possess that wonderful force and simplicity which entrance all classes on account of their finished style, and the pure English they contain. The ablest critics have proclaimed them to be the highest models of rhetorical composition.

The Independent Club, which ran Ruskin's campaign, said that the students of former times:

> failed to pay the meed of reverence to Wordsworth ... to De Quincey, in prose the modern Milton, and in power of gorgeous imagery not surpassed by any English writer ... that students of late years neglected the names of Thackeray and Dickens ... students of the present have hitherto been blind to the splendid services of living authors, of Tennyson, Browning, and Matthew Arnold...

And to the glittering list the Independent Club added Ruskin:

> ... whose rank in the realms of pure literature and of Art Criticism is finally fixed and who is beginning to be acknowledged as king and lord among social reformers.

Students had been misled by party feeling into electing men to the Lord Rectorship:

> ... on principles that are only valid for the election of representatives to the House of Commons. But the Lord Rector has not a single political duty to perform.

The custom was as hurtful in its effects on the University as it was absurd.

The Liberals rejoined that every vote for Ruskin was a vote for the advancement of the Conservative cause, although the Conservatives had no candidate.

A letter was circulated that was apparently from Ruskin to the secretary of the Art School, Chesterfield, Derbyshire, in answer to an invitation for him to lecture there. Ruskin seems to have replied:

> I could not if I would go to Chesterfield, and I doubt whether I would if I could. I do not hire myself out like a brainless long-tongued puppet for filthy ducats. You want me to make money for you: therefore you will tolerate advice. Hath not Chesterfield a steeple abomination;* and is it not the home of that arch-abomination-creator, Stephenson? To him we are indebted for the screeching, howling, shrieking fiends, fit for Pandemonium, called locomotives, that disfigure the loveliest spots of God's land.

The Ruskin side denounced the letter as a forgery. One of the Ruskin broadsides did however say—mysteriously—that the Liberals had extorted the letter from him "by arts they have not dared to defend."

Some students asked Ruskin to define his political views about Conservatives and Liberals. He replied:

> What in the devil's name do *you* have to do with either Mr D'Israeli [*sic*] or Mr Gladstone? You are students at the University, and have no more business with politics than you do with rat-catching. Had you ever read ten words of mine with understanding you would have known that I care no more for Mr D'Israeli or Mr Gladstone than for two old bagpipes with the drone going by steam, but that I hate all Liberalism as I do Beelzebub, and that, with Carlyle, I stand, we two alone now in England, for God and the Queen.

The letter appeared in the newspapapers, and a commotion followed. Ruskin looked ridiculous.

The result was: Bright: 1,128, Ruskin 814.

Gladstone's and Disraeli's inaugurations had been in the very large Kibble Chrystal Palace but Bright's was to be in the smaller St Andrew's Hall. The professors decided that they and their friends would have the best seats and the students would have to stand. Students held protest meetings. A former student later wrote:

> Wild proposals were made to defeat the Senate—that the hall be rushed and the best seats be occupied; that the meeting be boycotted; that Bright should be asked not to come, and so on.

The Senate gave in.

> On the day of Bright's inaugural address all was orderly in St Andrews Hall. Unusually so; for the students, proud of their victory, disciplined themselves.

The students were on their honour to be merciful to the defeated powers.

---

* The steeple of the parish church is strangely twisted.

Students—as usual—sang at the beginning, vigorously if not melodiously. Each member of the platform party, as he appeared, was greeted with cheering and stamping of feet. This was in contrast to the rowdy and unduly prolonged cheering at the start of Gladstone's installation. Bright began to speak quietly but became animated. He gestured and his hand came down sharply. In front of him was the ancient mace, resting horizontally on a stand as is the custom. His hand struck the mace. The head of the mace came away and crashed down among the newspaper reporters below the platform. His hand was bleeding. Someone produced a handkerchief and the wound was bound up.*

One other small incident happened. Two loud cracks came from the back of the hall. Some of the spectators were alarmed. But it was only the sound of benches snapping. People in the audience, in a kind of explanation, passed the broken pieces over their heads to the platform party. A professor stooped down and accepted the pieces, to enthusiastic applause.

Bright, when approached to stand for Rector, had been lukewarm. He seemed more enthusiastic after the installation was over. His diary says:

> To St Andrew's Hall: a very fine room and a great audience. First ceremony: admitting to the degree of LL.D. I was first 'capped', as the ceremony is called. After others had been 'capped,' I took the Chair and began my speech. The hall is good to speak in; the audience was attentive; and I spoke with ease and freedom - and the whole passed off better than I had feared.

He spoke extempore. The Principal, the Rev Dr John Caird, suggested to Bright that one passage was so fine that it must have been rehearsed. Bright replied that he did not prepare his speeches but thought out what he wanted to say and in what order. He gave some extra thought to special topics in his speech but did not write anything down.

Bright became Rector when he was near the end of his political career. But he was to continue campaigning for reforms in Ireland ("Force is not a remedy," he said). He disagreed with Gladstone's proposals for Home Rule in Ireland and left the Government in 1882.

---

* The mace suffered on at least two other occasions. During the Reformation it was stripped of religious emblems. And in 1971 it was in the Chapel for a service when it slipped from its usual secured position and fell to the floor. The head was damaged. How this accident happened was never made clear. The University Court decided that the mace—a most precious object and a very rare survival of fifteenth-century silver work—would not be used on ordinary occasions. Another mace, a modern one, is used instead. And the Rector's Mace, also modern, is used when he or she is present.

# A Whiff of Anti-Catholic Prejudice

Henry Fawcett (Glasgow University Archives)

*Henry Fawcett, social reformer and Liberal (1833-1884)*

*Elected 1883*

Fawcett was blinded when he was 25 years old: pellets entered his eyes from a gun fired by his father, who suffered from cataracts. His blindness was no impediment to his work but it was an impediment to his political advancement. Fawcett loved fishing, skating, riding, and walking and believed that blind people should act and be treated as if they had sight.

Fawcett was an MP and Professor of Political Economy at Cambridge University. He wrote and spoke on a huge range of subjects, for example: pauperism, strikes, the enclosure of commons, the condition of farmers and farm workers and of the labouring classes, finances of India, local taxation, and proportional representation. He was in favour of votes for women. When he was Postmaster General he introduced the parcel post, postal orders, and cheap telegrams. His wife, Millicent Garrett, was a notable suffragette and reformer.

This was an election which had a whiff of anti-Roman Catholic prejudice.

One of his opponents, who was proposed by the Conservative Club, was the Marquis of Bute, an immensely wealthy philanthropist, scholar, linguist, and patron of the arts. He gave to Glasgow University the Bute Hall. This great Gothic Revival structure is at the heart of the buildings which had, not long before the rectorial election, been erected for the University on Gilmorehill.

Bute became a Roman Catholic in his twenties. A leaflet was printed during the election campaign without the usual mention of its source and without a printer's name. It gives some clues why Bute was not chosen. The leaflet attempts sarcasm in giving "reasons why we should vote for the Marquess." They include:

Because he affects ... Saint Kentigern* and Breviaries.

Because he once laid the foundation stone of a Jesuit College, and thus gave conclusive evidence of his liberal tendencies in education.

The other points include:

Because it would please the Senate.

Because it is our only chance of getting a Tory Rector.

And last: Because he gave a subscription to the College Buildings relatively [sic] smaller than those of many Glasgow citizens.

Bute was, however, elected to the rectorship of St Andrews, unopposed, in 1892 and re-elected, with a comfortable majority over his only opponent, in 1895. He gave to the students there a large sum towards the cost of a building for the union.

In nominating Bute at Glasgow the Conservative Club said, among many other things, that the Marquess had:

... not only gained for himself a distinguished position in the ranks of literary men, but has also proved himself a munificent patron of learning. A Scotchman by birth he has evinced in a high degree, that true spirit of patriotism which has shed such a lustre on the annals of our country.

Another broadside from the Conservatives said:

It is a scandal to the University, and a disgrace to the Students, and particularly to that enlightened section of them which professes to be 'intelligent' that the MARQUESS OF BUTE should ever have been opposed. Consider his munificence to the university, his splendid abilities and rare attainments...

The Conservatives then turned their attention to Fawcett, saying:

So far as we can discern, the principal, if not the only reason, for voting for him is that he is a member of the Liberal Government, but, gentlemen, is that itself a sufficient qualification for election to the rectorship? No one could say that Mr

---

* Or Saint Mungo, patron of Glasgow.

Fawcett is a statesman, and he holds so extreme Republican and Democratic ideas, that he could not be entrusted with the management of any department of the state affairs except such an one as the Post Office..."

The other candidate standing against Fawcett was John Ruskin, art critic and social commentator, who had stood in 1871 against Disraeli and in 1880 against John Bright.

Fawcett died before he could be installed and deliver his Address. A monument to him is in Westminster Abbey and other memorials were set up, for example a scholarship for blind students at Cambridge University.

# Revered former Professor Steps In

Edward Lushington (Glasgow University Archives)

*Edward Law Lushington, former professor of Greek at the
University (1811-1893)*

*Elected 1884*

Lushington was an academic at Cambridge University and took the post in
Glasgow because the pay was good. The class of Greek was for years the
biggest of all, and the professors' pay was closely linked to the numbers of
students they had. Other academics at Cambridge took chairs at Glasgow
for similar reasons.

A historian of the University wrote of Lushington:

> He was a man of fine intellect, with a beautiful and sympathetic soul, a profound
> scholar and an excellent teacher, singularly courteous, considerate and fair-minded,
> but reticent and undemonstrative. He encouraged the dull and stimulated the brilliant
> ... His control of his class—often more than a hundred—was marvellous. He had a
> soft, sweet voice which was never raised, but stillness prevailed; no student ever

ventured upon an impropriety. Occasionally something might suggest pedal satisfaction;[*] 'Silence, Gentlemen, if you please,' and there was silence.

His brother-in-law, Tennyson, wrote of him:

> And thou art worthy; full of power,
> And gentle; liberal-minded, great,
> Consistent; wearing all that weight
> Of learning lightly like a flower.

Lushington was appointed professor in 1838 and held the post for 37 years. He was the person most closely linked to the University to become Rector since Adam Smith had done so—a tribute to the love and respect felt for him.

His election was unique. His predecessor died in November 1884 and the rules laid down that voting should take place in a specified period and this period had not yet expired. The political clubs and everyone else agreed that Lushington should be nominated quickly and be unopposed.

---

[*] "Pedal satisfaction" was a drumming of the feet or heels.

# The Winner has fewer Votes than the Loser

Lord Lytton (courtesy of the National Portrait Gallery)

*Lord Lytton, poet, diplomat, and former Viceroy of India (1831-1891)*

*Elected 1887*

Lytton had been a diplomat in 10 European capitals. He was a noted poet, under the pen name Owen Meredith, and novelist. His poetry is forgotten but some of it was well received when it was published. It has been described as too derivative, for example of Browning.

Lytton's service in India, from 1876 to 1880, was eventful. One of his first duties was to proclaim Victoria as Empress of India. Disraeli, the Prime Minister, wanted to please Queen Victoria and to warn the Russians that they should keep their hands off India.

Lytton failed to prevent the Second Afghan War. Famine ravaged the south and west of India, but Lytton acted to help the populace and prevent more famine. He also reformed the system of recruitment to the Civil Service and dismantled internal Customs duties and regulations.

His opponent for the Rectorship was Lord Rosebery, Liberal, who had been approached to stand in 1883 but had declined. He said that he did not much like being a Rector because they entailed rectorial Addresses.

The result was unsatisfactory. Each candidate had two nations but Rosebery had 22 more votes than Lytton did. It was up to the Chancellor, Lord Stair, to give a casting vote. Stair was a Conservative and Rosebery a Liberal, so Stair voted for Lytton. It was a political decision: the whole election was political. But Liberal students were outraged.

A pamphlet issued by the Liberal Club at the next election, in 1890, said that the Chancellor had wantonly disregarded the wishes of the majority, that Lytton had been foisted on the students by unfair means, and that:

> ... public opinion was roused to a conception of the flagrant injustice of a privilege capable of being so unworthily and unwarrantably exercised, and so utterly at variance with the principles of popular representation, freely accepted by all parties of our time. [*]

Lytton was appointed Ambassador the Paris in 1887, a post he much enjoyed because he had a great affinity with the French. He died of a heart attack while writing. Lytton was the first Earl of Lytton. His father, Rector 1856-1859, was the first Baron Lytton.

---

[*] The reference is to universal male suffrage.

# How a skilled Campaigner
# Won the Day

Arthur Balfour (Glasgow University Archives)

*Arthur James Balfour, Conservative statesman and philosopher,
later first Earl of Balfour (1848-1930). He was Prime Minister
from 1902 to1905*

### Elected 1890

Balfour was of an ancient Scottish family; he was a landowner, an aristocrat, and an intellectual. His paternal grandfather made a fortune in India as
a contractor. Balfour was, when nominated, a former Secretary of State
for Scotland and was currently the Chief Secretary for Ireland. His policy
of suppression in Ireland brought him the nickname Bloody Balfour—from
the people who wanted Home Rule.

His mother was one of the mighty Cecil family: his uncle was Lord
Robert Cecil, later Lord Cranborne and later still Lord Salisbury and Prime
Minister. Uncle Robert promoted Balfour's career. Indeed when Salisbury
resigned as Prime Minister, his place was taken by none other than

Balfour. This nepotism was the origin of the phrase "Bob's your uncle," meaning "Everything is sorted out, everything all right."

He was the child of his background—the great landed families, Eton, Trinity College, Cambridge, and the club of Cambridge intellectuals called "the Souls." He was charming, witty, an able Minister, and a good debater. He wrote *Defence of Philosophic Doubt* and *The Foundation of Belief* and lectures on theism and humanism. But Neville Chamberlain wrote: "He always seemed to me to have a heart of stone." Winston Churchill remarked on his "cool ruthlessness" and wrote:

> Had his life been cast amid the labyrinthine intrigues of Renaissance Italy, he would not have required to study the works of Machiavelli.

The other candidate was the Earl of Aberdeen, for the Liberal party. He had been twice Viceroy of Ireland and had been governor-general of Canada. In both countries he was loved and admired. He was to be made the first Marquis of Aberdeen. He was laird of Haddo House, Aberdeenshire, for 64 years. Aberdeen and his wife were philanthropists. They also wrote autobiographical works called *We Twa* and *More Cracks with We Twa*.

This election saw the debate, to be repeated many times, about whether the incumbent should take an active part in looking after the interests of students. And the problem of Ireland was an issue, as in other elections of this kind, for nationwide politics were always in the background.

Balfour, nominated for the rectorship by the Conservatives and the Liberal Unionists, won hands down. The victory was due mainly to the efforts and skill of one person, a member of the Union's board of management and future president of the Students' Representative Council. The *Glasgow University Magazine* wrote:

> The very life and soul of the Unionist organisation was the Conservative secretary, Mr R. S. Horne, who gained golden opinions from all parties for his conduct of the election.

He was to become Chancellor of the Exchequer and successively Sir Robert Horne and Viscount Horne. The statesman and Prime Minister Stanley Baldwin described him as "that rare thing, a Scots cad". Horne became Rector of Aberdeen University in 1921.

The *College Unionist*, campaign paper for Balfour, said:

> The man who votes for Aberdeen ... commits himself *in toto* to Mr Gladstone's Home Rule [for Ireland] policy whose central idea is that Ireland should be given up to the agitator and the moonlighter,* to be governed by herself apart, by a Parliament of her own, despite the outcry of the whole of the educated and industrial population of the country....

Balfour, said the *College Unionist*:

---

\* In Ireland, one who commits agrarian outrages by night.

has been the backbone of the Unionist cause ... the champion of true freedom and liberty in Ireland. He is the embodiment of the policy founded on the fact that the maintenance of law and order are the first essentials for the government of Ireland or of any other country, and that by remedial measures she may be made prosperous and happy...

He was:

... one of the foremost men in the Kingdom....Mr Balfour's great power is in the versatility of his genius...a distinguished scientist, a scientific critic of music, a brilliant litterateur, a powerful metaphysician... the most distinguished living Scotsman.

He was given a great reception when he arrived in the city to be installed and to deliver his Address. One of his biographers wrote:

No praise is more hearty and genuine than the appreciative cheers of young voices; and as Mr Balfour permitted himself to be escorted, like some newly-crowned monarch, from the station to the University, the hearty bursts of unrestrained enthusiasm which met him at every point, must have put new life and strength into him.

The title of his Address was *A Fragment on Progress*. He said:

Those who look forward to a period of continuous and, so to speak, inevitable progress are bound to assign some more solid reason for their convictions than a merely empirical survey of the surface lessons of history.

The *Times* said:

He has shown himself an able debater, a capable and resolute administrator, and a trenchant platform speaker ... Mr Balfour's rectorial address shows that he possesses his full share of the literary taste and cultivation that mark the most promising of our younger politicians of all shades of thought ... His address is carefully thought out, deftly framed and adjusted in all its parts, and teeming with apt phrases and felicitous illustrations.

He succeeded his uncle as Prime Minister in 1902 and had some successes but the Conservatives were defeated by a landslide in the general election of 1905. He became unpopular with the party for what was thought to be his unhurried casualness and in 1911 had to yield the leadership to Andrew Bonar Law.

As Foreign Secretary in a coalition government he was responsible for the Balfour Declaration of 1917 which declared British support for the establishment of a Jewish national home in Palestine, provided that safeguards could be reached for the rights of the "existing non-Jewish communities there." He became Earl of Balfour in 1922.

# Colonial Civil Servant, Mathematician, Conservative Party Organiser

Sir John Gorst (Hunterian Art Gallery)

## *Sir John Gorst, lawyer and politician (1835-1916)*

### *Elected 1893*

Gorst went to New Zealand in his youth as a public servant and was caught up in Maori affairs. When Maoris rebelled in 1863 he and his family narrowly escaped with their lives. He returned to Britain, became an MP, and reformed the Conservative Party's organisation. He held minor Government posts: Solicitor-General for England, Under-Secretary of State for India, and Financial Secretary to the Treasury. The Conservative Club said he was also a distinguished mathematician and described him as:

> ... a statesman whose chief desire has been to bring lasting good to the millions of our wage earners, by a just and true and honourable system of legislation ... and the beneficence of whose far-sighted measures will still be felt when the illusory dream of Home Rule [for Ireland] has been dissipated from the minds of the people of these realms.

His opponent was Herbert Henry Asquith (see page 99.) Gorst left Parliament in 1906 and the rest of his public life was spent in writing about education and health, especially children's health. He was thought of as failing to fulfil his potential in public life.

# The Great Imperialist

Joseph Chamberlain (Glasgow University Archives)

*Joseph Chamberlain, radical statesman (1836-1914)*

*Elected 1896*

Not all rectorial Addresses are of interest now, or even when they were delivered. Chamberlain's Address, however, is of interest: it sums up a political creed about imperialism. It was delivered in 1897—a most appropriate time. That was the year of Victoria's Diamond Jubilee and the climax of the Empire.

The background to the Address has a familiar air to us now—worries about Britain's relative decline in its economic and political power. Britain had been supreme among industrial nations, but Germany and the United States were becoming formidable rivals. The Empire needed to be revitalised to keep Britain's position sound, at home and abroad. Still to come were the Boer War, which cracked the Imperial spirit, and the First World War, which was to destroy the old Europe. Chamberlain expressed ideas that are now deeply unfashionable, even repugnant, and that is another point of interest.

He was the son of a shopkeeper. He did not go to a great public school, nor to Oxbridge. His power base was Birmingham, where he dominated municipal government and where he made his fortune from manufacturing screws. He dressed elegantly—far too elegantly—with a frock coat, monocle, and orchid, just as his son Austen was to do. The aim was to show that he was as fine a fellow as any aristocrat.

Chamberlain the politician was a great splitter. He was a leader of the radicals in Gladstone's Cabinet of 1880 to 1885 and seemed likely to inherit the leadership of the Liberal Party. But he quarrelled with Gladstone in 1886, partly over Home Rule for Ireland and partly because he mistrusted Gladstone. The Liberal Party split and was to be ineffective for the rest of the century.

Chamberlain led the Liberal Unionists from 1889 but he was in the political wilderness. The Conservative Prime Minister Lord Salisbury in 1895 offered him any place in the Cabinet he wanted. To everyone's amazement he chose the Colonial Office, a job that was thought of as a dead end. He did it with restless energy, even having electric light installed in the Colonial Office building. He believed that the British were the greatest governing race the world had ever seen. He also thought that the Empire's purpose was technical and economic improvement. Chamberlain "put himself at the head of the imperialist sentiment which swept the country during the 1890s," wrote the historian Robert Blake.

Chamberlain was nominated by the Conservative Club and stood against Augustine Birrell, lawyer, MP, and essayist. The Conservatives said, unctuously, that the Liberal Club had tried to find someone to stand against Chamberlain: "but no one was willing to deprive Mr Chamberlain of what they recognised to be an honour that he had thoroughly earned." The Liberals said that their man was an eminent lawyer, a great parliamentarian, and a splendid essayist.

Chamberlain had a huge reception in Glasgow, as often happened when a great man arrived to be installed as Rector. Students turned out in fancy dress and flocks of people tried to shake Chamberlain's hand. He always took care in preparing speeches but this time he knew he was following a great tradition and took special care. One of his biographers wrote: "He meant to read his address—an intention which made his friends nervous, needlessly as it proved." He had made himself so familiar with his text that nobody could remember an Address so perfectly delivered. His theme was patriotism. He looked back on the changes that had happened since he had gone into public life nearly 30 years before.

> I have consistently sought—it may be sometimes with faltering steps and by mistaken roads—the greatness of the Empire and the true welfare of the people at large.

It was untrue that we had not the strength to sustain the burden of Empire—that the "weary Titan was struggling under the too vast orb of his fate." He said that our special interest, our duty, our national mission was to develop and colonise in order that we might gather strength in order to sustain the burden of Empire.

We do not lack efficient instruments for our great purpose, and we can still count on the energy and devotion of our countrymen, and on their ability and their confidence and respect of the people they are sent to govern for their good.

On the bleak mountains of the Indian frontier, amid the sands of the Soudan, in the swamps and forests of Western Africa—wherever the British flag floats, Englishmen, Scotsmen, and Irishmen are today fronting every danger and enduring every hardship, living as brave men and dying as heroes, in the faithful performance of duty and the passionate love of their country. They ask from us that their sacrifices shall not be in vain! If such be then the spirit of our people, why should we shrink from our task, or allow the sceptre of Empire to fall from our hands through craven fears of being great?

He declared his "faith in our race and in our nation." He said:

I believe that, with all the force and enthusiasm of which democracy alone is capable, they will complete and maintain that splendid edifice of our greatness, which, commenced under aristocratic auspices, has received in later times its greatest extension; and that the fixity of purpose and strength of will which are necessary to this end will be supplied by the natural patriotism which sustains the most strenuous efforts and makes possible the greatest sacrifices.

Chamberlain was to continue his career as a great splitter of parties. In 1904-1906 he led the Tariff Reform League, which wanted protection for British industry from German competition. Protection, the League said, was essential to development of a system of imperial preference. The League divided the Conservative Government and contributed to the Liberals' overwhelming victory in the general election of 1905. Chamberlain was struck down by paralysis in 1906 and his political career was ended.

# Prime Minister who married an Heiress and who had Derby Winners

*Lord Rosebery, Liberal statesman and landowner (1847-1929). Prime Minister 1894-1895*

## Elected 1899

Rosebery was, as a politician, an enigmatic personality. He was called in his own lifetime, in a biography published in 1923, "the man of promise." Winston Churchill said of his adherents and admirers:

> At first they said: 'He will come.' Then for years: 'If only he would come.' And finally, long after he had renounced politics for ever: 'If only he would come back.'

His reputation was great but his achievements few—at least in politics. Perhaps one reason was that he had lots of other interests.

Rosebery's horses won the great classic races, including the Derby three times; two of those wins were in his two years of the premiership. His racing colours were primrose and pink: his family name was Primrose and his choice of pink is presumably from the "rose" in his title. His racing did not endear him to Nonconformists.

He produced speeches and essays on all kinds of subjects—for example, Scottish history, the Turf, Robert Burns, William Wallace, and oratory (he himself was an excellent speaker). He wrote books on Robert Peel, William Pitt, Napoleon's last years, Lord Randolph Churchill, and the early life of Chatham. He travelled. He loved shooting.

He married Hannah Rothschild who was the only child of Baron Mayer de Rothschild. At the wedding, the bride was an orphan: she was given away by Disraeli. The marriage into one of the wealthiest and most influential families in Europe established Rosebery's political and social position more firmly. But the *Jewish Chronicle* said the wedding was "a lamentable occurrence" to be bewailed in sackcloth. "We mourn, we deplore, this degeneracy," the *Jewish Chronicle* said, "and we pray to God fervently to spare the community a similar grief." No other adverse comment seems to have appeared in the newspapers.

Lord Rosebery gave a dinner at Dalmeny, his house near Edinburgh, to mark their homecoming. The speeches of welcome were perhaps florid and exaggerated, but heartfelt. Rosebery said:

> My wife, as you know, is a Jewess by race, an Englishwoman by birth, and, today, by adoption, you have made her a Scotswoman.

His wife became a great Liberal hostess. He took an important part in organising Gladstone's crucial Midlothian campaign, at a cost to Rosebery, it is said, of £60,000. And that reinforced Rosebery's claims to high office. He later said:

> One of the minor results of the Midlothian Election was to close to me any London Club of which I was not a member.

He was blackballed from the Travellers' Club. He said:

> As I was already a member of eighteen this was of less consequence.

One of his homes was Mentmore Towers in Buckinghamshire, an opulent mansion in the Elizabethan style. It had been built by his wife's father. Mentmore was full of wonderful treasures—paintings, ceramics, silver, furniture, and books.* In 1896 he bought up, for one meal, every out-of-season strawberry in the country. The cost would have kept a family of four for more than a year. But he was one of the 12 men in the country with an annual income from land of more than £100,000.

A Scotsman and Glasgow graduate wrote of him:

---

\* Mentmore and most of its contents were sold in 1977 after the death of his son. The house then became owned by the followers of the guru Maharishi Mahesh Yogi, the promoter of transcendental meditation. Followers of the Maharishi say they are able to perform levitation or 'yogic flying', and Mentmore acquired the nickname of London's Third Airport.

I used to attend political meetings of all sides, and heard Gladstone many times, the old Duke of Argyll, the Marquis of Salisbury, Mr Chamberlain, and others, but though all were eloquent, and some made great orations, none could approach Lord Rosebery.

He had the most exquisite voice, an incomparable choice of words, and could reach heights of passion and of scorn. The lightest tone reached everyone in a large hall where other well-known speakers were bawling themselves hoarse in a vain effort to reach the back benches.

He was one of the few aristocrats I ever saw who looked like one, for I have seen bearers of noble names whose appearance suggested the village grocer or roused the desire to offer them a shilling to carry one's bag. His face was heavy, but was illuminated at times with a vivid and really sweet smile. His glance conveyed that sense of aloofness which I have noticed in some men of great intellect and in statesmen whose life had been spent in dealing with great affairs. He seemed to me the only man of my time with any vision, and I have always mourned that his speeches in the Lords urging reform of that House and of the Army were derided by Lord Salisbury [several times Conservative Prime Minister] and his followers.

Rosebery entered the Cabinet in 1885 and was twice Foreign Secretary. He succeeded Gladstone as Prime Minister in 1894. The Government was defeated the next year on a minor matter. Rosebery, as the Prime Minister, could have won a vote of confidence, or he could himself have resigned. In fact he announced the resignation of the entire Government. A general election followed and the Liberals lost. Rosebery stayed leader of the Liberal opposition until 1896. His Liberal Unionists supported the Boer War while Sir Henry Campbell-Bannerman and the radical wing of the Liberal Party opposed it. Rosebery gradually moved to the right of the Liberal Party and he always remained an imperialist. The conflicts within the Liberal Party were damaging.

His opponent for the Rectorship was Lord Kelvin, for the Conservatives. Kelvin was born William Thomson in Belfast but Thomson's father was appointed Professor of Mathematics at the University and the boy was taken to Scotland when he was eight. He became a student at the University at the age of 10 and went to Cambridge University at the age of 16. He was made Professor of Mathematics and Natural Philosophy at Glasgow in 1846 at the age of 22. He held the chair for more than 50 years.

Kelvin produced a profusion of inventions. The patents made him very wealthy. Honours given to him included a knighthood, the Legion of Honour and several other foreign orders, a clutch of honorary degrees, Fellowship of the Royal Society, and membership of innumerable other learned societies. The peerage came in 1892. Kelvin is buried in Westminster Abbey next to Isaac Newton. There is a statue to him in Kelvingrove Park, Glasgow, at the foot of the slope that leads from the river Kelvin, from which he took his title, up to the main University buildings of Gilmorehill.

Lord Kelvin's prestige in the University was extraordinarily high and Rosebery's emergence as his rival was resented by many people. All this was symbolised by an article in the *Glasgow University Magazine*. A duel was fought with swords, the *Magazine* said, by a supporter of Lord Rosebery and a supporter of Lord Kelvin.

> A heated argument took place between R. H. Begg, the notorious Tory, and La Torre, the Liberal enthusiast.[*]

Begg raved "at random" against Rosebery:

> La Torre's southern blood rose to fever heat as he tried to justify the selection. Instantly, immediately, suddenly, Begg designated his opponent with a name which cannot be here repeated.

Two hours later La Torre's seconds called upon Begg, who at once named his seconds. It was agreed the duel would be held in the Union. Begg, strong and a notable swordsman, chose swords and betting was all in his favour.

> Begg was evidently in splendid form. The white of his eye protruded, his arm quivered, his knees shook, and his teeth clattered together. He looked very brave, as indeed he always does, and his appearance inspired the spectators with keen appreciation. We have seldom seen so fine a specimen of humanity—tall, broad shouldered, powerful, short-winded, eloquent, and a fine-looking fellow all over. ... He employed the minutes before the call of time in abusing his opponent and putting out his tongue.

As they crossed blades, Begg:

> ... called loudly for the *Magazine* journalist, as he always likes his doings recorded ... every time La Torre almost hit him, out went the Tory's tongue. The fight was furious. Begg began to dictate the words he wanted printed in the *Magazine,* and we feel constrained to publish them.
>     'Begg, with great agility, bounded round his man. No comparisons of the merits of the men was possible... Then like an arrow from the bow, the president's blade flashed through the air. La Torre's cheek fell [i.e. he had been cut.] The blood rushed from his face. He leaped in the air ... He fell before the might of his conqueror'.

The "duel" has been called the last duel to be held in Scotland and has been re-enacted in the university precincts. This article in the *Magazine* has been treated seriously but is almost certainly a joke

It is hard in our times to perceive the importance that rectorial elections used to have in politics. Rosebery's campaign and success in 1899 do however show what could happen. Rosebery's election as Rector enhanced his prestige among his followers in the party. A rectorial election could be a success or a setback for a party in the country at large.

Rosebery was a Liberal Imperialist during the Boer War. The Liberal Party at the time of this election was in difficulties. British troops in South Africa had met disaster. "The jeering delight of the Irish at the news of

---

[*] Both were fourth-year students, Begg in law and the Italian La Torre in science.

every British defeat", wrote Rosebery's biographer Robert Rhodes James, "inflamed equally the Conservatives and the Liberal Imperialists, while the supine leadership of Campbell-Bannerman created an intense personal bitterness between the separate Liberal sections."

Kelvin became Chancellor of the University in 1904 but died in 1907 and was succeeded by Rosebery—the man who had defeated him for the Rectorship.

Rosebery was a Conservative or an Independent in 1909-1910. He achieved a remarkable score of being Rector of all four Scottish Universities.

# Boer War Supporter—
# or pro-Conservative Pendulum?

George Wyndham (Glasgow University Archives)

*George Wyndham, Conservative statesman
and man of letters (1863-1913)*

*Elected 1902*

When he was elected Rector Wyndham was a coming man. He was Under-Secretary for War when the South African war broke out in 1899. British forces suffered defeats at the beginning, and Wyndham defended the Government's record. He became Chief Secretary for Ireland in 1900, where his policy was maintenance of the Union and the promotion of economic development. He was sympathetic to the Irish.

He stood against John Morley, writer, editor, and Liberal statesman. It is hard to assess whether Wyndham's victory was because the students liked his stance over the Boer War and Ireland. It is, however, the case that his immediate predecessor and his immediate successor were Liberals which may indicate that the students were in a conservative mood when they chose Wyndham. Moreover, Morley was an apparently strong candidate.

Wyndham was to sponsor reforms to the tenure of Irish land in 1903. He resigned in 1905 over an attempt to bring about partial Home Rule there and his career was effectively finished. He was worn out by six years of overwork. His writings were on poetry of Shakespeare and Pierre de Ronsard and other subjects but politics drew him away from literature. He died aged 49.

# Conservatives play the Scottish Card, but it Fails

Herbert Asquith (Glasgow University Archives)

*Herbert Henry Asquith, Liberal statesman (1852-1928).*
*Prime Minister 1908-1916. Later Earl of Oxford and Asquith*

## Elected 1905

Asquith was the first Prime Minister, apart from Disraeli, who did not come from the landed classes. He was always called Herbert in his earlier years but switched to Henry from the time he met his future wife Emma Tennant, who had brilliant gifts, an original mind, and a strong character.

The other candidate for the rectorship was a Scot, the Marquis of Linlithgow, Conservative, who had been Governor-General of Australia and Secretary for Scotland. An extraordinary leaflet appeared during the campaign. It was anonymous and apparently was in support of Linlithgow but is in fact a brilliant spoof, calculated to make Linlithgow's candidature look foolish. The writer takes a Scottish nationalist line and parodies it. Nevertheless the leaflet does reveal that nationalist feelings were strong

—otherwise the spoof would not have worked. The first motion in the House of Commons for Scottish Home Rule had been moved 16 years before, in 1889 .

Asquith was a barrister and was MP for East Fife (for 32 years) and later for Paisley. When he was Home Secretary in the 1890s he acted against sweat shops and child labour and reformed the system of factory inspection. He advocated one man one vote, wanted monopoly holdings of land to be broken up, sought to end the exploitative employment of Chinese workers in South Africa, and above all campaigned for Free Trade.

The Liberal Party was riven by disputes about the Boer War (1899-1902). Was Britain's imperialist action justified? Or were the Boers being treated shockingly? Asquith went with the imperialist side and upset many members of his party.

Linlithgow was the seventh earl but was elevated to Marquis. He held junior offices in Conservative administrations and became Governor of Victoria (1889-1895).

He returned to Britain in 1895 and was Paymaster-General; and in 1900 was appointed the first Governor-General of Australia. He was very reluctant to ratify a measure of 1901 that said immigration was to be for whites only. Linlithgow resigned in 1902, saying that his salary was not enough to meet his expenses in office. He became Secretary for Scotland in 1905.

Lord Linlithgow was the representative of an ancient Scottish family. But his achievements did not quite match up to Asquith's, and Asquith's qualities, as described by his backers, would adorn an archangel.

Asquith, said one of his propaganda sheets, was:

> ... of the best type of our public men—unostentatious, scrupulously honourable and fair to his opponents, free from bitter personalities and envenomed partisan animosities, always discussing questions on the loftiest planes, just, comprehensive and considerate in his views, single-minded in his aims, devoid of desire for personal aggrandisement, loyal, steadfast, devoted to his country, and always placing its interests before those either of party or person... a democrat of democrats ... at once an idealist and a political reformer ...

and so on and on.

The spoof leaflet says, in part:

> We desire to call the attention of all Scottish students of this University to one very strong claim which the Marquis of Linlithgow has on our support in this Rectorial Election—a claim which will no doubt be overlooked or belittled by our opponents, but which to Scotsmen should be sufficiently powerful to make them give him their votes on this point alone....
>
> The Marquis of Linlithgow is a Scotsman; and we contend that this alone is sufficient reason for his election. Mr Asquith may be 'the mighty man of State' that the Liberal magazine names him; he may have served the country well, and have won fame as a speaker and a statesman—*but he is not a Scotsman.* We have here two

candidates for office—one a Scotsman, the other an Englishman. Should we, under any circumstances, reject our own countryman?

## Lord Linlithgow was honest and honourable.

And with such a fair representative of our native land suing for our honours, why should we go to England for our Lord Rector? Do we love England more than our own country? Does England love us, or even deal justly by us? Let us glance at our history and we shall soon discover the 'justice'. In the year 1603 the crowns of Scotland and England were united under a Scottish king. But was this a benefit to Scotland? History tells us that all the nobility of the land flocked to London, taking with them the wealth of the country, and from this time all through the reigns of the Stuarts Scotland was treated as a conquered country. ....

When our present King ascended the throne, the English, in spite of the loud dissent of Scotland, insisted on naming the King, Edward VII. He is not Edward VII of Scotland, but Edward I.

It is easy to see, from these few instances out of hundreds, how much cause we Scotsmen have to love our English friends. What have we gained? Trade? Rest assured that our trade has been gained in spite of, not through the English alliance. England has done nothing for us; so why should we honour her? Let us look to ourselves. Give Scotland's honours to Scotland's sons. Even though the Englishman [Asquith] should be a little cleverer than the Scotsman [Linlithgow]; even though he has done more work for the country, and has won greater renown in the doing of it—after all, Scotland is Scotland, and not Britain.

## The Liberal camp's propaganda said:

The authors of this astounding tract have done well in concealing their identity. We do not know whether it has been issued by the Conservative Club or not. At any rate it is not issued in their name. It may, perhaps, come from some patriot's club or other; but more childish nonsense has not been issued in the whole campaign.

## Butter would not melt in the Liberals' mouth.

## The Liberals went on, in a mock sanctimonious vein:

None are prouder of their country than we, none rejoice more in the great men who have been born therein, men whose work has cut a deep channel in the stream of knowledge ... But we as firmly maintain that while we are truly Scotch, we are nonetheless members of the wider nation—Great Britain. We heartily reject the narrowness which would insist we cannot be British as well as Scotch....

## And the Liberals went further, unctuously:

We wonder how English and foreign students at our University will take the pamphlet. Let them be assured that the Liberal Party, while truly appreciating the value of nationality, does not hold any such sectarian views as the pamphlet gives utterance to.

Campaigns traditionally included specially written songs. These efforts, often weak parodies of well-known songs, were not really meant to be performed. Here are, as examples, some specimens from *The Linlithgow Song Book*. They are not the worst examples that could be chosen.

There is a pub in London town—London town,
And there old Asquith sits him down—sits him down,
And drinks his dram and murmurs mournfullie
   About that faithless Varsitie.

*Chorus*

Fare the well for I must leave thee,
Do not let the parting grieve thee,
For remember that the greatest ass must go—must go.
Adieu, deluded friends, adieu, adieu, adieu,
For Lord Linlithgow stays with you—stays with you;
So I'll hide my head in cinders and in soot,
   And own I've fairly go the boot.

The next one was to the tune of *Scots Wha Hae*. It included these verses:

Wha wad guard Britannia's laws?
Fights he in Linlithgow's cause!
Fa's he? Then a hero fa's—
Death! 'tis victory!

Fierce the strife, the warfare long;
Bosoms heave, be arms as strong!
Fight! and yours the triumph song -
   Yours the victory!

Asquith's audience at his Installation was divided by gender: men at the front, women at the back. This was on the instructions of the Acting Principal who came in for much criticism for what he had done. That kind of thing was still going on in the 1950s. The Professor of English held his "ordinary" or first-year class at 9 a.m. and 10 a.m.: the first session for women (then called Queen Margaret students) and the second for men.

Asquith was to be Chancellor of the Exchequer from 1905 to 1908 (he introduced old age pensions). He succeeded Henry Campbell-Bannerman as Prime Minister in 1908. During his long term as Prime Minister he introduced the Parliament Act of 1911, which cut the power of the House of Lords; and had to face the suffragettes, acute troubles in Ireland, and the build-up the First World War. For most of his career he was against votes for women.

He formed a coalition Government in 1915 to prosecute the war. A dark moment came in 1916. Some Conservatives and some Liberal colleagues led by Lloyd George thought he was not vigorous enough in prosecuting the war and ousted him from the premiership. Lloyd George became Prime Minister.

The rift between the two men continued, although Asquith was leader of the party again from 1923 to 1926. The Liberal Party was weakened and was never again to be the main opposition to the Conservatives.

# A most Superior Person

Lord Curzon (Glasgow University Archives)

*Lord Curzon of Kedleston,*
*Conservative statesman (1859-1925)*
*Elected 1908*

Curzon annoyed the students by repeatedly postponing his installation. They mocked him and three mass meetings called for his resignation. The two sides were reconciled.

Curzon was a devoted public servant, a great Viceroy of India, a restorer of ancient and beautiful buildings in Britain and India, a most eligible bachelor in his youth, and an eminent figure in political life for more than 30 years. He always wanted to be Prime Minister but the prize eluded him.

His father was Lord Scarsdale, whose mansion, Kedleston Hall in Derbyshire, designed by Robert Adam, is now owned by the National Trust. The family traces its ancestry to Robert de Courson, from Courson in Normandy, who came over with the Conqueror.

Curzon went to Eton and Oxford and became an MP when he was 27. He travelled widely in the Orient and was under-secretary for India in 1891-1892 and for foreign affairs in 1895. He became Viceroy of India in

1898 when he was only 39. He was a reforming Viceroy. He quarrelled with Lord Kitchener the Commander-in-Chief in India: the issue was control of the army there. A power struggle followed. Kitchener won and Curzon resigned in 1905. On his return to Britain he found himself in a kind of limbo. The Liberal Party had been returned to power in 1905 and his political prospects, since he was a Conservative, were not good. (The Liberals were to be in power until a Coalition Government was formed in 1915.)

This was a bad time for Curzon, who was embittered by the political setbacks and the bruising quarrel with Kitchener. He took a revived interest in art and archaeology. He loved to collect antiques, works of art, and old buildings. And he wanted to keep himself in the public eye. That is why he let his name go forward for the Chancellorship of Oxford University: he was elected, defeating Lord Rosebery by a big margin, and he did a lot of excellent work for the University.

He also let his name go forward for the Rectorship of Glasgow, although in this case his motives were more complicated than obtaining a high-profile and prestigious post. He had hesitated about accepting nomination for Rector but learned that his old foe Sir Henry Campbell-Bannerman, the Prime Minister, was to be nominated by the other side. Campbell-Bannerman had blocked his return to political life. Curzon had been given an Irish barony when he was made Viceroy but when he came back from India he expected the usual earldom of the United Kingdom as a recognition of his work and status. Campbell-Bannerman refused to give it him and these matters rankled deeply. Curzon accepted the Glasgow nomination. He wanted to get revenge by defeating Campbell-Bannerman but his enemy died. Curzon wrote to a friend: "Damn the fellow, he has done it deliberately."

One of his rivals for the rectorship was David Lloyd George, the "Welsh wizard," who was Chancellor of the Exchequer and a future Prime Minister. Curzon confided to a friend that "the little Welsh bruiser [Lloyd George] may leave me a mangled and eviscerated corpse." The other rival was Keir Hardie, pacifist, parliamentarian, Scotsman, and the virtual creator of the Labour Party.

Curzon and Lloyd George did their best to score off one another in their propaganda. The two were to be opponents for years ahead. Both knew that the contest would be close.

The Conservative Club described Curzon as scholar, author, traveller, scientist, orator, and statesman. Socialism, said the Conservative Club, means repression and robbery. The Conservatives quoted, against Keir Hardie, a description of him by the leader of the university Socialist Party: "a Proletarian, an ex-Miner, an Agitator, a Socialist." The Conservative Club said he was an agitator, pure and simple.

Not only is the nomination of Keir Hardie an unwarranted and impudent intrusion into the arena of University Politics, but it casts a slur upon the dignity of the Rectorial Chair, which the Conservative Club is pledged to maintain, and in addition is altogether out of keeping with the high traditions of our *Alma Mater*.

And Lloyd George was "aptly described as a political hooligan," was "notorious as Leader of the Extreme Radicals" and was "the Rankest Pro-Boer in the Commons." (Lloyd George was nearly lynched at Birmingham Town Hall for his pro-Boer sympathies and had to be disguised as a policeman to escape.)

The Liberal Club, campaigning for Lloyd George, said that their man:

... shames the mincing snobbery of the aristocrat [Curzon] no less than the malevolence of the demagogue [Hardie]. Unlike the former, he had neither rank nor fortune to give him a start; unlike the latter, he did not spend his time in whining against circumstance. But he fought his way to the top by sheer ability and force of character, and now holds the second office under the Crown, and a record which the most brilliant among his brilliant colleagues may well envy. Surely an irresistible appeal to the old Scots spirit!

During the Liberal Party's tenure of office:

... the finances of the nation have been established on a sound basis; old-age pensions have become a reality at last; and, most of all, the Liberal party has **done** what no other great political party ventured to **propose,** viz., to attack that demoralising monopoly, the Liquor Traffic. Does not the courage of the leaders in standing up manfully against the Brewer call for the whole-hearted support of all not deep in the slough of indifference...?

As for Lord Curzon, we cannot conceive that the students of the most Democratic of the Scottish Universities will seriously consider him ... We have ever been proud to despise official pomposity, and consider nothing so despicable as priggishness and snobbery ... The measure of the vote given to Lord Curzon will measure the desire of the students of to-day to disavow the past, and will reveal how far a tawdry snobbishness has displaced love of character, merit, and grit.

Osborne Mavor (who later took the pseudonym James Bridie, by which he is now known), was a brilliant figure in student life. He wrote in his autobiography of the campaign:

We of the Liberal Club had chosen as our champion Henry Campbell-Bannerman. It was of Sir Henry that R. B. Cunninghame Graham said: "He has all the qualifications for a great Liberal Prime Minister. He wears spats and he has a beautiful set of false teeth".

But on the death of Campbell-Bannerman the choice of the Liberal Club fell on Lloyd George. Bridie was not pleased and later wrote:

He had just become Chancellor of the Exchequer and nobody could understand why. He did not seem to us a weighty person. Though we did not lay great stress on scholarship and gentility among ourselves we liked a savour of them in our Lord Rector and Lloyd George did not appear to us to reach pass marks in these qualities. Nor did we like Welsh Nonconformists... We thought he could very well have stayed at the Board of Trade and that it was weak of Asquith [the Prime Minister] to kowtow to the Welsh Nonconformists. We thought that his boots were too big for him and that he would presently fade out and be heard of no more. But he was all we could get, and with heavy hearts we set to work to make the best of him.

It was during this election campaign that Mavor, Walter Elliot (see p. 154) and others devised the great anthem of Glasgow University students, *Ygorra,* which goes:

Sala, sava, sala sava,
Cora bella, cora bella,
Ching, ching, ching ho,
Varsity ygorra, varsity ygorra
Ygorra, ygorra, ygorra!

The tune is borrowed from the song "My Dear Love" by Guiseppe Giordani (1753-1798), who wrote music for operas and ballets. (see p. 223) On special occasions, a person's name was put in the last line of *Ygorra* to honour him or her. For example, the students sang it for their much-loved Principal, Sir Donald MacAlister, and the last line went: "MacAlister ygorra ...etc." The word *Ygorra* was used as the title of the Charities Day ("Rag Week") magazine.

The story goes that a hymn of praise to Lloyd George was sung at an Eisteddfod. A garbled and meaningless version (the original was of course in Welsh) reached the people who ran the *Glasgow University Magazine.*

Mavor and Elliot adapted the garbled version and persuaded the Liberal Club to use it in the rectorial campaign. Mavor and Elliot claimed that the original Welsh words meant:

Hail to the saviour of his people!
He is a man of war and at the same time of peace.
He is the Protector of the Poor.
Lloyd George is a very great man indeed.

The song lived on for many generations but seems now to have died out.

Curzon was the winner of the Rectorial election, but by a very small margin. Keir Hardie was nowhere. Curzon wrote:

I met the little Welshman [Lloyd George] afterwards and half expected him to direct that angular elbow towards my eye. To my astonishment, all he did was cackle with laughter and say: "Trust the Gaels to choose a Lord. They're even more snobbish than the Welsh."

Curzon had been installed as Chancellor of Oxford University shortly before he became Rector of Glasgow. He took a great deal of interest in Oxford University: he reformed the college finances, raised funds, attended ceremonies, and wrote an average of 24 letters a day about the University's business. His job at Glasgow was in contrast not close to his heart. He thought the students there "rather a wild and uncouth lot." Repeatedly he postponed his installation and Address, sending messages saying that his back was bad, or that he had been in a car accident and was confined to bed, or that he was going to South Africa for the sake of his health. Some of these excuses were genuine. At last he promised them faithfully he would appear—and sent the students a message saying a Governmental crisis, over reform of the House of Lords, obliged him to stay in London.

"We were not," wrote Bridie, "accustomed to be treated in this fashion by mere ex-Viceroys." Three mass meetings of the students called for his resignation. Students held a public procession during which they mocked their Rector as being Rostand's Chanticleer—the cock who believed that unless he crowed the sun would not rise. The implication was that Curzon believed if he left London for two days the sun would cease to rise on the British Empire. The English political cartoonists took up the idea and portrayed Curzon as a puffed-up and ridiculous cock. He hated that. He remarked: "Really it is intolerable that they should lecture and hector a Lord Rector in this fashion."

The calls made by meetings of students for Curzon's resignation put the Students' Representative Council in a quandary, for the SRC is the official channel for the views of students. The SRC consulted the Town Clerk of Glasgow. His opinion was that these matters were properly for the SRC. A plebiscite was held and the student body exonerated the Rector by a large majority of intentional discourtesy.

Curzon was lampooned for his perceived haughtiness:

> My name is George Nathaniel Curzon;
> I am a most superior person.
> My cheek is pink, my hair is sleek
> I dine at Blenheim once a week.

But Bridie also said that Curzon "seemed to us a singularly amiable and patient person."

He ran into trouble at a party for some students. Bridie wrote:

A semi-circle of presidents and secretaries was disposed in front of Lord Curzon's chair ... Johnny Mowat [vice-president of the Students' Representative Council] and I were wandering about the room discussing great matters. As we passed the apex of the semi-circle we heard the Rector say, "I suppose the dull moments of my speech [the Address] will be enlivened with bursts of song?" Johnny Mowat's flying elbows opened a space between the secretary of the Temperance Society and the president of the Bible Students' Union. His large, pale face and fiery, red-rimmed eyes confronted the statesman and, in his somewhat metallic *tenorio robusto* voice, he observed: "You'll have to see that there are no dull moments in your speech." Lord Curzon bridled. He said, "Ah! Shall I hand it to you to revise before I deliver it?" "No,' said Johnny. "I've no time. I'm working for my final. But Mr Williamson [honorary secretary of the SRC] will be very glad to do it for you".

Curzon did give an Address, although it came only nine months before the end of his term of office.

Curzon was to have a celebrated affair with Elinor Glyn, a novelist and actress, who was dazzlingly beautiful, cultivated, and intelligent. When they met she was famous for one of her steamy novels which included amorous tusslings on a tiger skin. The book was naturally a best-seller. This titbit went around:

> Would you like to sin
> with Elinor Glyn
> on a tiger skin?
> Or would you prefer
> to err with her
> on some other fur?

The verse goes much better in an English accent than in a Scottish.

Curzon, soon after they met, sent her a tiger skin. He had shot the animal himself.

She fell in love with him at first sight. She wrote to a friend that Curzon was "my King and I his grovelling slave, ever ready to kiss his hands, lick his beloved toes." Curzon's wife Mary had died—the climate of India had harmed her health. Elinor Glyn's husband died in 1915. Curzon and Glyn were free to marry. They had known each other for eight and a half years. Curzon, however, wanted a male heir, but Elinor was 51. Moreover, she did not have the sensual beauty that Curzon liked. In 1916 he married Grace Duggan, an American widow. Curzon had not warned Elinor Glyn that the engagement was to happen. She learned about it from an advertisement in *The Times*.

His first wife, Mary Victoria Leiter (1870-1906), was the daughter of Levi Zeigler Leiter, who was a co-founder of a great department store in Chicago, Marshall Field's. They were Pennsylvanian German and Moravian Brethren, not Jewish as is sometimes said.

When they married he received a lot of money from her family; and he spent some of it on Kedleston. She hated the place and his family. In India she had a household of 800 servants. Curzon wanted her to be referred to as the Vicereine but there was trouble about that with the establishment as no other wife of a Viceroy had borne that title.

When Curzon married Grace Duggan the gossip was that he had again married for money. That was not true. Grace spent extravagantly and that gave people the wrong idea. She spent on credit. Her debts were formidable.

Curzon returned to politics in 1915 and was Foreign Secretary from 1919 to 1924. He wanted to succeed Bonar Law as Prime Minister in 1923 but Baldwin succeeded. It was a crushing blow. Curzon described Baldwin as "a man of the utmost insignificance." In fact he was passed over because it was politically impossible to have a Prime Minister in the House of Lords and because his colleagues in the party did not want him anyway.

Curzon as Foreign Secretary was largely responsible for the settlement at Lausanne, which was a tidying-up of frontiers and rights in the Balkans, the Aegean, Greece, and Turkey. He also intervened in the issue of the Rhineland, where France was encouraging separatism.

Curzon was made a Marquis in 1921: status and peerages were important to him.

He already been given a viscountcy. But he had no son, only three daughters. Grace had many miscarriages and never gave him the male heir he wanted. He managed to fix it that some of his titles went, on his death, to his relations. That took a lot of trouble and expense.

# Suffragettes interrupt the Installation

Augustine Birrell (Glasgow University Archives)

*Augustine Birrell, Liberal statesman, lawyer, biographer, and essayist (1850-1933)*

*Elected 1911*

Birrell had a long and distinguished career as a parliamentarian, with a special interest in education and Ireland, and as an author. He was President of the Board of Education from 1905 to 1907. He was Chief Secretary for Ireland from 1907 to 1916 and helped to found the National University of Ireland in 1908 with colleges in Dublin, Cork, and Galway. The aim was a representative Roman Catholic university to balance Trinity College Dublin, the bastion of the Protestant Ascendancy.

Birrell had been defeated for the Rectorship in 1896. Birrell's competitor this time round was Lord Charles Beresford, the obligatory Conservative but not an outstanding figure. Beresford was a son of the Marquis of Waterford and was to be the first Baron Beresford. He was a high-ranking naval officer who also sat as a Conservative MP.

The Installation was disrupted by suffragettes, who were especially active at that time. Almost every year from 1869 a Bill was brought before Parliament to give women the vote. The campaign was closely connected with the campaign to give married women rights over property. Without the vote, said the campaigners, the law on married women's property would not be reformed.

Men's automatic rights to their wives' property and earnings on marriage was finally removed in 1882. But the issue of votes for women remained. Mrs Emmeline Pankhurst had founded the Women's Franchise League in 1889; it became the Women's Social and Political Union in 1903. The suffragettes, when the Installation was held, had already taken to violent tactics but had not yet started going on hunger strike.

The installation was held, as usual, in St Andrew's Hall and began with the usual din from the students as they gathered. Stewards were scattered around the building. Birrell had spoken hardly half a dozen words when a cry went up: "Votes for Women." The cry was repeated in other parts of the hall. The stewards seized the interruptors and unceremoniously removed them, to howls and cheers from the audience. About a dozen women were treated in this way.

As the speech went on, the interruptions went on. A woman was removed from the gallery amid so much uproar that the Rector said:

> Gentlemen, I am almost persuaded that you have come here today to hear the women and not me. I really think you might try what the effect of leaving them alone would be.

The Principal, Sir Donald MacAlister, told the audience:

> It is quite clear that there are some persons who have intruded into this room for the purpose of preventing you from hearing your Lord Rector. I ask you not to play their game.

Later protestors were removed with as little disturbance as possible. The *Glasgow Herald* noted:

> Apart from the disturbances caused by the suffragettes, the Lord Rector was accorded a much more courteous hearing than some of his predecessors obtained.

The Rector was taken in procession back to the University's main building at Gilmorehill.

Then a cry went up: "Now for the suffragists." The command "Line up" was given. Several hundred students, singing, whistling, and carrying sticks and missiles, marched along Gibson Street and Woodlands Road, and reached the western end of Sauchiehall Street.

The Women's Social and Political Union had a shop in Sauchiehall Street. The mob sent a volley of stones smashing through a glass door and a plate glass window. A mass of students swept into the shop. Books and pamphlets were scattered. Flags and other emblems of the suffragettes were seized. Students jumped on the counter, dancing and shouting. A solitary woman stood on a balcony at the rear of the shop, motionless with fear. The rioters left.

The woman who had stood on the balcony walked, with two other women, to the front of the shop, stepping through the broken glass. She shouted: "Cowards, cowards", but her words were lost in the shouting and cheering. A big crowd of onlookers had gathered and the police were unable to get through while the destruction was going on.

Other ugly incidents happened in the centre of the city. Another suffragettes' premises, in West Campbell Street, was stoned and its windows broken. Advertisements for a suffragist meeting were wrecked. Several men were arrested at these other incidents.

Birrell's later public life was undistinguished. When he was Chief Secretary for Ireland, he failed to foresee the Easter Rising of 1916, admitted his negligence, and resigned. His political career was over and he left Parliament in 1918.

Books by him include lives of Charlotte Brontë, William Hazlitt, and Andrew Marvell, but he was best known for two volumes of essays: *Obiter Dicta* and *More Obiter Dicta.** These two books are charming and their scholarship is unobtrusive. He was able to write entertainingly on a dull subject.

The suffragettes won their cause when women aged over 30 were given the vote in 1918 and women between 21 and 30 were given the vote in 1928. The first country to give women the vote was New Zealand, in 1893. Women did not vote in Switzerland, in national elections, until 1971.

---

* "Obiter dicta" are remarks by a judge which are meant as asides and not to be taken as an integral part of the judge's opinion or verdict.

# French President chosen as Sign of Friendship

## *Raymond Poincaré, French statesman and President of France (1860-1934)*

### *Elected 1914*

The students' choice was a gesture of solidarity and friendship to France: the First World War had broken out only two months before. He was un-opposed—something that happened very rarely. Poincaré's term was extended beyond the usual period because of the war and also so that he could deliver his Address in the customary way.

Candidates for the rectorial election of 1914 had been lined up: a Socialist, a Conservative, and a Liberal. But the First World War broke out, the political clubs declared a truce, and a joint invitation from the Liberals and the Conservatives went to the President of France. He was the first foreigner to hold the office. Edinburgh University, by contrast, chose as

Rector in 1914 Field Marshal Lord Kitchener, hero of Khartoum and Secretary for War.

Poincaré had had a long career in politics, being elected a deputy in 1887 when he was aged 27. He was appointed a Senator in 1903. He headed a right-wing coalition Government in 1912, a Government which sought to reform the electoral system and to raise France's international prestige. He was elected President in February 1913 and served for seven years. President Poincaré intervened in politics more than any of his predecessors since the 1870s.

One of Poincaré's staff wrote a message to the students in French, published in the *Glasgow University Magazine* in 1914. It says, in translation:

> Among the distinctions conferred upon Raymond Poincaré since his accession to the Presidency, his election as Rector has certainly been among those that have particularly touched him... The President is the personification of the national honour of France and the rights of Man.
>
> The University of Glasgow has carried out an act of good and sincere friendship towards a faithful Ally. The two peoples have fought long and bitterly, but that has been like a man and a woman who know that one day their love will be the stronger. Let us hope that the reconciliation will be eternal for the greater good of liberty, justice, and civilisation.

Poincaré's installation and Address took place on November 13, 1919, very close to the first anniversary of the Armistice. Almost every single person in the audience had lost a relation or friend in the War. The Address was full of emotion. Here are some passages:

> I was above all deeply touched to find, in my election, a fresh mark of that 'auld alliance' which, in days of yore, united both our peoples, and has received from these last years a revival of strength.
>
> It is Scotland that, many centuries ago, sowed the first gems of the *Cordiale Entente*; and there is no Scot, there is no Frenchman, who does not remember the words of Shakespeare:
>
>> If that you would France win,
>> Then with Scotland first begin.
>
> No one has had more and better opportunities than I, of witnessing the deeds of valour and devotion performed during the past four years, on the soil of France, by the men and women of Scotland, and I am glad to assure them today of the gratitude of my fellow-countrymen.
>
> As to the Scottish soldiers, I had long known of their reputation: 'Lions in the field and lambs in the home'.
>
> The youth of your Universities, and especially those of Glasgow, have enlisted enthusiastically. Their minds had been formed by masters who had inspired them with the sense of responsibility and with firmness of purpose: they were thus prepared for victory. The Scottish battalions have shared in the hardest fights, and have everywhere behaved with an indomitable gallantry.
>
> How many valiant Scots are ... lying in the soil of France, after fighting for the common ideal of both our nations? To the mothers and widows of these heroes, I give the assurance that their image will ever be engraved in the memory and the heart of my country, and that the French women will take care of their graves as if they were those where their own husbands and children are sleeping.

Is it not a Scot who was Commander-in-Chief, during the greatest part of the war, of all the armies of the British Empire which were fighting in France and in Belgium?...

And I will add without any flattery that Field-Marshal Haig has embodied, during this long war, all the finest qualities of your nation. I saw him in the most tragic hours, and I presided at times over important conferences where he gave proof of as much clear-sightedness as moral energy.

I do not forget the decisive part the British Navy has played in the war, and I know the great contribution Scotland, and in Scotland, Glasgow, has furnished as well in the recruitment of the crews as in active shipbuilding. Both by sea and by land has the Scottish youth, with the French youth, bravely defended right and freedom.

For a French Rector of a great Scottish University, the only means of not being too unworthy of the title he had received from the spontaneous kindness of the Students will consist in devoting the remainder of his life to this brotherly co-operation of both our peoples.

I willingly pledge my faith to you, Ladies and Gentlemen, that I will never forsake a task the greatness of which I know, and which concerns not only the future of our nations but also the very fate of mankind.

The University Chapel, which is in one wing of the western quadrangle, was dedicated in 1929 to the glory of God and in memory of the 755 sons of the University who died in the First World War. Their names are recorded on the walls. The names are also recorded on the walls of the 404 members of the University who died in the Second World War.

James Bridie wrote in his autobiography, *One Way of Living,* that at the outbreak of war in August 1914:

... nearly every Highland student in Glasgow enlisted in Lochiel's Camerons. One day, in the winter of 1914, I was standing on Laffan's Plain, near Aldershot, with the Ninth and Fourteenth Divisions of Kitchener's army. I was with the Fourteenth. The melting snow was over my boot tops and I, with twenty thousand other men, was soaked to the skin. We had been there for three hours, waiting for Lord Kitchener ... What with the sleet and the steamy fog it was impossible to see anybody but the battalion in front. But we kept, in our misery, a vague impression that the plain was full of soldiers. The seeping sleet fell, silently blanketing all sounds but occasional grunts of distress and invocations to the Redeemer from the suffering troops. Suddenly, from miles away, I hear *Ygorra*. The Camerons were singing it to keep warm.

At the Battle of Loos, wrote Bridie:

Lochiel's Camerons went over the top dribbling footballs and singing a song that puzzled their officers very much. I am told a piper played the accompaniment. Their chaplain wrote to the papers about it after the War, and the song he had managed, by listening carefully, to transcribe in some sort of mangled version, was ... *Ygorra*.

Poincaré from 1922 to 1924 was again Prime Minister, the first former President of France to lead a Government. He took charge of foreign affairs and pursued an ardently nationalistic policy. He sought to enforce the Treaty of Versailles, especially in Germany's reparations, but his aims were frustrated. From mid-1926 to mid-1929 his Government carried through stringent financial economies and stabilised the franc.

# A Memorable Address by an Ailing Man

Andrew Bonar Law (Glasgow University Archives)

*Andrew Bonar Law, Conservative statesman (1858-1923). Prime Minister 1922-1923*

*Elected 1919*

Bonar Law was a young Glasgow clerk in 1879 when he heard Gladstone's great rectorial Address in the Kibble Palace, the huge glasshouse in the Botanic Gardens near the University. Gladstone fired him with ambition to achieve the same honour and speak to a similar meeting. Bonar Law achieved both these ambitions.

He was one of two Glasgow businessmen to become Prime Minister: the other was Henry Campbell-Bannerman, who held the post from 1905 to 1908. His father was a Presbyterian minister of Scottish descent in New Brunswick, Canada. When his mother died and his father remarried, the boy was sent to live with well-off relations, on his mother's side, in the Glasgow area. He made money in Glasgow, first as a banker and then as a partner in a firm of iron brokers.

Bonar Law entered Parliament in 1900, when he was 42, became leader of the Conservatives in the Commons in 1911 and was Colonial Secretary (1915-1916), Chancellor of the Exchequer (1916-1918), Lord Privy Seal (1919), and Leader of the House of Commons (from 1916).

Bonar Law liked a meal of boiled chicken and rice pudding with ginger ale (he was a teetotaller.) He was a heavy smoker and immune to the charms of music and literature but played bridge and chess very well. His given names were Andrew and Bonar but "Andrew" was never used. His friends called him Bonar. He was always referred to not as Law but as Bonar Law, as if it were a double-barrelled name lacking only a hyphen. He is an indexer's nightmare.

When President Raymond Poincaré of France was elected to the Rectorship in 1914, the political clubs had agreed to drop their own candidates. Among them was Bonar Law. An attempt was made, when the next election became due in 1919, to continue this apolitical approach. The Students' Representative Council held a meeting of the political clubs in the hope of an agreement on a single candidate to be returned unanimously. The move failed.

Bonar Law's main opponent Gilbert Murray, a strong Liberal, was Professor of Greek at Oxford University and a public figure. Murray had been appointed Professor of Greek at Glasgow in 1889 when he was 23. It was a prestigious post, he was inexperienced, and the students were tough. He wrote to his wife about his early lectures:

> It was an awful strain ... It seems that the whole work is policing. You have, so I'm told, never to look at your book, and never to look at one man for more than a few seconds. You keep your eyes wandering up and down every corner of the room, watching for insubordination. Of course I shall beat them in the end, but it is such degrading work.

He was on a sleeper train to London at about this time and found himself sitting up suddenly in his berth and saying in firm tones: "I insist on silence." A clergyman quavered from the upper berth: "I beg your pardon, sir, I have been told that I snore."

He made his mark as a teacher. One of his former students, Lord Lindsay of Birker, philosopher and educationist (the former Sandy Lindsay), said:

> When I was a student at Glasgow, professors gave their best to their ordinary classes. The wonderful impression which A. C. Bradley [Professor of English] and Gilbert Murray made on the students of the University was made through their ordinary classes, not on a mere handful of people who took honours in English or Greek ... That tradition ... produced in me the impression that anyone could teach honours subjects but it required one's whole imagination and energy to teach the ordinary class.

He was Regius Professor of Greek at Oxford from 1908 to 1936. He was not only a great scholar but was a prominent activist for the League of Nations.

The other candidate was Bertrand Russell (Earl Russell), mathematician, philosopher, controversialist, and later a Nobel prizewinner for literature and campaigner for nuclear disarmament. Bertrand Russell's name was put forward by the Socialist Club. The club originally wanted to nominate Karl Liebknecht, who with Rosa Luxemburg was a founder-member of the German Communist Party in 1918. He led an abortive revolt in Berlin in 1919—the Spartacus Rising—in which Rosa Luxemburg took part. At about the time the invitation from the Socialist Club arrived, Liebknecht was murdered by army officers. The next choice was Rosa Luxemburg, but she too was murdered by army officers. What could the Socialist Club do? Russell was chosen as the most controversial and exciting person the committee could think of. He accepted at once. He had been an active pacifist during the First World War. For this Trinity College, Cambridge, deprived him in 1916 of his fellowship there. His pacifist beliefs brought him imprisonment in 1918. He was already a highly distinguished academic figure.

Bonar Law got 1,073 votes, Murray 726, and Russell 80. Murray would have valued the honour very much. He also was defeated four times when he stood for one of Oxford University's parliamentary seats. Russell's vote was small because of political and social feelings at the time.

Bonar Law's election by the students gave him even greater pleasure than his honorary Doctorate of Civil Law from Cambridge University, especially since he was a Conservative and Glasgow was a centre of Liberalism and Socialism.

The subject he chose for his Address was *Ambition and Success*. Friends noted that he appeared more anxious about this speech than about any other he had given, but his oratory did not reach the heights of Gladstone's, his admired model. By the time Bonar Law delivered his Address in March 1921, he was exhausted: he had been in high political office for six difficult years. A senior civil servant mentioned Bonar Law's condition to the Prime Minister, Lloyd George, in the January of that year. Lloyd George said: "B. L. ought to take a drink. Unfortunately he is a teetotaller ... failing drink, the only remedy for Bonar is a wife." (He was a widower.) Both ideas were out of the question.

Bonar Law perhaps knew that he was dying. The historian Robert Blake (Lord Blake) wrote in *The Unknown Prime Minister*, his biography of Bonar Law, that the subject, *Ambition and Success*:

> ... seemed a surprising choice for someone who was widely but erroneously believed to be wholly without that quality. His address ... contained no startling new thoughts, and does not lend itself to quotation.

The man looked grey and strained. His voice failed him now and then. He spoke, as he always did, without notes but this time his marvellous memory failed him several times and at one point and he was silent for about two minutes. His audience, boisterously, tried to fill in the gaps and that disconcerted him even more. But his speech was received with great applause.

There were celebrations of every kind, at which he had to be present—torchlight processions in cold and dank weather, luncheon parties, and even dances. Bonar Law was suffering from high blood pressure and in the same month his doctor advised him to take several months' rest. He retired in 1921. In spite of ill health he was Prime Minister from October 1922 to May 1923. He resigned from ill health and died the same year.

# Rectorial Address that Rang around the Country

*Lord Birkenhead (Frederick Edwin Smith), Conservative statesman, orator, wit, and lawyer. (1872-1930)*

## *Elected 1922*

Birkenhead's Rectorial Address became hugely controversial and of all the Addresses ever made was the one which made most impact on the public mind. It took a tough and unfashionable line about several issues but especially about the League of Nations; and right-thinking people were shocked. One phrase stood out, "glittering prizes for those with sharp swords", and was used as shorthand for the whole speech. Birkenhead was dogged by the controversy until the end of his life.

    F. E. Smith made a name for himself as a barrister in Liverpool and entered Parliament for a Liverpool constituency. His maiden speech lasted an hour and was full of witticisms and invective. He became famous for the brilliance of his rhetoric.

He was fond of sporting a red flower in his buttonhole and holding a long cigar. He had a prodigious income at the height of his career at the Bar but was a great spender. He loved socialising, staying up late, cards, and horses.

He came from Birkenhead, close to Liverpool, and Liverpool had a large Roman Catholic population of Irish background. As a Tory he was therefore sympathetic to the Orange cause. He entered Parliament in 1906.

As a lawyer Birkenhead defended Ethel le Neve, mistress of Dr Crippen the wife-murderer, and acted in other sensational cases. During the Irish crisis of 1914 he opposed Home Rule and was the Crown prosecutor in 1916 in the case of Roger Casement, an Irishman who plotted an uprising in Ireland and sought German help. Casement was hanged for high treason. Birkenhead played a major part in the Irish settlement of 1921. The main aim of his Irish policy was the preservation of Protestant rights in Ulster. He was made Earl of Birkenhead on being appointed Lord Chancellor in 1919. He wanted to be remembered for his important work on reforming the law, especially land law.

The others standing were:

Sir John Simon, lawyer and Liberal statesman. He had been Solicitor-General, Attorney-General, and Home Secretary. He was to be Foreign Secretary, Chancellor of the Exchequer, and Lord Chancellor.

H. G. Wells, novelist and writer of short stories; pioneer of science fiction, and progressive thinker. He was an advocate of free love and a practitioner of it. He was backed by a confederation of clubs.

Birkenhead received 1,165 votes, Simon 530, and Wells 353. The students returned a Conservative; but at the General Election in that year Glasgow returned one Liberal, four Conservatives, and 10 Socialists. The students, as might be expected, did not represent a cross-section of Glasgow's population.

The title of the Address was *Idealism in International Politics.*

He was heavily sarcastic about the League of Nations.

Untaught by previous experience; undeterred by the shattering refutation of their beliefs which the Great War brought with it, the Idealists immediately had the originality to exploit its outbreak for their own controversial purposes. It was indeed unfortunate, they admitted, that the war should have occurred at all, and especially war so savagely conducted and flung over so enormous an area of the world's surface. But, after all, it had its bright side. For it was to be a war to end war. This time, at least, when once the ploughshare, according to the correct tradition, had ousted the weapons of war, there was to be no further declension into primeval savagery. And so we were to have a League of Nations consisting in time of all the nations, great and small, in the world; equipped with military and naval force, and therefore able to make good its decisions against a recalcitrant member.

While I thought and think that there was and is still a modest area within which the League of Nations may make useful contribution to the harmony of the world, the larger claims made on its behalf have always seemed to me frankly fantastic. Its framers forgot human nature as absurdly as they neglected history. What in the history of the world has ever happened which afforded foothold for expectations so megalomaniac?

He spoke of the Roman Empire:

... teaching the entire world through the whole of its stern, dominating, and Imperial sway, that might was right, and that a sharp sword in the hand of a disciplined soldier was the most persuasive argument in world diplomacy.

Birkenhead attempted to apply to human societies the Darwinian theories of evolution and the survival of the fittest. Marx, at the other end of the political spectrum, attempted to do the same thing. That exercise is tempting but sterile.

Politically, economically, and philosophically the motive of self-interest not only is, but must be, and ought to be, the mainspring of human conduct ... Mankind subsists precariously upon this globe on the terms of constant and contributory toil. The experience of thousands, perhaps hundreds of thousands, of years has shown that the desire of self-advancement is the only adequate incentive for that standard of labour and achievement which each individual must be encouraged in the common scheme to afford.

The peroration of Birkenhead's Address said:

The world continues to offer glittering prizes for those who have stout hearts and sharp swords ... It is for us who in our history have proved ourselves a martial, rather than a military, people to abstain, as has been our habit, from provocation; but, so equipped, to march with heads erect and bright eyes along the road of our Imperial destiny.

This kind of remark was perhaps inappropriate so soon after the First World War; many people in his audience were likely to take some offence at the martial tone of what he said.

The phrase "glittering prizes" as sometimes used today originated from that speech. It was not however invented by Birkenhead. The newspaper writers and other commentators had probably neither heard nor read with the care the whole speech but picked up a few paragraphs from it.

Lord Curzon, a very senior Tory, said that Birkenhead:

... has angered all thinking and serious people by his Glasgow Rectorial Address ... The women voters are said to detest him.

Birkenhead's biographer John Campbell wrote:

The reaction to F.E.'s words was immediate and sustained. To the new orthodoxy of the soft left, to all the *bien pensants* of the League of Nations Union and other bodies which believed, as a fervent article of faith, that all that was necessary to avert war was to talk peace, and held that great armaments by their very existence were the cause of war, F.E.'s blunt scepticism and reiteration that, on the contrary, the only way to preserve peace was to be prepared for war came as a blasphemous affront. For a decade or more after the Treaty of Versailles, even those who had little belief in the efficacy of the League of Nations found it prudent to pay lip-service to its great potential. Alone among leading statesmen, F.E. expressed his doubts; for his effrontery he was reviled as a warmonger for the rest of his life. For daring to suggest that good intentions might not be enough, he was denounced from pulpits and from pacifist platforms up and down the country, and ostracised even by those of his own party who almost certainly, in their hearts, agreed with him.

A meeting of the League of Nations Union was held soon after the Address; Birkenhead was a vice-president. A member sought to have him removed from the post but the chairman said that Lord Birkenhead was a man of exuberant vitality. "Not all the things the noble lord said were absolutely consistent." The call for resignation was not successful.

The students listened attentively and quietly to the Address. The text is not vivacious nor amusing as the audience might have hoped for —Birkenhead did have a great reputation as an orator and wit. Indeed many passages might be thought obscure. Perhaps the students were quiet because they were doing their best to hang on to his every word and follow his argument.

But there is another reason for the quiet behaviour—a reason that reflects credit on the students. Their much-respected Principal, Sir Donald MacAlister, had been dangerously ill. Two days before the ceremony the doctors told his wife Edith that it was out of the question for Sir Donald to attend: the audience would be too noisy and disturbing:

> If you allow the Principal to go to it, you will probably not get him home alive. Any excitement might kill him.

His wife wrote that he refused to stay away and that he said:

> It is my duty to be there. I can't possibly let the students down. If it kills me it can't be helped. I'd sooner die than shirk what I ought to do.

Lady MacAlister told the President of the Students' Representative Council, Gavin MacCallum, what had happened and asked him if it would be possible to ensure a quiet Rectorial. He returned that evening with the President of the Union, Ronald M. Macphail. They said that they had held an emergency mass meeting of the students in the middle of the day and that the students, one and all, had pledged themselves to make no disturbance.

The *Glasgow Herald* reported on the ceremony:

> The contrast of the two sides of the proceedings deeply impressed everyone who was privileged to be present at the great gathering in St Andrew's Hall. On the one hand there was the boisterous enthusiasm preceding the installation, a period of privilege dear to the heart of students, and on the other the earnest attention with which the Lord Rector's closely woven address was followed during the better part of an hour. There was a striking absence of those light-hearted flippancies with which the Rectorial Address is usually interspersed.

Sir Donald wrote to the president of the Students' Representative Council:

I want to express to you and to your colleagues, and the whole body of students whom you represent, my grateful acknowledgements for the manner in which the arrangements made for the Rector's installation were carried through. I heard nothing but admiration expressed by the distinguished company who honoured us by their presence, for the attitude of self-respect and self-control maintained by the students during the delivery of their Rector's address. It was a model for other generations, and other places, to copy.

Birkenhead was to be Secretary of State for India from 1924 to 1928. His high spending in the end forced him to give up politics and make money in the City. He led life to the full and died aged 58.

# The Dandy who wore an Orchid and a Monocle

*Austen Chamberlain, Conservative statesman,
later Sir Austen (1863-1937)*

## Elected 1925

Chamberlain was knowledgeable about flowers, often had an orchid in his buttonhole, wore a monocle, and dressed immaculately. The students teased him about the monocle. He was son of the politician Joseph Chamberlain, who had become Rector 1896, and half-brother of Neville Chamberlain, Prime Minister from 1937 to 1940. Austen Chamberlain's manner of dress was an exact copy of his father's. His father adopted it to proclaim his respectability and status, although the top people tended to dress informally, even sloppily.

Austen Chamberlain was Foreign Secretary when elected. He was soon to be joint winner of the Nobel prize for peace in recognition of his work in negotiating the Locarno Pact. (The other winner was an American diplomat.) The Locarno Pact was between Britain, France, Belgium, Germany, and Italy and its aim was to prevent aggression and ensure peace in Europe. Chamberlain was soon also to be made a Knight of the Garter. He had been Chancellor of the Exchequer, Secretary of State for India, and leader of the Conservative Party. He was from a political dynasty and was trained like a racehorse for the Prime Ministership but he was not ruthless enough.

Hundreds of the students at his Installation wore monocles, which were especially put on sale in the Union. But Chamberlain rather spoiled the effect. When on the platform he signed the oath that he would do his duties in the office: he had to take off his monocle and put on a pair of ordinary glasses. When he had signed, he took off the glasses and put back the monocle.

His opponents were G. K. (Gilbert Keith) Chesterton, novelist, poet, journalist, essayist, and one of the founders of Distributism, and Sidney Webb, one of the founders of the London School of Economics and of the Fabian Society and an indefatigable social researcher. The Liberal Club proposed Chesterton and the Labour Club proposed Webb.

The outcome was: Chamberlain 1,242; Chesterton 968; Webb 285.

One of the meetings of the Chesterton campaign was held at the Union, which occupied what is now called the McIntyre building. A student who was present, Jessie S. Smith (Jessie Duncan) wrote later:

> Because I was a Protestant I couldn't dream of voting for a Roman Catholic [as Chesterton was], and, as a friend of mine had asked me to join the Conservative Association—half-a-crown or five shillings was the sub.—I couldn't vote for a Liberal, so I bought a monocle to vote for Sir Austen. At that time the Liberal crowd had easily the most interesting supporting speakers and this particular meeting was to have the great G.K.'s sister-in-law, Mrs Cecil Chesterton, as speaker.

The person chairing the meeting mentioned that Mrs Chesterton's husband had paid the supreme sacrifice during the War.

> There was a sad lament [Jessie Smith recorded] from an Opposition member in the left gallery whose 'Boo-Hoo' and the rubbing of his eyes (very bad taste but frightfully funny) was abruptly stopped by several Liberal supporters who were about to throw him into the arena, when a sensible steward signed to them to carry him out feet first.
>
> When this interruption was over, the chairman hastily called on Mrs Cecil to speak. She immediately began her supporting talk on behalf of 'Gilbert.' Guffaws greeted this familiarity with such a remote, large, and famous figure. At once, Mrs Cecil replied: 'All right, I'll eat my apple.' There actually WAS an apple on the right hand corner of the chairman's desk. This she picked up, and proceeded to eat, to the embarrassed consternation of an audience who were abruptly silenced. Back went the apple ... her talk began. Beside me on the left, however, was a resourceful student with a walking stick. Out came a knife opened at both ends. One blade was inserted into the end of the stick, the other left dangerously open. Deftly he whipped the stick over the chairman's desk, wriggled it like a magnetic fishing rod, stuck the open blade into the apple and, before the chairman or Mrs Chesterton realised what was happening, he

was holding aloft from his vantage-point the disciplinary apple. Cheers and more guffaws brought the meeting to an untimely and face-saving end.

Chesterton's friend Hilaire Belloc told a meeting in favour of Chesterton that the first reason for not voting for Chesterton was that he had written some of the best poems of our time. There was something nefarious and disreputable about good poetry, and it was up to the students to show their displeasure of it.

Hugh Roberton, an eminent musician, later Sir Hugh, spoke for Webb and said he had fault to find with all three candidates. "You wanted a Lord Rector and you have selected three Englishmen." He said Chamberlain was a man with a monocled eye and a manacled mind.

A strong tradition in the election campaigns has been the staging of "stunts", dramatic incidents to attract attention to a candidate. Here, as an illustration, are some of them from this era.

The Liberals captured two Conservatives and took them to a shooting lodge at Aviemore, Inverness-shire, 11 miles from the nearest railway station. One of the captives was kept there until polling day. The other was released because he had to go to an interview for a job, but he undertook to take no more part in the campaigning. The Conservatives replied by kidnapping two leading Liberals; one was kept prisoner on Inchmarnock, an island in the Kyles of Bute, and the other in Largs, Ayrshire.

Kidnapping became such a threat that some people went about with bodyguards or took elaborate precautions, doubling on their tracks. Conservatives lay in wait outside the union in a downpour to trap some Liberals but failed. They sheltered under the walls of the building but buckets of water were thrown on them from above.

The *Bulletin*, a Glasgow newspaper now long deceased, wrote:

The extraordinary feature of the installation was its peacefulness. The stock phrases of 'student exuberance' and 'the wild ebullitions of youth' need not be taken from the well-worn cupboard of jargon ... Certainly there was some form of demonstration—the singing of *Ygorra* on the slightest provocation, the chorus of moans and periodic yodellings from lusty groups tucked away in the dim recesses under the galleries, and plenty of amiable chanting of unimpeachable ditties... Nobody was even pushed off a bench. Not a sock was removed; not a missile harder than soft words flew through the air.

The address was on the efforts of Europe for peace, the rise of the League of Nations, and the hopes of nations. Chamberlain finished:

Soon we shall commit to a younger generation the care of the lamp now once more dimly burning within the Temple of Peace.

The *Bulletin* said:

It was hopeless to expect from him more than an exposition of things as they are, and a cautious hope that the League [of Nations] will endure and work out its own salvation. His point of view is static; he is temperamentally a little fearful of development.

The President of the Students' Representative Council and the honorary secretary of the union made a traditional request of the Rector: that he use his influence with the Principal to obtain a day's holiday for the students so that they could celebrate the occasion properly. Shouts went up from the audience: "Ask a week, Austen." It was a day.

Chamberlain continued as Foreign Secretary until 1929 and was First Lord of the Admiralty in 1931. He told his party leader, Stanley Baldwin, after the general election of 1931 that he did not want to hold high office again: his aim in this was to clear the way for his half-brother Neville to become Prime Minister, which happened in 1937. Austen had died suddenly two months before.

# Scottish Nationalist almost Defeats the Prime Minister

Stanley Baldwin (Glasgow University Archives)

*Stanley Baldwin (1867-1947), Conservative statesman, later Earl Baldwin. He was Prime Minister when he was elected.*

## Elected 1928

The result of the election was remarkable. Baldwin was the hot favourite for many reasons. Tories had been returned in the previous three contests. Liberalism was on the wane. A Socialist candidate had been nominated only twice before and had done badly. No Scottish Nationalist had been nominated before. And Baldwin was after all the Prime Minister. But the margin of his win turned out to be very narrow. The Scottish Nationalist did extraordinarily well.

Baldwin was Prime Minister from 1923 to 1929 and from 1935 to 1937. He was leader of the Conservative Party for 14 years and was Prime Minister for half that time. His premierships were marked by the General Strike (1926) and the Abdication crisis (1936). He helped to end the

General Strike peacefully and got rid of Edward VIII without getting rid of the monarchy.

The Scottish nationalist candidate was the flamboyant R. B. (Robert Bontine) Cunninghame Graham, writer, adventurer, and political figure. The others were:

E. Rosslyn Mitchell, who was a graduate of Glasgow, a solicitor, a former town councillor, and at this time the Labour MP for Paisley. He had been president of the Students' Representative Council.

Sir Herbert Samuel, later Lord Templewood, a Liberal statesman and a philosopher. He was from a banking family. By the time of the election he had been Postmaster-General and Home Secretary—not offices that were a match for Baldwin's. Samuel was later to be Home Secretary again.

Cunninghame Graham was a Scotsman. His early years were spent as a rancher in Argentina but he was Liberal MP for a Scottish constituency from 1886 to 1892. He became first president of the Scottish Labour Party in 1888, of the National Party of Scotland in 1928, and of the Scottish National Party in 1934.

Cunninghame Graham was an accomplished orator. He wrote many travel books but his best known works were essays and short stories. His appearance was unforgettable: tall, lithe, and elegantly bearded and moustached. He had had to sell the ancestral estate at Gartmore, near Aberfoyle, because when he inherited it the debts were heavy. He himself was not inclined to economise.

The *Glasgow Herald* wrote:

> His career has been incredibly full of romance and adventure both in the wide spaces of the earth and in the narrower arena of industrial and political turmoil at home. ..
>
> Well travelled in his youth in southern continents, to which he later returned, he has written brilliantly—and perhaps enduringly—about places as far apart as Mexico and Morocco; and the Latin civilisations of South America and Islam in North Africa have drawn from him a slim but incomparable bibliography. As a Liberal member of the House of Commons, where his passage was turbulent, as a Socialist candidate in Camlachie [in Glasgow]; as one who shared bruises and imprisonment with John Burns [the Socialist leader] in the Battle of Trafalgar Square [during a demonstration against unemployment] ... he has been a picturesque and unique figure.

Cunninghame Graham's candidature was announced to the students by the writer and Scottish nationalist Compton Mackenzie in a public speech. Mackenzie, as he stood on the platform, was frightened. He had been suffering from pyorrhoea and all his teeth had been taken out a few weeks before. His false teeth had only just been fitted and he did not know if they would stay in place or if his voice would be affected. Cunninghame Graham had addressed huge meetings in Trafalgar Square. This time he said:

I would not face these 'Ephesians'* for anything, not that I mind a rough meeting or opposition, but Glasgow students go to make a row, quite apart from what they may think.

The meeting began with clamour but in a few moments Mackenzie had won their attention with his fervour for the cause of Scottish nationalism. Moreover, he treated barracking in a friendly manner, unlike many other distinguished speakers.

The backers of Cunninghame Graham were artful. They had no money to hire halls for public meetings so instead they forcefully took over the meetings of other groups. One of the students who ran Cunninghame Graham's campaign was John MacCormick. He was to run the successful campaign for Compton Mackenzie in 1931, was to be a great leader of the Scottish Nationalist movement, and was elected to the rectorship in 1950.

MacCormick wrote about the 1928 campaign:

> The distinguished politicians who visited the Union to speak for our opponents knew very little about University affairs and were wholly ignorant about the office of Lord Rector. Early in the campaign I discovered that they could all be completely stumped by a simple question, asked on a point of order halfway through the first sentence of their speech: 'Mr Chairman, has the speaker any right to address this audience unless he can tell us what are the duties of Lord Rector in a Scottish University?
>
> The ensuing uproar increasingly became one united shout from the audience —'Answer the question! Answer the question!' which, apart from the noise, the poor speaker could seldom do.

The total poll was 2,644. Baldwin took three nations, but Rothseiana by only eight votes, Loudoniana by 21, and Glottiana by 69. Cunningham Graham won Transforthana by 32. (The other candidates did poorly). In the global vote, Baldwin had 1,044 and Cunningham Graham 978. The Scottish Nationalist candidate would have carried the day if only a handful in each nation had voted for him instead of the Conservative.

It was said that the "flappers" tilted the scales: women voted for Baldwin in a higher proportion than the men did. This may have been because the Conservative Government in this year granted votes to women aged between 21 and 30. In any case at this period a higher proportion of women students turned out to vote than did men students. Students who had supported Baldwin's rivals thereafter called Baldwin the "first Lady Rector".

It was a great moral victory for nationalism. Compton Mackenzie wrote much later that he could remember no such moment of exhilaration in his life as when he heard the result. He said the shock to public opinion was tremendous.

> An evening or two later, there was a great meeting in St Andrew's Hall, addressed by the Duke of Montrose, Cunninghame Graham, Hugh McDiarmid, John

---

* Jolly companions, roysterers.

MacCormick, and myself. The enthusiasm was immense, and I do not believe there was anyone in that huge audience who was not convinced that the National Party of Scotland would soon sweep the country.

Montrose took an active part in public affairs; he was also a marine engineer and naval architect.

Baldwin did not make much impact on student life, but he was present (with the Chancellor, the Principal, and other notables) when the Union building was opened at the foot of University Avenue. The former Union building at the top of the Avenue was handed over to the Queen Margaret Union (the women's union). The QM has since moved on to modern premises. The original union building has been renamed the John McIntyre building after the original donor. It is occupied by the Students' Representative Council and a bookshop, and some classes are held there.

Baldwin said on the occasion of the opening of the new building:

All of you, especially the students in their later years here, will never really feel at home in these magnificent surroundings. Their whole heart will be in that rabbit-warren up the hill.

He also said:

I want the future of the Union to be even greater and more distinguished than in the past, and you will have to work hard to do that....
    It always strikes me that in Glasgow it will be impossible for a prig to emerge, I think he would die, and that is a very good thing.

His political persona was of a conciliator. His public persona was of a man who loved cricket, farming, his pigs and his pipe. But these were simply the technique of propaganda, "like the orchid of Mr Chamberlain or the ringlets of Disraeli", according to a chairman of the Labour Party. He liked music and art, but not the modern art of his time.

Baldwin's family was powerful and enormously wealthy—they manufactured iron and steel. He was educated at Harrow and Cambridge and went into the family business. He did not enter Parliament until he was 40 and for many years seldom spoke there. He became President of the Board of Trade in 1921. From that comparatively lowly job he leaped to being Prime Minister, succeeding Bonar Law. Baldwin's competitor Lord Curzon was a much more glamorous figure and people were surprised that Baldwin pipped him. It was rather like John Major winning over Michael Heseltine in 1990. It was said that Curzon was ruled out because he was a member of the House of Lords. On the other hand, Curzon's colleagues did not really want him as Prime Minister.

Baldwin's wife is alleged to have told her marrying daughters that on their wedding nights they should "think of England".

Baldwin in his later career was accused of betraying the ideals of the League of Nations—for example, over the Italian invasion of Abyssinia and over the Spanish Civil War. He was opposed to Britain's rearmament and was regarded as one of the guiltiest of the "Guilty Men" who failed to recognise the threat from the Nazis. When the Second World War came he was vilified. George Orwell described him as "simply a hole in the air." Winston Churchill said of him in 1947, the year he died, "it would have been better if he had never lived."

He had failures of judgement in foreign affairs but was popular at home.

# Nationalist Victory tainted by Anti-Catholic Feeling

Compton Mackenzie with the Duke and Duchess of York, the future King George VI and Queen Elizabeth (Glasgow University Archives)

## Compton Mackenzie, author and Scottish Nationalist, later Sir Compton (1883-1972)

### Elected 1931

Compton Mackenzie is one of only two people to win on a mainly or solely Scottish Nationalist ticket. Other factors came in: he was also famous as an author; and the student who led his campaign was brilliant and dynamic. And Mackenzie was a Roman Catholic, which told both for him and against him

He was a flamboyant, theatrical character and a prolific writer of plays, novels, essays, poetry, and autobiography. The autobiography runs to 10 volumes. An early work, the novel *Sinister Street,* made his name and he was hailed as a rising talent, even a genius, although some people criticised him for using such words as "tart" and "bitch". He was converted to

Roman Catholicism in 1914. He served during the First World War in the Dardanelles and in Greece, chasing spies and working for British Intelligence. In the 1930s his reputation as a writer was not as high as it had been when he was young but he was immensely popular with the reading public. Mackenzie founded *The Gramophone,* the oldest surviving magazine of its kind in the world.

The other candidates for the rectorship were a Conservative, a Liberal, a Socialist, and a political maverick. Mackenzie was not a likely winner: he was well known as a Scottish Nationalist speaker but as well as being a Roman Catholic he was English-born and English-reared. His victory was brought about partly by political sentiment in Scotland. During the 1920s the level of unemployment in Scotland was never less than 14 per cent. In the 1930s world trade collapsed; and Clydeside, with its heavy industry such as shipbuilding and engineering, had come to depend on world trade. Shipbuilding especially was badly hit. The level of unemployment during those years averaged more than 25 per cent. Economic calamity helped to foster the Nationalist movement and helped the Labour Party in municipal politics to displace middle-class rule. And it was the boredom, despair, and deprivation that fostered street gangs and strikes.

Mackenzie also owed his victory to the ability, energies, and talent of John MacCormick, who ran his campaign. MacCormick was to be a most influential figure in the Scottish National movement.

Candidates for the rectorship did not appear but left the management of their campaigns to their principal backers, an ancient convention that survived well beyond the mid-twentieth century.

Mackenzie reaped votes through his literary reputation, but after the victory this aspect of the result was rather played down by the nationalists. He received messages of support from literary figures who were well known at that time: John Drinkwater, poet, playwright, and critic; St John Ervine, playwright, novelist, and biographer; and Walter de la Mare, poet, novelist, and writer of short stories.

In the previous election Stanley Baldwin, the Conservative Prime Minister, received 1,044 votes and R. B. Cunninghame Graham, the Nationalist candidate, was only 66 behind. Cunninghame Graham's vote was more than twice the combined vote for Lord Samuel, the Liberal, and Rosslyn Mitchell, the Socialist. That result gave a boost to the Nationalist cause in the country at large.

When Mackenzie's candidacy was announced, the press and the public took more than usual interest. *The Inverness Courier* was outspoken:

> Who are Mr MacCormick and Mr Compton Mackenzie or any leading light in their trumpery party that Scotland should trust them and place its destiny in their hands? The first-named, a callow inexperienced youth of twenty-odd years with only the "gift of the gab" to recommend him, the second, a writer of English novels of a not

particularly elevating kind who, after a lifetime spent in England has taken it upon himself to shed the light of his presence upon Scotland, and instruct us poor ignorant Scots what we ought to do and how we ought to do it ... They have vapoured and pranced and postured, but have they done anything of the slightest practical value for the country or the people whom they aspire to instruct?

Mackenzie's backers laid out his principles. If elected he would attend every meeting of the University Court. His counsel and aid "will be available at any time to each individual" student. (In fact he did not attend the Court in the way he had promised, soon losing interest.)

He was the representative, his backers said, of a movement that was striving for the regeneration of Scotland as a vital force in European culture:

> Compton Mackenzie is the representative of a movement, the members of which genuinely believe that the cause of disarmament and world peace would be enhanced by a delegate from Scotland in the League of Nations.
>
> Compton Mackenzie is the representative of a movement which stands definitely for self-government for all nations in general and Scotland in particular.
>
> Compton Mackenzie is one whose outlook is not that of the party politician but rather that of the artist, and, above all, one who is a writer and a personality of world-wide distinction.

His rivals were:

Sir Robert Horne (Conservative), who had been a prominent figure in student life at Glasgow University in the early years of the century. He trained as a lawyer, went into Parliament, and was holder of several Cabinet posts culminating in the Chancellorship of the Exchequer in 1921-1922. He refused to serve in Bonar Law's government of 1922 and spent the rest of his parliamentary career on the back benches. He was given a peerage in 1937. He had many business interests. It was said that he never fulfilled his early promise.

Tom Johnston (Labour), a journalist, was one of a group of Labour MPs who were returned in the 1922 general election when the west of Scotland "went red." Clydeside was to acquire the nickname "Red Clydeside." Johnston wrote in 1909 *Our Noble Families*, a devastating critique of the landed classes. He was at that time editor of *Forward,* the newspaper of the Independent Labour Party. Johnston was to be Secretary of State for Scotland during the Second World War.

Sir Oswald Mosley (New Party). He had already been an MP as a Conservative, as an Independent, and for Labour but he was standing as leader of the recently-launched New Party. He was later to be founder in 1932 of the British Union of Fascists and in 1948 of the Union Movement.

Gilbert Murray (Liberal). He had been Professor of Greek at the University between 1889 and 1908 but had gone on to be a teacher at Oxford University. Murray was a candidate for the rectorship in 1919.

The voting was: Mackenzie 849, Horne 762, Murray 581, Johnston 110, Mosley 21. Mackenzie won Glottiana, Rothseiana, and Transforthana, and Horne won Loudoniana.

It was the Nationalists' first electoral victory of any consequence. Horne's coming second was especially piquant because he had been one of the most prominent Conservative opponents of Scottish home rule. Mackenzie told his mother:

I am the first Catholic Rector to be elected since the Reformation and the first literary man since Macaulay, but he was a politician as well. Even Sir Walter Scott was defeated twice.

Mackenzie wrote in his autobiography:

I was amused by a somersault turned by Sir Robert Bruce in the *Glasgow Herald*.[*] On the morning of the Rectorial election there was a leader reminding me that I was standing as a political candidate and would receive from Scottish youth the answer that my ridiculous advocacy of Home Rule deserved. On the following morning there was a leader to warn me against supposing that my election had the faintest political significance. My election was due to the support of the Irish Catholic vote.

Soon afterwards, the editor of the *Daily Record*, David Anderson, wrote to him that not only in the *Glasgow Herald* but also elsewhere the credit was given:

... to the Roman Catholic vote for your return as Lord Rector....the 'vote' feeling has become very definite. From my point of view it is a tremendous pity that this religious red herring has been drawn across the whole issue, and threatens to destroy the merits of your victory.

John MacCormick wrote in his autobiography *The Flag in the Wind* about Mackenzie's win:

It was a Pyrrhic victory which, owing to the malice of our enemies, did as much harm as good. Mackenzie being a Roman Catholic it was immediately put around by those who envied our growing strength that it was really a Catholic rather than a Nationalist triumph. They went further and insinuated that many of the leading members of the National Party were Catholics and that Home Rule would be synonymous with Rome Rule ... The lie that our Party was under Catholic control took firm root and spread all over the country like some foul weed.

The phrase about Home Rule and Rome Rule is a strong echo from the Irish national movement of the previous hundred years.

Gilbert Murray was philosophical about his defeat, writing that "this was just one more instance of a world epidemic of nationalism." But Scottish nationalism was not at all like the nationalism that was simmering in Germany and Italy.

Mackenzie's sister Fay wrote to her mother about the installation in St Andrew's Hall:

---

[*] Bruce was its editor.

A lot of ceremonies took place—none of which I heard at all as the students were all shouting, talking, singing, whistling, and cat-calling through it all... Bless his heart, he was dead white and obviously very nervous, which had the effect of making him look about twenty-five, and when he gave us his charming smile he looked about nineteen. It is a most remarkable tribute to him that during the long reading of his address, the students were practically silent—there were just a few harmless interruptions. I understand from the Principal of the University that this is simply incredible: the unfortunate Baldwin was not allowed to be heard at all and Curzon they treated in an even rougher way ... They just broke the benches when he was speaking, and threw them about!

A dinner was held in the Union. The first toast after the loyal toast was given by one of the candidates defeated by Stanley Baldwin in 1928, Rosslyn Mitchell, who proposed the health of the *Alma Mater* and spoke for 55 minutes. The Principal muttered: "He is giving us the Rectorial Address he would have delivered if he had been elected."

Mackenzie's rectorial Address included the remarkable passage:

There is perhaps at this moment sitting in this hall a student who when ten trienniums have passed will stand where I stand now and be triumphant in the golden noon of this country's new life.

There was such a person in the hall—John M. MacCormick. Twenty years later, not 30 years later, he stood on the very platform where Mackenzie had stood, wearing the same gown, being installed in the same office.

Most of Mackenzie's best work was done by the 1930s. He spent his last years in Edinburgh as a much-admired figure. His best-remembered work nowadays is *Whisky Galore* (1947), which was made into a film.

# The Tradition of Political Voting is Interrupted

Sir Iain Colquhoun (Glasgow University Archives)

## *Sir Iain Colquhoun of Luss (1887-1948)*

## *Elected 1934*

Landowner, man of affairs, Knight of the Thistle, DSO and bar, seventh baronet and 28th Chief of Clan Colquhoun, Laird and Baron of Luss. His ancestor Humphrey de Kilpatrick or Kirkpatrick obtained a grant of land on Loch Lomondside during the reign of Alexander II (1214-1249).

Colquhoun had been an explorer and soldier. During the First World War he killed a German officer with his sword.

Colquhoun was put forward as a non-political candidate. His backers issued a newspaper called *The Non-Political Lord Rector*, which declared:

We oppose the idea that the Rectorate must necessarily be held by a politician or a man who can be politically labelled. Against statesmen, as such, we hold no brief. But we do object to their election on party-political grounds.

The newspaper had a point: the previous five rectors had been politicians or politically aligned. From time to time, however, the student body made a strong statement by choosing a different kind of candidate, such as the President of France, Raymond Poincaré, at the beginning of the First World War, the pacifist Dick Sheppard two years before the outbreak of the Second World War, and the African nationalist and freedom campaigner Albert Luthuli in 1962.

The *Non-Political Lord Rector* also said:

> Sir Iain Colquhoun has two qualifications for the Rectorate. The first (and it alone should be necessary) is that of personal worth. The second, equally important in our present circumstance, is that he stands for a principle—the principle of freeing Rectorial elections from the political incubus which restricts and ruins them.

He had served on the University Court as Rector's Assessor when Compton Mackenzie was Rector. When the Principal, Sir Robert Rait, was ill in 1935 and 1936 he presided over the University Court and he was strongly committed to the University's interests. Sir Iain later gave the University some land on Loch Lomondside as a field station for the Zoology Department.

Other contenders:

Sir Stafford Cripps, lawyer and Labour statesman. Cripps was at this time associated with left-wing movements. His backers said that if you voted for Cripps you voted for peace and you were expressing sympathy with the unemployed. He was described as having one of the keenest brains and being one of the most eloquent orators in the country. Cripps was to campaign against appeasement of Hitler. After the Second World War he became Chancellor of the Exchequer and pursued a policy of "austerity," a word that went well with his thin lips and pince-nez.

R.B. Cunninghame Grahame, who had stood as a Scottish Nationalist in 1928 but lost to Stanley Baldwin.

Ignacy Jan Paderewski, pianist, composer, and former President of Poland, backed by the Distributist Club. Paderewski began to play when he was three years old. As a virtuoso he appeared in many European countries and in the United States. His popularity enabled him to campaign during the First World War for Poland to be given back her independence (she had been swallowed up by her neighbours, especially Russia.) He became President of Poland after the War but returned to music.

Sir Archibald Sinclair (later Viscount Thurso), Liberal statesman. Sinclair had served in the army, went into Parliament in 1922, and was to be leader of the Liberal Party from 1935 to 1945. He was to be Secretary for Air from 1940 to 1945. He would hold the Rectorship from 1938 to 1945.

The Conservative Club did not put up a candidate against Colquhoun because that would have split the Conservative vote.

The leaflets and newspapers carried their usual uninhibited propaganda. Of Cunninghame Graham the Colquhoun camp said:

> We have the very greatest respect for the remarkable personality and literary genius of Mr R. B. Cunninghame Graham ... We might willingly vote for R. B. Cunninghame Graham, author, traveller, and sportsman; but for R. B. Cunninghame Graham, Scottish Nationalist, never!"

The Colquhoun camp quoted passages from Cunninghame Graham's writings—passages that criticised some aspects of Scottish life and manners. He said that at street corners groups of men stood spitting. Spitting was, he said, a national sport. Women and children were afraid to pass these men by. These men were "not quite civilised, not yet quite savages, a set of demi-brutes." If a woman in a decent dress went past, they said: "There goes a bitch."

He also said that:

> 'Thank you' and 'If you please' were terms unknown. In railway trains we spit upon the floor and wipe our boots on the cushions, just to show our independence; in [tram]cars and omnibuses take the best seats, driving the weaker to the wall like cattle in a pen. In streets we push the women into the guttters. 'It's only just a woman' being our excuse.

The poorest man in Scotland, he said, could read and write, knows history, geography, and arithmetic.

> Still, in the social scale of human intercourse, the bovine dweller in East Anglia is a prince compared to him ... No doubt the [Scots]man is better educated than his southern colleague, but as you see him once, and have no time to learn his inward grace, his lack of outward polish jars on you.

The *Student Socialist* said about Paderewski:

> You give your vote to Distributism if you give it to Paderewski; you are registering a desire for Scotland to become a land of peasants again...

That was a dig at the Distributist Club's Irish connections and its policy of "three acres and a cow." (See Appendix A.)

And the *Student Socialist* said of Colquhoun:

> He is one of the landowners that make walking or camping in the Loch Lomond district a tantalising annoyance by prohibitions ... He is a survival of a parasite class in Scotland, the 'lairds' ... He occasionally walks around in a kilt with his bare feet.

Colquhoun took all nations. Voting was Colquhoun (Non-Political) 770. Paderewski (Distributist Club) 487, Cunninghame Graham (Scottish Nationalist) 340, Sinclair (Liberal) 207, Cripps (Socialist) 185. Turnout was 44.2 per cent.

Of all students, 44.2 per cent voted, but of the women 64.8 per cent voted and of the men 37.5. Distributists were Paderewski's backers—and the Distributists were strongly associated with Roman Catholicism. After the election two of the Distributists' former presidents said Paderewski's cause had been damaged by "the stirring up of religious bigotries".

# As War looms, a Pacifist is Chosen

Dick Sheppard (Peace Pledge Union)

*The Rev Dick Sheppard, pacifist (1880-1937)*

*Elected 1937*

Very many rectorial contests had been basically about domestic party politics. This contest was about burning international issues. It was an era of idealism and campaigning, of Nazism and Communism, of nationalism, of the Spanish Civil War, of the Italian invasion of Abyssinia, of the Japanese rape of China. And above all it was an era full of fear about an impending war—fear felt especially strongly by the young.

H. R. L. ("Dick") Sheppard was a leading pacifist and founded the Peace Pledge Union in 1936. He was a popular preacher, had a modern outlook on the Christian life, and was the first person in the country to make a religious broadcast. He was successively Vicar of St Martin in the Fields, London, Dean of Canterbury, and Canon of St Paul's.

Sheppard wrote a letter to the national Press on October 16, 1934, asking for the signatures of men and women who would subscribe to the words "I renounce war, and never again, directly or indirectly, will I support or sanction another." None of the dailies printed it, with the exception of the *Manchester Guardian*, the *Daily Herald*, and the *News Chronicle*—papers of liberal consciences or on the left. But the response was immediate and powerful, solidified the pacifist movement, and brought about the Peace Pledge Union.

The students at Glasgow included many whose fathers or close relatives had fought—and perhaps died—in the First World War. Sheppard was chosen as the first pacifist rector. Some candidates after the Second World War were to have the label of peace attached to them, for example Emrys Hughes MP in 1953, but these candidates were "fellow travellers", people close to the Communists.

His rivals for the post were Emeritus Professor W. Macneile Dixon, who had taught English at the University and who was backed by the Scottish Nationalists and Distributists, Winston Churchill (Conservative Club), and J. B. S. Haldane, biologist and Communist (Popular Front.) The *Student Pacifist* wrote:

> Pacifists reject the revolutionary's theory that violence and tyranny are justified when used for a good cause. On this point they part company with communists, fascists, and all others who believe that the world can be bludgeoned into the likeness of Utopia. Their political philosophy is democratic.
>
> War was always wrong, and war-makers have always been men of criminal intentions; science has now provided the war-makers with the power of putting their intentions into destructive action on a scale which was undreamt of even a quarter of a century ago.

Some eminent people addressed meetings in Sheppard's favour, including C.E.M. Joad the philosopher and controversialist, Aldous Huxley the writer, Middleton Murry the writer, critic, and pacifist, Rose Macaulay the novelist, and the Rev George MacLeod, who was a leading campaigner in Scotland for Sheppard's pacifist cause. (MacLeod was to become rector in 1968). Messages of support came from Bertrand Russell the mathematician, philosopher, and campaigner for peace, and from Laurence Housman the novelist and dramatist. Rose Macaulay wrote:

> Those who would like Britain to give a lead must vote for Dick Sheppard. Those who think it safer and wiser to remain barbarians with tomahawks had better vote otherwise.

The backers of Churchill wrote:

> The Universities of this country have the reputation of being a breeding-ground for the more revolutionary of political theories. Undergraduates, confident of their intellectual superiority over those whose views have been formed in the bitter school of experience, feel it their duty to remake Britain and then the world according to theories which promise the sun, moon, and stars and a glorious political Utopia. But despite this superficial layer of blood-red exuberance for creeds which point the way to the unalloyed bliss of the promised land, we feel assured that there is a sanity inherent in all of us that is bound to assert itself in the direction of Tory principles.

The Conservatives said that Macneile Dixon stood for narrow nationalism, Sheppard for altruistic idealism, and Haldane for a dangerous infatuation: the "destruction of Fascism and the advent of some form of Communism, the universal panacea for all the ills of the world." They enlarged upon Churchill's achievements and qualities. But Churchill's career at that time was in the doldrums, which was admitted by the Conservative Club: "To-day finds him as the stormy petrel of politics..." The Conservative Club also said: "The present situation is fraught with peril. We must at all costs avoid being drawn into a general conflagration."

Macneile Dixon was put forward by his supporters as:

> ... the Scottish candidate for a Scottish position, a man of real culture and varied practical interests, and a protagonist of student rights for more than thirty years.

He was willing to take his position seriously by attending every meeting of the University Court and being always available to students. "He knows that Scotsmen have difficulty in getting jobs when up against Oxford and Cambridge."

His campaign newspaper, *The Scot*, said of Churchill:

> A politician who smells bad even to his own Tory party, a turncoat English politician, and his sponsors want him as Lord Rector of this Scottish university. What a hope, gentlemen! What a hope!

Of Sheppard:

> A man who believes it is wrong to fight under any circumstances. And his sponsors, in all good faith, think that he will be elected by you; you who are the descendants of a race known throughout the world as fighters 'par excellence.' Ye Gods!

Haldane's message to the students said in part:

> The world is living in the shadow of the next war. The Fascist Governments of Germany, Italy, and Japan are waging war to-day. Our Government is not carrying out its duty under International Law to govern them. Its policy of supporting Fascism by forbidding the sale of arms to those who are fighting it, whether in Abyssinia or Spain, while refusing to carry out provisions of the Covenant of the League [of Nations] against aggressors can only lead to further wars, even more serious than those which are now being waged in Spain and China...
>
> I have worked on human and animal metabolism, but I have not seen the findings of biochemistry applied to assure an adequate diet to the children of Britain. The time has come when the national standards of adequate diet could and should be drawn up and applied, when defence against disease should be undertaken by the nation on as great a scale as defence against war.

The campaign newspaper for Haldane was called *The Student Front*, the "Official Organ of the Unity Committee Against War and Fascism." That phraseology is reminiscent of the jargon of the Soviet bloc during the Cold War.

Of Sheppard's supporters *The Student Front* said:

> They seem to think that it is enough to recoil from the horrors of war. They would guile the public into believing that if they loathe war they must support Sheppard.

They pretend that they have a monopoly of fastidious disgust and abhorrence of meaningless slaughter. Their campaign is based on reasons utterly false and arguments which are not relevant. There are many non-pacifists who recoiled from war, but who believe that the fundamental cause of war is not the wickedness of mankind but the greed and rivalry of small groups of men who direct the economic and imperialist machine. The only effective way to put an end to war once and for all is to destroy or improve that machine so that disputes either do not arise or are settled without resort to force. But force may be necessary to achieve this end.

During the campaign Sheppard wrote:

Glasgow is going well—a free fight in which my pacifist crowd seem to be splendidly militant. To-day they phone that the issue is between Winston and me with the betting on me—I am sure though that they are being optimistic.

Sheppard received 538 votes, Macneile Dixon 364, Churchill 281, and Haldane 220. Sheppard won all nations. The turn-out was 32.83 per cent. Sheppard was the first clergyman to be elected since 1686.

The "establishment" was upset. *The Scotsman* wrote that it was a remarkable example of what a keen and united minority could accomplish when the majority was apathetic and divided. The *Glasgow Herald* thought Sheppard "not quite in the tradition of University Rectors." The votes cast for him were idealistic and romantic, "symptomatic of the spirit of the new world and of young people's dissatisfaction with the old."

George Lansbury the Labour politician said:

Glorious news. This is a great sign of youth's revolt against barbarism and resolve to follow [the] advice of Christ to fight evil with good. God bless and strengthen you.

At Sheppard's home in London the telegrams of congratulation were arranged like a red carpet from his study to the door. "He was moved and excited beyond words," wrote one of his biographers. "This was, he believed, the verdict of youth on his crusade."

Sheppard was elected on October 23. He said: "Now it doesn't matter if I die this week." He died in his sleep on October 31. He had suffered for many years from asthma. He once wrote: "I still pray 'Give us this day our daily breath.'"

# The Election is Caught Up in World Affairs

Sir Archibald Sinclair (Glasgow University Archives)

*Sir Archibald Sinclair, Liberal statesman,
later first Viscount Thurso (1890-1970)*

*Elected 1938*

Sinclair's ancestors were important people in Caithness. Sinclair served in the army from 1910 to 1921 and entered Parliament in 1922. When chosen as Rector he had been leader of the Liberal Party for three years.

The University was, in the weeks before the rectorial election, briefly on the remote periphery of dramatic international events—Neville Chamberlain's appeasement of Hitler and the dismemberment of Czechoslovakia. These events led directly to the outbreak of the Second World War.

This was a very confused election. No Conservative candidate was named, perhaps because national politics were in a state of turmoil over appeasement. Many students were therefore left without a party and were "floating". Were they to vote for the Liberal man? Or were they to vote for the man backed by the Roman Catholics in the Distributist Club? Or the pacifist? Or not at all? These questions were muddling enough, but a far greater issue appeared.

Polling was to be held on October 22. The Prime Minister, Neville Chamberlain, came back on September 30 from his meeting with Hitler in Munich, waved a piece of paper at the aerodrome, and declared "Peace in our Time." The policy of appeasing Hitler had triumphed. Czechoslovakia was dismembered. On October 3 the German army marched into the Sudetenland, a part of Czechoslovakia with a large German population. Two days later the President of Czechoslovakia, Eduard Beneš, resigned, saying his country had been betrayed by the West. A huge debate went on in Britain—was the appeasement of Hitler justified? Had Britain and other countries betrayed Czechoslovakia?

Beneš was at once proposed as a rectorial candidate by the Scottish Nationalists. What happened then was extraordinary but has not been fully explained. It does seem that the British Foreign Office and the Czechoslovak Government were anxious to stop Beneš being chosen as Rector. Perhaps they feared it would anger Hitler. Pressure seems to have been put on the University authorities to block the nomination.

The Scottish Nationalists had a telegram saying: "Dr Beneš honoured to stand in rectorial election for principle of small democratic nations." It was signed "HALTON". Staff at the Czechoslovak Legation in London very soon denied that Beneš had agreed to stand and said that the name Halton was unknown to them. The Czechslovak Minister in London, Jan Masaryk, held that the telegram was a hoax and emphasised that Beneš would not accept nomination. Jan Masaryk was the son of Thomas Masaryk, first president of Czechoslovakia, the Father of the Nation.

The Czechoslovak Legation said:

> If Dr Beneš had consented to participate in such a political contest at the present time, *his action would have been open to misinterpretation in various quarters* [italics added].

A telegram said:

> Beneš under no circumstances candidate as officially stated before. Please stop his name being used without authorisation.

John MacCormick, a leading Scottish Nationalist and well known in the University, said:

> The approach originally made by the Nationalist Association to Dr Beneš was made with the full knowledge of the Czech Legation, and without discouragement by the Legation, and in a perfectly proper manner.

Archibald Sinclair sent a telegram to the Liberal Club: "Delighted to retire in favour of Beneš." The offer did him credit and won him goodwill.

Both the Liberals and the Socialists said they were willing to support Beneš if he stood without a party label.

The University authorities were in difficulties. They said there was no rule to ban the nomination of a candidate who had not given his consent. But the Senate stated that it was obliged to regard Beneš's name as authoritatively withdrawn from the election. His name, the Senate decreed, would not go forward.

The Scottish Nationalists asked: Who told the Foreign Office about our plans? Why had Beneš never replied himself to all their letters and telegrams? Had he received them? Who inspired the Hitler-ish demand of the Senate that we drop the candidature of Dr Beneš within a certain time? Scottish Nationalists were soon also to say:

Sir Hector Hetherington [the Principal] and the Senate have violated a student right that has been in existence for nearly 500 years.

Some of the sponsors of Beneš had withdrawn their names.

By subversive influence pressure has been brought to bear on some of the sponsors of Dr Beneš, which in fact would seem to indicate to us the poverty of the Senate's arguments.

A final twist to the story came late. The University authorities stated that Beneš's nomination papers were not in order. One of the signatories gave an address that could not be traced. He gave a matriculation number (the number he had on the roll of the university) but nobody of his name had that number. He said he was enrolled in a certain class but nobody of his name was enrolled in the class. Beneš's nomination was therefore ineffective.

The Scottish Nationalists and the Socialists, without their own nominee, declared their support for Sinclair. His programme said he was against "Fascism, aggression, and the current political thought that might is right." The Distributists put up Sir Henry Lunn, a Roman Catholic apologist and a pioneer of Alpine skiing. He was backed by "a united front against militant atheism, Communism, Nazism, Fascism, and social injustice." Lunn endorsed Chamberlain's policy towards Hitler.

The *Glasgow Herald*, from a Conservative and middle-class stance, declared that the Distributists probably cast their net too widely. The *Herald* revealed its special views in a convoluted sentence: if the Distributists:

... hoped to catch Conservative votes for a Gladstonian Liberal by emphasising their candidate's support for Mr Chamberlain's foreign policy—although it is by no means certain that the Premier would himself welcome this gesture—the sectarian nature of Sir Henry Lunn's candidature was much more likely to have the opposite effect.

In short, his Roman Catholicism and his Roman Catholic backing had put people off.

The leading pacifist movement, the Peace Pledge Union, put up Laurence Housman, novelist, dramatist, and poet who had advocated votes for women and who was a pacifist. The previous election, only a year before, saw the triumph of Canon Dick Sheppard, pacifist. This time the pacifist did poorly. All the comings and goings about Beneš had probably distracted voters from the issue of pacifism. The *Glasgow Herald* was of the opinion that Housman lacked a vivid personality.

A poor turnout, at 28 per cent, reflected the muddle. It was thought that the Conservatives stayed away because no candidate attracted them. Sinclair received 579 votes, Lunn 314, Housman 303. Sinclair took all nations. At that time women and men went to separate polling stations. Women were still somewhat segregated in the campus, but the separation also meant that the women were protected from the traditional fight outside the men's polling station.

> Sir Archibald Sinclair's return [said the presidents of the Liberals and the Socialists] is a positive affirmation that only by means of collective security can the forces of fascism be halted.

Sir Archibald Sinclair was leader of the Liberal party from 1935 to 1945 and Secretary for Air from 1940 to 1945. He became Viscount Thurso. His tenure of the rectorship was extended until 1945 because no election was held during the Second World War. Indeed his tenure was the longest since that of Sir John Maxwell from 1691 to 1717.

Beneš became the President of the exiled Czechoslovak Government, first in France and then in Britain, and in 1945 was re-elected President of Czechoslovakia. When the Communists took over in 1948 he resigned. He died three months later, a broken man. The Czechoslovak Government, when the Second World War was over, expelled all Germen speakers from the Sudetenland and settled people there from other parts of Czechoslovakia.

# Campaigner for the Poor and Hungry

Lord Boyd Orr (Glasgow University Archives)

*Sir John Boyd Orr, later Lord Boyd Orr, nutritionist and Nobel Prize winner (1880-1971)*

## Elected 1945

Boyd Orr was a leading figure in campaigning for the world's poor. One of the people who saw him in action said: "He had the fire of God in his belly and he belched." His devoted work was especially important after the end of the Second World War, when some European countries faced famine.

On leaving school he became a pupil-teacher but later went to the University, graduating MA in 1903. He planned to take a degree in Divinity and become a minister of the Free Church but gave up the idea. He was a schoolteacher for four years and then took a degree in medicine. Boyd Orr saw, during his ward rounds, the diseases of poverty and malnutrition, such as rickets, in the children from the slums. That inspired him to do a D.Sc in metabolic disease. During the First World War he won the MC and bar and DSO. He saw at first hand the poor health and physique of many soldiers.

Boyd Orr ran institutes for research into nutrition in Edinburgh and Aberdeen that were internationally renowned. An example of his interest in nutrition was his demonstration that in the 1930s the rate of infant mortality in Scotland was the worst in western Europe apart from Spain and Portugal. He carried out research into the nutrition of 1,500 children of unemployed miners in Lanarkshire and gave them skimmed milk: the milk was otherwise being dumped as unsaleable. It was years before school milk became the rule. He worked on the nutrition of animals in East Africa and the effects that had on the well-being of the Kikuyu and Masai peoples. That work raised his interest in the problems of feeding people in developing countries. He became a professor at Aberdeen University in 1942.

Boyd Orr produced seminal work that influenced governments: *Food, Health and Income* and *Hunger in the Midst of Plenty*. He lobbied the League of Nations and President Roosevelt on behalf of the starving and those threatened with starvation. His obituary in the *Times* says that he was a spellbinder who could bring conferences of Government officials to their feet cheering his forthrightness and sincerity. In 1945 a meeting in Quebec set up the Food and Agriculture Organisation of the United Nations and he was named its first director.

His opponents for the rectorship were Sir Thomas Beecham and Lord Lovat. No political figure stood—almost the first time that had happened for more than a century.

Thomas Beecham was one of Britain's most distinguished conductors and impresarios. His father was a millionaire from making Beecham's Pills, a proprietary medicine. Beecham, when he was a candidate at Glasgow, had had a distinguished career for nearly 40 years at Covent Garden, the Metropolitan Opera, New York, and elsewhere. He was to go on to found the Royal Philharmonic Orchestra. Beecham was noted for his candid remarks on musical matters and for his speeches after concerts. He is reported to have said: "A musicologist is a man who can read music but who cannot hear it."

Lovat was 24th chief of the Clan Fraser, 15th Baron, and a landowner and professional soldier. During the Second World War he was one of the founders of the commando forces. He achieved great feats of daring and bravery in leading raids on Lofoten and Dieppe. He was badly wounded in Normandy and had to leave the army. He briefly was a junior Minister in the House of Lords but resigned in 1945.

The University was full of ex-servicemen when the election was held. The students did not choose the soldier Lovat nor the musician Beecham but the peace-maker Boyd Orr, who at that time was not only heaped with honours but was one of the MPs for the Scottish universities.

Douglas Young, poet, dramatist, and scholar, addressed a meeting in the Union in favour of Boyd Orr's candidacy. Young was luxuriously bearded. At the end of the meeting, the chairman asked if there were any questions. A voice from the back: "Does Mr Young sleep with his beard ootside or inside the blankets?" He replied: "I think, Mr Chairman, this question should be addressed to Mrs Young."

Boyd Orr received 597 votes, Lovat 317, and Beecham 203. Boyd Orr won all nations. The turn-out was 32.1 per cent. On the other hand, 38.8 per cent of the women voted, and 28 percent of the men, which may have affected the result. The next year the graduates elected Boyd Orr as Chancellor. Soon after that he resigned the Rectorship.

Boyd Orr was director of the Food and Agriculture Organisation until 1948 but resigned in disgust over obstruction from Governments and officialdom. He was made a peer. He received the Nobel Prize for Peace in 1949 and gave the money to organisations working for peace: he was very conscious of the threat of nuclear war.

# A Former Student from the Golden Age

Walter Elliot (Glasgow University Archives)

## Walter Elliot, Conservative statesman (1888-1958)

### Elected 1947

Elliot was one of the leaders in Glasgow student life who became leaders in political life. His great colleague in student days was Osborne Mavor, a medical man who became a playwright and wrote as James Bridie. Their era is called the "Bridie era" and was from 1908 to 1914. That was when the Union debates and the *Glasgow University Magazine* were adorned by outstanding personalities and when Daft Friday, the great annual entertainment at the union, was held for the first time. This was perhaps the golden age of student life in Glasgow; but the 1950s and early 1960s were also brilliant. Indeed, all students believe their era was brilliant.

The mythology of the era of Bridie and Elliot has been learned by generations of students. The University Union, in an act of faith and homage, has commemorated James Bridie and Walter Elliot by naming libraries after them and both are also commemorated by portraits there in bronze. Mavor chose James after his paternal grandfather and Bridie after his paternal grandmother. Bridie was not only a playwright of eminence but also a founder and vigorous campaigner for the Citizens' Theatre in Glasgow.

Elliot and Mavor were glittering personalities, although a contemporary to whom I spoke about the era said that Mavor "aye had a big mooth." That however could be said of many student politicians and debaters at Glasgow University through the centuries.

Elliot became president of the Union in 1911. The *Glasgow University Magazine* said:

> It was especially true of Walter
> That custom could not stale nor time alter
> His basic ambiguity
> And frequent fatuity.

When he was Secretary of State for Scotland in the late 1930s Elliot was faced with surging nationalism, economic calamity, and indifference in Whitehall to what was going on in Scotland. For example, in 1932 during the Depression the Government decided to abandon the building on Clyde-side of a great passenger liner, named at that time No 534, on the grounds of economy. It was a crushing blow to Glasgow and the region.

> The question, [wrote Elliot] is not so simple from the point of view of workers on the Clyde. Government can scrap cruisers [i.e. liners] and claim the money for something else.

But, he said, the people of Scotland knew that officials were too apt to spend the money that was saved on carrying out work in England, such as bridges in London, while "there is more than enough unemployment in Scotland." Work on the ship was resumed and she was launched as the *Queen Mary*.

Elliot tried as Secretary of State for Scotland to improve the economy through such agencies as the Scottish Development Council, but without much effect. Nevertheless the agencies were a step towards greater Government intervention in the future. His greatest achievement was the transfer in 1937 of the Scottish Office from London to Edinburgh, with all the vital departments under one roof. That brought a much more streamlined and efficient system for the administration of Scottish affairs. He opposed Neville Chamberlain's policy of appeasement to Hitler.

The other candidates in the rectorial election were David Niven the actor; Tom Johnston, a Labour statesman who had been one of the most able Secretaries for Scotland (1941-1945) and who had been a candidate in 1931; and James Bridie, who was backed by the Scottish Nationalists. Albert Einstein declined an invitation to stand. It is sad that Elliot and Bridie were contenders for the Rectorship in the same year.

Elliot's campaign managers for the rectorial election emphasised his record as a scholar (MB ChB and DSc of Glasgow), soldier (MC and bar, service in both World Wars), politician and statesman (Minister of Agriculture from 1932 to 1936, Secretary of State for Scotland from 1936 to 1938, and Minister of Health from 1938 to 1940). He lost his parliamentary seat in 1945 by 88 votes. but was returned in 1946 for the Scottish Universities constituency. (The voters were the graduates of the Scottish universities.)

Mavor's supporters said in one of their publications during the campaign:

> The university is a home of humanity, culture and the arts of life—not a political arena.

To which the Elliot camp's leaflet, *Rectorial Record,* replied:

> A culture which is divorced from the reality of the community in which it exists is worthless. Those people who believe that 'culture' is an end in itself should build their fifth university* on the top of Ben Nevis and retire there to stagnate in peace and tranquility [*sic*].

*Rectorial Record* also carried an editorial that echoed thoughts expressed about these elections long before Elliot's time and long after:

> Apathy has been the distinguishing feature of all recent elections in the University, whether S.R.C. [Students' Representative Council], Union or Rectorial.... It would seem that the vast majority of students are interested only in attending classes and passing examinations and not in any other phase of university life...

The Mavor camp declared about their candidate:

> From his University days he had written plays for the Scottish National Players, and in 1931 his play 'The Anatomist' was successfully presented in London's West End. A long line of London successes has not availed to entice him to England ... As James Bridie he has put Scottish plays solidly on the European map, *Tobias and the Angel*, *Mr Bolfry*, *It Depends What You Mean*, and *Dr Angelus*, to mention only a few, having placed him among the very best Dramatists in Britain ... His services to the arts in Scotland, quite apart from the matter of prestige, can never have been surpassed.

His platform was declared in a leaflet:

> Four things he does not believe in: Socialism, Conservatism, Communism, ANY OTHER ISM. Five things he does believe in: Common-sense, Enjoying Life, The Arts, Youth taking the lead, GLASGOW UNIVERSITY.

Sir Seymour Hicks, actor-manager and author, wrote:

> Apart from being the foremost British dramatist of our own time, and an outstanding literary figure—he is loved by all, who know him, as a great human being—wise, kindly and just, with a heart beating with sympathy, for those who seek help and advice—it will be a joy to the countless thousands to whom he speaks and has spoken that so great an honour as election to the Rectorial Chair of your grand University has been proposed for him.

The great actress Dame Sybil Thorndike sent a message of support.

---

* There were four Scottish universities at that time.

Tom Johnston's campaign was, compared with the others, quite muted. Labour had won the general election of 1945 sweepingly; but national politics are not always reflected in the way the students vote. Moreover, money was lacking for the Johnston efforts (see Appendix B).

David Niven's campaign seems to have been only a stunt to publicise his current work—a film about Bonnie Prince Charlie. It was said that a cheque for £100 to his sponsors, probably from the film production company, was not actually spent on the purpose intended. Niven's commitment to Glasgow may not have been strong. A story goes that when he was in the army he asked to be posted to any Scottish regiment except the Highland Light Infantry, The City of Glasgow Regiment. The army sent him to the Highland Light Infantry.

Voting was: Elliot 1,022; Mavor 521; Johnston 448; Niven 30. Elliot took all the nations. Mavor and Johnston were each the runner-up in two nations. Of all students, 34.26 per cent voted. The turnout among men was 28.75 per cent and among women was 53.67 per cent. It seems that Elliot won both because of his connections with the university and because of his career as a politician: the Conservative vote in the West of Scotland was then still comparatively strong.

Bridie wrote most gracefully in the *Scottish Daily Express* after his defeat:

> With that consummate tact so characteristic of newspaper editors, the editor of this newspaper has asked me to pay a small tribute to the gentleman who knocked me for six at the rectorial election. I gladly comply, because I admire Mr Elliot more than I admire most people ... Mr Elliot is a large man ... British politics have failed to provide for him a sufficient niche...
>
> They squeezed Mr Elliot into the Ministries of Agriculture and Health and these narrow cells were pretty nearly burst wide open. That quiet provincial job for a quiet provincial Scotsman—the Scottish Office—came his way and rapidly reached an importance it had never reached before. The mistake of putting Elliot and Johnston, in quick succession, into the Scottish Office was hurriedly remedied and Westminster breathes again.
>
> It looked like pure chance whether he came into politics at all. After five years with the Scots Greys he was wounded and a little tired of war. He jumped at the chance of contesting Lanark and getting 28 days leave. His telegram of acceptance—'Yes. Which side?'—is a matter of history.

Elliot's campaign managers promoted their man in a rather reverential way. But the students, when he appeared among them for dinners or similar events, used to sing, to a version of the "Battle Hymn of the Republic":

> Wattie Elliot has a big beery nose
> Wattie Elliot has a big beery nose
> Wattie Elliot has a big beery nose
> And he takes it with him wherever he goes.

Elliot's installation was comparatively quiet. The *Glasgow Herald* wrote:

Mr Walter Elliot gained the day at the St Andrew's Hall when, after his installation as Rector of Glasgow University, he quelled a noisy audience and persuaded them to listen for half an hour to a 'lesson' on Scottish history.

The 'subjection' of the students was all the more notable because of the hilarity which preceded Mr Elliot's investment with the robes of office by Mr A. M. L. McFarlan, President of the Students' Representative Council—the first time that the ceremony had been performed by a student before students. There was the usual pre-ceremony entertainment ... Bugles, whistles, and cat-calls were silenced when Mr Donald Macmillan, secretary of the Students' Representative Council, asked the audience to respect the University mace. But the respite was brief, for 'hostilities' began again with the appearance of the platform party... They were subjected to a barrage of streamers and squibs, which, although there were no casualties, forced them to take evasive action.

Mr Elliot had the better of the preliminary skirmishes when, after finishing a sentence with a preposition and being advised to 'watch his grammar,' he replied—'I am a Doctor of Science and of Laws, but not of literature.'

Elliot was a diligent rector and loved to attend events run by his constituents. He was active in preparing the celebrations for the University's 500th anniversary in 1951, celebrations that were held after he had demitted office. During the Labour Governments of 1945 to 1951 he played the Scottish card with skill, attacking Labour's forgotten promises of home rule. He even criticised Labour for having three English-born MPs in Scottish seats..

The *Times* obituary said of Elliot:

> He brought to the House [of Commons] intense sincerity, zeal for ordered reform, and a mind at once robust and fertile.

The writer spoke of his:

> ... grasp of subject, his wide outlook, and his gift of ready and forceful speech.

# Scottish Nationalist Candidate Triumphs

John MacCormick (Prof Neil MacCormick)

*John M. MacCormick, Scottish nationalist leader and lawyer*
*(1904-1961)*

*Elected 1950*

The degree of self-government that Scotland has today is owed to a great extent to John MacCormick's tireless efforts over three decades. His election was a boost for the Scottish Nationalist cause.

He founded the Glasgow University Scottish Nationalist Association in 1927. The inaugural meeting of the Scottish National Association, which brought together four main groupings of nationalists, was held in 1928 at the Union building. The catalyst was the students' association.

When MacCormick was still a student he was one of the founders and was the first chairman of the National Party of Scotland. When it merged with the more moderate Scottish Party, MacCormick became the honorary secretary. When the National Party refused in 1942 to widen its ranks and embrace all parties who wanted some self-government for Scotland, he resigned and founded the Scottish Convention.

MacCormick launched the Scottish Covenant in 1949. The Covenant, which received 2,000,000 signatures, sought a federal parliament for Scotland with "adequate authority" over Scottish affairs. Defeat for MacCormick at Glasgow University would be seen on all sides as a sign that the movement had lost its impetus and would have been a severe blow to the Covenant.

At the general election in the same year as MacCormick was chosen, Labour won 46.2 per cent of the votes, the Conservatives 44.8 per cent, Liberals 6.6 per cent, and the Scottish Nationalists only 0.4 per cent.

MacCormick was always known as "King John". During the inaugural meeting of the Scottish Nationalist Association in 1927, one of the speakers was, naturally, MacCormick. Somebody at question time asked: "Will an independent Scotland be a Republic?" A voice from the balcony said: "No, it'll be a Kingdom and they'll have King John in charge of it." And the nickname stuck for ever afterwards. Maybe it survived because of an unconscious association with the name of Count John McCormack, an Irish-born singer of opera, Lieder, and sentimental songs. Count John retired from the stage in 1928 but broadcast during the Second World War, left recordings, and was still famous long afterwards.

John MacCormick was in the tradition of fast-thinking public speakers who were bred in numbers over many generations at Glasgow University Union debates:

> Not many men can succeed in unpremeditated speech—the thoughts only half-a-sentence ahead of the words that provoke them. But this was John MacCormick's special talent and his audience never failed to be moved by it. Through most of his life his Scottish audience grew in size and influence, its sympathies captured by his personality.

Some of the obituaries of MacCormick said that he achieved little. But the river of Scottish nationalism goes underground from time to time and emerges again. What MacCormick and his colleagues did was crucial. And his dreams have indeed become reality.

Almost all the holders of the rectorship for more than 150 years had been politicians. Among the few exceptions were a President of France (Poincaré, was a politician but chosen in very special circumstances), a pacifist campaigner (Sheppard), and a philanthropist and man of science (Boyd Orr). And Compton Mackenzie, Scottish Nationalist. For the students to choose a nationalist, as they did with Mackenzie and MacCormick, was breaking away from a dominant tradition.

It has been pointed out that between 1931 and 1950 the rectorial elections went to people outside politics or to politicians with strong Scottish links. These decades were dominated by the Depression, the rise of Fascism, and the Second World War. Perhaps the students had lost some of their earlier interest in and faith in the party system.

At the time of MacCormick's election to the Rectorship the economy of Glasgow was different from what it had been in the desperate 1930s. Unemployment was on average only 3 to 3.5 per cent. But that was double the unemployment in the country as a whole. And *per capita* incomes in Glasgow and the west of Scotland were about 10 per cent lower than the country as a whole. The great industries—the building of ships and locomotives and the manufacture of machine tools—were going into decline. Young people tended to drift away in search of work or better pay. All this meant that the people felt Westminster was being unfair to Scotland.

John MacCormick's candidature in 1950 was backed not only by the Scottish Nationalists but also by the Liberals and the Distributists. His opponents were:

Rosamund John, who was a British film starlet. She was perhaps the earliest of the candidates whom one can tactfully describe as "colourful."

Lord Inverchapel, a former diplomat, nominated by a "non-party, independent" group. His campaign was run by men in Maclay Hall, a hall of residence. He was put forward as a Scot, living locally, having the time to take part in the life of the University (he was 67 and retired), and one who would actively represent the student body. He was an international figure, having been (as Sir Archibald Clark Kerr) the British Ambassador to Iraq, China, the Soviet Union, and the United States.

He was an immensely distinguished diplomat and at the peak of his career was followed by a media circus, but he had some quirks. He made considerable play of his links with Scotland and indeed was of Scottish ancestry. Yet he was not born there, nor educated there, and he did not live there except on short holidays. He was born Archibald Kerr Clark but changed his name, perhaps to make it sound more Scottish.

He played down the fact that he was born in Australia. In his early entries in *Who's Who* he pretended to be five years younger than he was. When that deceit was discovered he omitted from his entries his date of birth.

During the election his distinguished political friends Bob Boothby and Harold Nicolson went to Glasgow to speak on his behalf. Messages of support came from international figures such as General Dwight D. Eisenhower, future President of the United States. Inverchapel was disappointed by his defeat but was pleased that he had polled more votes than the Tory and Labour candidates.

Sir David Maxwell Fyfe, Conservative Minister (later Lord Kilmuir), was born in Edinburgh, served in both World Wars, and was a Member of Parliament and lawyer—he was Solicitor General and Attorney

General and he was a prosecutor in the Nuremberg trials of Nazi war criminals. He was one of the leading personalities of the European Movement and the European Assembly. Maxwell Fyfe was later to be Home Secretary and Lord Chancellor.

The Rev George MacLeod who was to become Rector in 1968. He was nominated by the Labour Club.

Douglas Fairbanks the film actor was a potential candidate but in the end did not stand.

MacCormick received 661 votes, Inverchapel 636, Maxwell Fyfe 632, MacLeod 305, and John 14. The nations voted two for MacCormick and one each for Inverchapel and Maxwell Fyfe. A few votes differently cast would have brought a very different result. MacCormick led Inverchapel in Transforthana by only 19 votes. If Inverchapel had captured that nation he would have had two nations and MacCormick one. Inverchapel would have won the election.

The Maxwell Fyfe propaganda sheet was called the *Rectorial Record*; the fourth edition of it was hijacked on its way from the printer's and overprinted with a pro-MacCormick slogan. A prominent supporter of Maxwell Fyfe was George McNicol, who was captured during the campaign, put in a cage borrowed from the Glasgow Zoo, displayed in the centre of the city, in George Square, and fed with buns. The students of Aberdeen University, where he was later to be Principal, perhaps treated him with more respect.

One of the propaganda sheets was *A Cross for MacCormick*, the cross being both a saltire and a cross on a ballot paper. It was a most persuasive document, with articles or messages of support from the author Neil Gunn; a leading Liberal, John Bannerman; the director of the Kelvingrove Museum and Art Gallery, Tom Honeyman; James Bridie; and Compton Mackenzie.

Bridie wrote:

> He is the Scottish National movement at its sanest and best, and without him we could have whistled long enough for the slightest consideration of our ideas ... It was MacCormick who, many years ago, almost single-handed, struck the first effective blow for Scottish Nationalism, by securing the election of Compton Mackenzie as Lord Rector.

The campaign produced two songs, or snatches of song, that caught on and even survived for several years afterwards. One was sung to a tune adapted from "John Brown's Body" and in a mock posh, or "pan loaf", or Kelvinside accent:

> Soliderity for Mexwell
> Soliderity for Mexwell
> Soliderity for Mexwell
> And we're all going to vote for MEXWELL FAIFE

The other was to the tune of the 'Bonnets of Bonnie Dundee':

To the Lords of the Senate twas Elliot said:
You'll need a new rector to reign in my stead
And there's no better man you can take it from me
Than John M. MacCormick MA LL.B

Chorus:

Here's to MacCormick, our rector to be,
Here's to the man who will set Scotland free,
Though our troubles are legion and few are our joys,
MacCormick's the man who will stand by the boiz .

It is a surprising thought that Elliot the Conservative would countenance MacCormick the nationalist, but Elliot was a loyal Scot and did a great deal for his country.

One of the leaders of the election campaign was Ian R. Hamilton, a rebellious but brilliant student who had run a magazine called the *Gilmorehill Girn*, suppressed by the University authorities. MacCormick later wrote in his memoirs that Hamilton during one of their meetings expressed his impatience at the way things were going for the Scottish Nationalist movement. Hamilton then suddenly exclaimed:

We must do something dramatic, something which will call the attention of the world to our movement ... surely there is something we can do which will hurt no-one yet make the Government in London a laughing-stock. Politicians will be even more sensitive to ridicule than to violence. Something like taking the Stone of Destiny back to Scotland.

And indeed Hamilton and friends, the next Christmas, took the Stone from Westminster Abbey. They did not steal it, they said. It was Edward I who had stolen it. They were reclaiming it.

MacCormick's election came the year before the University celebrated its five hundredth anniversary. The person most important in founding the University, William Turnbull, Bishop of Glasgow, was born in Bedrule, Roxburghshire. One of the highlights of the celebrations was the carrying of a torch in relays of students from Bedrule to the Cathedral. That was followed by a torchlight procession from the Cathedral to the University's main buildings.

The next day was the installation and Address in St Andrew's Hall, an event that did not add lustre to the quincentenary celebrations. When the Rector entered and sat down, a firecracker exploded under his seat. He faced a clamour of rattles, whistles, trumpets, and more firecrackers. Bags of flour were thrown at him. A kilted piper marched through the hall. A rope was stretched between the galleries; two students clambered along it.

A cardboard replica of the Stone of Scone, placed on the speaker's table, was removed by an official. Somebody put a live goose on the platform—an action that drew a rebuke from the Rector. A student in running gear presented him with a flaming torch—a reminder of the torchlight procession that had taken place the day before. Scottish Nationalists put two burning braziers at the front of the gallery and would not allow them to be interfered with. MacCormick was tolerant although he said later it was the noisiest event of its kind he had ever known.

# A leading Figure in the Arts

Tom Honeyman (Glasgow University Archives)

*Tom Honeyman, promoter of the arts and a significant figure in the cultural life of Scotland (1891-1971)*

*Elected 1953*

His knowledge of art was vast—especially because, when an art dealer, he was working directly with artists and their descendants or representatives. Honeyman qualified in medicine at Glasgow University, served as a doctor in the army during the First World War, and practised medicine until 1929 when he became an art dealer. He was director of the Glasgow Museums and Art Galleries from 1939 to 1954, initiating some outstandingly successful exhibitions.

He was a founder of the Citizens' Theatre; another founder was his friend James Bridie. Above all he was crucial in persuading Sir William Burrell the shipping magnate and collector to bequeath his immensely valuable works of art to the city—the Burrell Collection. Honeyman was awarded the St Mungo Prize which was for people who made Glasgow "more beautiful, more healthful, or more honoured". He lectured all over the world to Scottish societies and cultural groups.

One of his notable deeds was to buy Salvador Dali's great work Christ of St John of the Cross, for £8,200. At the time both the painting and the price paid came in for much vicious and ill-informed criticism. But its value now is very substantial. And Honeyman acquired, with the painting, the right to reproduce it, which turned out to be a valuable asset. It has been said that the sales of postcards showing the painting have brought in enough money to cover its cost. He resigned his directorship of the museums and art galleries, he told me, because of "corporationitis"—he was fed up with certain town councillors.

Other candidates: John M. Bannerman, a prominent figure in the Liberal Party; Lord Bilsland, a banker and businessman who did a great amount to help Scottish industry and development; Emrys Hughes, a left-wing Labour M.P. who, in spite of his name, sat for a Scottish constituency ("Who's your man? Hughes your man, for rector and for peace"); Albert Pickard, a Glasgow eccentric and self-publicist; and Lady Tweedsmuir, Conservative M.P..

Lady Tweedsmuir was the widow of John Buchan (Lord Tweedsmuir), writer of adventure stories and biographies, an MP, and a Governor-General of Canada. She was the candidate suggested by the Conservative Party headquarters but the choice was not a good one: she did not have enough calibre and was not well enough known to succeed

Honeyman received 744 votes, Tweedsmuir 372, Bilsland 366, Bannerman 241, Hughes 70, and Pickard 37.

Honeyman was elected on a "working rector" ticket and was diligent but did not leave a great mark. The Students' Representative Council occupied Pearce Lodge, which is a fragment of the seventeenth-century College building. SRC meetings were held in a large room on the top floor. Honeyman wanted the room to be elegantly fitted out and furnished but the idea came to nothing.

Honeyman's installation was very noisy but no more than that. The noise was mainly a response by the audience to the presence of "heavies" from the University Athletic Club who had been brought in by the Students' Representative Council, the organiser, as stewards. They would have been better to have stayed away.

He was conducted by the students in a torchlight procession from the middle of the city to the University's main buildings, as many of his predecessors had been. And like them he was in a carriage which was drawn by students. But that was the last occasion on which a carriage was used. His successor, R. A. Butler, went in an open car.

# Hooligans disgrace the University

R.A. Butler (Glasgow University Archives)

*Richard Austen Butler, Conservative statesman,
later Lord Butler (1902-1982)*

*Elected 1956*

Butler's installation was the scene of disgusting behaviour. Students pelted him with eggs, tomatoes, flour, and lavatory rolls and squirted fire extinguishers at him. His speech was drowned by noise. Many dignitaries walked off the platform, including three professors. Newspapers all over Britain and all round the world carried the story. The University was shamed.

The front page of the *Daily Express* had a photograph that showed Butler who had just been hit on the face by a bag of flour; the Principal, Sir Hector Hetherington, with lavatory paper on his head and shoulder; and the Rev Dr John Foster, Professor of Church History, with flour on his head and tomato juice on the sleeve of his robe. Meta Ramsay, honorary secretary of the Students' Representative Council, who later became

Baroness Ramsay of Cartvale, received a direct hit from a flour bomb. A huge cabbage knocked out a photographer.

Nobody knows why Butler stood there and took it. His remarks later about the subject were ambiguous and diplomatic, but that was typical of the man. Sir Hector did not walk off: he thought that would have been rude to Butler the guest.

A paper in the Netherlands, *De Telegraaf,* had the story and a photograph on its front page, with headlines that need no translation: BUTLER'S TOMATENDOOP IN GLASGOW and MINISTER MIKPUNT IN STUDENTEN JOOL.

The *Kansas City Times* also thought the story was worth the front page:

> Richard Butler, Deputy Prime Minister, Is Pelted With Flour, Soot and Eggs in Traditional Glasgow University Semi-Riot....But He Just Keeps on Talking.

The *Gazzetta del Populo,* Turin, reported:

> At the English university of Glasgow the installation of Mr R. A. Butler produced an unusual display of excitement.

Reporters and photographers who were present from the Glasgow papers passed the story to the national news agency the Press Association, which in turn passed it on to the international news agencies such as Reuters. That is why the coverage was national and world-wide.

The *Times* said in a leading article the morning after the debacle:

> A mob of young roughs insulted their new Rector and guest, Mr Butler, and dragged the name of their university in the mud for all the world to see. 'Shocking' is the word used by the Senior Glasgow Magistrate to describe the pelting of the speaker and others with rotten fruit, bags of flour, and rolls of toilet paper. It is the right word and in marked contrast to the extraordinary statement made by Sir Hector Hetherington, the Principal and Vice-Chancellor of Glasgow University. He has blamed the Press, saying to the reporters: 'If you were not here, it would not happen.' If Scottish undergraduates are such exhibitionists that they throw decency to the winds when they know that their behaviour will be reported, then the sooner higher education stays south of the Tweed the better ...
>
> If young men, not privileged to enjoy the status of undergraduates, caused any similar trouble, they would be jumped on severely in the courts and with the full backing of public opinion. There is no reason why students should have the impudence to regard themselves as above the law and they should be treated with as little leniency as is extended to any other more or less juvenile delinquents.

Sir Hector later wrote in a reply to a letter from an academic in Cambridge:

> I do not know why *The Times* should have wanted to bite so hard. But it will do no great harm. Of course I did not make the rather silly remark that is attributed to me. I did say that if the newspaper men had not been there in such force the thing would not have been so bad, which though unproveable is true. But it was a little bit of bad temper that made me say this, and since controversy with the press is about the least profitable of exercises I decided to leave it alone.

The acting Lord Provost, John Blackwood, said:

The hall is in a shocking mess and we shall have to present a bill to the students. Two years ago we spent £20,000 in redecorating and reseating the hall.

A cutting from the *Kansas City Times* was sent to Sir Hector by an academic at the University of Texas who was a graduate of Glasgow and Harvard. He said he would keep very quiet about his Glasgow degrees until his colleagues had forgotten about "the perfectly lamentable rectorial affair".

Letters came to the University from, among other places, Hove, Sussex; Moor Park, London; Nottingham; Prestwich, near Manchester; Llanelli, South Wales; Newbury, Berkshire; Southport, Lancashire; Scone, Perthshire; Bedford; Horden, Co Durham; Capel, Surrey; Tain, Ross-shire; and Reading, Berkshire. Some of the letters were on lined paper. Some had many words underlined. One suggested that the guilty students should be soundly thrashed. Many of the letters were angry but many were sympathetic. The Rev Dr E. Evans, from near Skipton, Yorkshire, wrote expressing his sorrow and saying : "I remember Asquith's installation in 1906 or 1907: there was a fair row (in which I did not take part) but we did hear the speech, and there were no eggs, tomatoes, or pease meal."

The *College Courant,* a magazine published by the Glasgow University Graduates' Association, said:

It was a contemptible exhibition of vulgarity and bad manners, of which graduates must be thoroughly and angrily ashamed.

But, said the *College Courant*:

... no one will contend that all Glasgow undergraduates, or even a large proportion of them, partook in the disgusting revels. ...The installation was a vulgar show, but there was no lack of vulgarity in the publicity given to it. In our view the most august of British dailies [i.e. the *Times*] treated it with pomposity, bad temper and sarcasm in the worst of taste.

Nor is only the press to be blamed for making the worst of a bad show. Senior members of the university, who should know better, said in public, and not always in the heat of the moment, things that would have been better left unsaid.

The great majority of students, immediately after the event, seem to have wanted the guilty brought to justice. But when the process of justice began, the student body closed ranks. Amnesia was prevalent. A handful of students were fined by the University Court, but only a handful. The archives record their names.

Nobody paid much attention to what was in the Address in all the tumult during and after the event. The Rector did say:

Britain may no longer be the world's workshop, but we lead all countries in the quality of our products and in the range of our inventive genius. We lead all others in the development of aircraft and the application of nuclear power for peaceful purposes. We look forward to a new form of energy which promises unlimited power from sea water. Britain has always ruled the waves.

A little while ago I forecast that we should be capable in this country of doubling our standard of living in the next 25 years... We stand on the threshold of an expansion of wealth unprecedented in the history of mankind. Within a generation—your generation—standards of living in many lands can be revolutionised.

Butler was of a liberal cast of mind, was an excellent Minister, and was one of the most progressive and thoughtful Conservative leaders. Yet he twice failed to achieve the highest office.

He was Minster for Education 1941-1945 and was the architect of what became known as the Butler Education Act. It introduced the 11-plus examination and reorganised secondary education. He was Chancellor of the Exchequer from 1951 to 1955 and after that held slightly less important posts until he became Home Secretary in 1957. He was Foreign Secretary 1963-1964.

Anthony Eden resigned from the Prime Ministership in 1957 and Butler was expected by many people to succeed him. But Harold Macmillan got the job. Macmillan resigned in 1963 and again Butler was expected to succeed. But Sir Alec Douglas-Home got the job.

Butler's rivals for the rectorship were: Lord Attlee, Labour statesman and former Prime Minister; Ernest Hemingway, writer; and Lord Gibson, judge (as chairman of the Scottish Land Court). Voting was: Butler 1,132, Attlee 897, Gibson 759, Hemingway 410. Butler took all the nations.

The layout and writing of Lord Attlee's leaflets, pamphlets, and newspapers in this campaign were perhaps the most professional in the history of the University. He was, said his supporters, the first truly distinguished international figure to accept nomination in post-war years, a claim that cannot be denied. His newspaper, the *Clarion,* enumerated his career in the First World War, social work in the East End of London, leadership of the Parliamentary Labour Party in the 1930s, and deputy premiership during the Second World War.

As Prime Minister from 1945 to 1951 he led a Government which changed the face of British society and gave this country a new, more honoured world status.

The *Clarion* also, as was inevitable, referred to students who were promoting the causes of other candidates. The pamphlets produced for rectorial elections for at least a century have abounded in these references, whose full meanings are now almost all lost but which were often very defamatory. Here, for the record, is an example of this genre. The *Clarion* said:

The truth must be told about the grafters, the careerists, and the drunks who minister to Lord Gibson.

[Hugh] Reilly and [Kenneth] Fee have much to answer for. [Donald] Wintersgill is a sheep whom we, in all charity, would like to see avoid the slaughter. Let him live to drink another day.

Reilly, Fee, and Wintersgill were leading figures in the Students' Representative Council and the Scottish Union of Students. Fee had been editor of the University magazine. Reilly became a most respectable lawyer and Fee a most respectable teacher and campaigner for Scottish nationalism. Wintersgill became a journalist.

Attlee had messages of support from Mrs Eleanor Roosevelt, Aneurin Bevan, Professor Denis Brogan, Lady Megan Lloyd George, daughter of the Liberal former Prime Minister, Bertrand Russell, and Tom Johnston, a former Secretary of State for Scotland.

One of the students supporting Attlee wrote to the Labour party's branch in Saffron Walden, which was Butler's constituency, asking for what the student called "the dirt" on Butler, but no reply came. That student became an eminent doctor in Canada.

Gibson was an eccentric. He tended to make unexpected judgements from the bench and defend them to the newspapers and whoever else would listen. A young graduate of Glasgow who went into the Scottish civil service in the mid-1950s was told by one of his seniors that Lord Gibson's odd behaviour was one of the big headaches the civil service had to cope with.

For example, the President of the Court of Session, Lord Clyde, severely rapped Lord Gibson's knuckles in a statement of January 1956—a statement unanimously endorsed by the other Lords of Session.

Gibson had refused to give effect to a judgement of the Court of Session but he was over-ruled by his two fellow-members of the Land Court, who were both laymen. The language he used was, Lord Clyde said, extravagant and unjudicial:

> Persistence in his attitude could only damage the credit and the respect which the Land Court must maintain if it is to perform its role ... The assertion of the Chairman on this matter is one which he should never have made. I have made these observations in the hope that a deplorable situation created by the Chairman at his own hand will not arise again.

Gibson produced £1,000 of his own money for the running of his campaign—a most unusual happening but not unique. Part of the money went on the buying of an ancient car that gave out flames from its exhaust and served very little purpose in his campaign. Someone climbed up a wall in Gibson Street, close by the main buildings, and added "Lord" to the street sign. "Lord Gibson Street" survived for years.

Gibson had been president of the Students' Representative Council and became a Labour MP. One of his causes when he was an MP was the eradication of warble fly, which lays its eggs on the skin of cattle. The eggs, when they hatch, damage the hide, which loses much of its value. The Tory Club made much fun of his speeches on warble fly.

Lord Gibson was run as the only "working rector" candidate. His backers were mostly office-bearers of the Students' Representative Council. Support also came from the Distributist Club.

Hemingway was promoted by Maclay Hall and other halls of residence. He was delighted to be asked and sent a cheque to his backers. The covering letter, which must be valuable now if it has survived, said the money was for "the slush fund", a phrase not common then in British English.

The amount of the cheque is not known at this time. Hemingway did better than expected by the pundits, but Maclay Hall had a solid body of men and they were effective. The candidate's international fame was thought to have produced votes.

Butler's performance as Rector was a disappointment to the students. He was fully briefed by the Students' Representative Council before he went into his first meeting of the University Court: he was told he was entitled to chair the meeting and the students expected him to do so. When he came out of the meeting he said that he had not taken the chair but that Sir Hector had done so "because he knows all about the business." He did not understand the Scottish university system, nor did he learn about it.

He did enjoy being Rector in spite of what happened when he was installed. He was at that time depressed. His first wife had died and he had lost his chance of being Prime Minister. He found his term of office a kind of therapy. Butler told Douglas Alexander, the President of the Students' Representative Council, that he felt accepted and respected by the student office-bearers. He said this in a genuine and moving way. He relished the egalitarianism and straightforwardness of the Scottish students.

The Students' Representative Council held a large formal dinner for the Rector at the Central Hotel, which at that time was the best in the city. Sir Hector later enjoyed telling the story that the President of the Students' Representative Council arrived by taxi, the Registrar and Secretary of the University Court by tramcar, and the Principal and Vice-Chancellor by foot.

Another lavish dinner was held at the St Enoch Hotel, now demolished. The Students' Representative Council was the host but the Rector was to pay the bill. The SRC sent the bill, which was for £300, two days later to Butler at the Home Office, but it crossed in the post with a note from the Rector.

Butler's note said: "Lovely dinner—herewith a cheque for £150 to cover it all." The people who ran the SRC could only marvel at a fixer even better than they were themselves, for Butler knew exactly what he was doing.

The political journalist Anthony Howard wrote about the St Andrew's Hall incident in his book *RAB, The Life of R. A. Butler* (he was usually referred to as Rab):

Rab, no doubt, fully deserved the tributes that various newspapers paid him for the calm he had displayed in trying circumstances. But soon there began to be an undertow of criticism, particularly within the Conservative Party—fuelled in part by the absurd pictures of Rab that went around the world ... but provoked also by some curiously ill-judged comments, making light of the whole episode, that he chose to make afterwards. Somehow the announcement, 'I understand youth. I have children of my own and I like to feel I haven't lost touch', was not quite what the Tory party wanted to hear.

How much damage the whole Glasgow episode did to Rab's long-term prospects within the Conservative Party it is hard even now to judge. But, given that pictures are far more emotive than words, and that the image they presented immortalised the Right's impression of him as a well-meaning but ineffective reformer being satisfactorily brought up short against the social effects of his own policies, it was probably not minimal.

It was the last rectorial installation to be held in the magnificent St Andrew's Hall, a venue for all kinds of public gatherings such as political rallies and for concerts (the acoustics were excellent.) Never again, after that display, would the authorities of the University and the City let the installation and Address be held there. The ceremony since then has been held in the Bute Hall of the University. Decorum has prevailed: the very long tradition of rowdiness has come to an end.

And a tragedy happened: St Andrew's Hall was gutted by fire in 1962, although some of the noble facade remains.

Why did the riot happen? It was not simply a few hooligans getting out of control. Behind the much-publicised event was tension within the student body—tension which had existed for many decades and which indeed still exists, to some extent, but which at that time was unusually strong.

Activists in student life made their names through taking part in the political debates at the Union (which had only men as members) and the Queen Margaret Union (which had only women as members). Or they made their names through holding office in Athletic Club, or the Students' Representative Council, or the *Glasgow University Magazine*. Becoming well-known often led to being voted on to the Board of the Union or of the Queen Margaret Union, the ultimate prize.

It was a fact of "corporate life" that leading members of the Students' Representative Council and leading members of the Union did not get along well. The two bodies were rivals.

At this period the Union was overcrowded. It was built in the late 1920s when men students numbered 3,800; they were now 4,900 and rising. An extension to the building was badly needed. The only way to achieve that was with money from the Government through the University Grants Committee.

That was one of the roots of the trouble. The Union's annual general meeting had for generations passed a resolution that the Union would always be all-male, voluntary, and independent. That commitment was adhered to fiercely. The Queen Margaret Union did not want nearly as strongly to adhere to its rule that only women could be members.

The Union's principles came under threat. The University Grants Committee would not give money for an extension to the Union building unless all students could use the premises—and that was impossible to reconcile with the Union being all-male and voluntary. The alternative was perhaps a bigger and better Refectory, an eating place run by the University. But the Union Board opposed that idea "if this Refectory is likely to compete with the catering facilities of, or in any way weaken, the Union."

Leading figures in the Students' Representative Council were privately happy to contemplate the Union losing its old status. All this debate meant that there was more than usual antagonism between the Students' Representative Council and the Union.

Butler's installation and Address were seen as affairs of the Students' Representative Council; and a few leading members of the Union—not the Board and no more than a small number of men—decided to disrupt the event. And that action contributed towards the hooliganism and vandalism.

The Students' Representative Council had some inkling, a week before the ceremony, that rowdiness might happen. Someone suggested at a meeting of its executive committee that Mr Alexander, who was a final year student of Divinity and who would be in the chair as President of the SRC, should calm down the audience at the beginning by giving a short prayer. He refused to let the Divine Name be used in this way. Other members of the committee pushed the point. He said: "Back me or sack me." The proposal was dropped.

That was as well. Before the installation ceremony began the Rector and the president and the honorary secretary of the Students' Representative Council were waiting behind the scenes at St Andrew's Hall, ready to go in procession down a central aisle of the auditorium and up on to the platform. The platform party was already assembled. The Rector and the officials of the S.R.C. could hear a distant murmur coming from the audience beyond some closed doors. Miss Ramsay (the honorary secretary) said to one of the staff: "That sounds like a quiet meeting." The member of the staff looked strained and gave the stunning remark: "These doors are sound-proofed."

The rowdiness was an undercover operation in the war between the Students' Representative Council and some members of the Union. The bad feeling is expressed in a cartoon published in the *Glasgow University Magazine* of November 1958. It show the president of the Union and the president of the Glasgow University Athletic Club as Gunpowder Plotters: their target is the offices of the Students' Representative Council.

In the end, the Union and the Queen Margaret Union agreed to abandon their single-sex rules and voluntary membership. In return the Union received an extension to its building and the Queen Margaret Union received a new building. All students have to join one or other of the Unions. This has meant a shift in student life. No longer does the Union have the very dominant role that it used to have.

The two Unions have evolved different characters. The Union is at present seen as the rightful place for hearty, beer-drinking men and the Queen Margaret Union for the less machismo men. These are of course stereotypes. The Union has lost some of its traditions and has gained accommodation; the Queen Margaret Union has lost much of its character and traditions and has moved from its venerable former home, now called the McIntyre Building, to a modern building. Former members and office-bearers of the Queen Margaret Union have expressed strong regrets at what has happened there. The Students' Representative Council has moved into the McIntyre building.

# Tradition of Politicians as Rectors comes to an End

Lord Hailsham (*The Guardian*)

*Lord Hailsham (Quintin McGarel Hogg),*
*Conservative statesman and lawyer (1907-)*

### Elected 1959

Hailsham was the last of the conventional political figures to hold the office. It was the end of a tradition that had lasted almost without interruption since 1820. The tradition does not seem likely to be revived. Instead of politicians the electorate tends to prefer "celebrities" from television.

Hailsham when he was candidate had been an MP or a member of the House of Lords since 1938. He had held many posts in Government and the Conservative Party, including those of First Lord of the Admiralty (1956-1957), Minister for Education (1957), and chairman of the Conservative Party (1957-1959). He was Minister for Science from 1959 to 1964.

Who was to be the Conservative candidate, after R. A. Butler's term came to an end? Harold Macmillan, who had been Prime Minister since 1957, declined—"prudently," said Hailsham's biographer. Lord Hailsham allowed himself to be nominated. He was unwell and in low spirits at the time when voting was held but he rallied. Butler told him that the students had "no intention of submitting you to the same tortures as they did me". Butler added: "What is needed is a continual work of diplomacy in the interests of *these charming students.*" (Italics added.)

Hailsham's opponents were Billy Butlin, later knighted, and "the pacifist divine," Michael Scott.

Butlin was one of the pioneers of holiday camps, establishing his first in 1936 at Skegness, Lincolnshire. He worked during the Second World War for the Ministry of Supply, using his skills in catering and providing mass accommodation. After the war he opened more holiday camps and hotels. He was a collector of antique silver, especially flamboyant gilded silver. Butlin was on a "working rector" ticket.

Michael Scott was an Anglican missionary and a campaigner for social and political justice. He had worked in a leper colony in South Africa and in slum areas of London, being at that time close to the Communists. He was in India for a while and was much influenced by Gandhi. He helped in exposing South African oppression of black people and in Britain was briefly imprisoned for his part in demonstrations against nuclear armaments. He also was on a "working rector" ticket. One of the students who supported him was Donald Dewar of the Labour Club.

Voting was: Hailsham 1,428; Butlin 1,182, Scott 493. Hailsham carried every nation. The turnout was 48.8 per cent.

Hailsham's rectorial address was not given in St Andrew's Hall, which had held many rectorial events. St Andrew's Hall had been where Butler had given his address three years earlier, to scenes of appalling behaviour. Instead, Hailsham spoke within the University precinct, in the Bute Hall, where loutishness was much less likely. In any case the students were unwilling to risk another dreadful embarrassment. The event went off with propriety. Hailsham however bemused some of his audience when he was speaking by occasionally taking off his mortar board, apparently at random, and bowing. This is in fact the custom at Oxford, Cambridge and other universities when the speaker mentions the words "Chancellor" or "Vice Chancellor." It was a practice then little known at Glasgow.

The rectorial address was entitled *The Need for Faith in a Scientific Age.* He had been appointed Minister for Science (not OF Science). Its content was rambling. The peroration ran to 315 words in one sentence:

When I survey the emotional, the intellectual, the moral, the political, even the physical litter and chaos of the world today, when truth has almost ceased to be regarded as objective, when kindness is made to depend upon political, class, or racial affiliations, when only the obvious stands in need of publicity; when I look at popular pin-ups, playboys, millionaires, and actresses with the bodies of gods and goddesses and the morals of ferrets lurching from one demoralising emotional crisis to another and never guessing the reason; when I view the leaders of great states, the masters of immense concentrations of power and wealth, gesticulating like monkeys and hurling insults unfit for fishwives; when I reflect on the vapidity of so much that is popular in entertainment, the triteness of so much that passes for profundity, the pointlessness and frustration of the popular mood on one side, and the brutality and cynicism on the other; when I consider all this, I can only reflect, without complacency but with a profound sense of thankfulness and peace, not that I am not as other men are, but being as other men are I have become in addition a citizen of no mean city, where decency and orderliness prevail, where objective truth is honoured, beauty admired, and kindness and human feeling universalised to cover the whole compass of suffering humanity, with a mission to carry on into the modern world the traditions nurtured and fostered in Greece, Rome, and Jerusalem, which I hold sacred, believing that these alone, at least in my own experience, can sanctify and therefore civilise the restless and destructive spirit of chaos and mutual hatred which, allowed to develop uncontrolled in modern conditions, could well annihilate the human species upon the planet, or alternatively undo the process of evolution itself and plunge mankind back into the animal status from which it arose.

Hailsham's career after the election was also notable. He inherited a viscountcy but renounced it in 1963, when the leadership of the Conservative Party was vacant, and went back to the House of Commons in a by-election, aligning himself for the leadership. But the leadership went to Alec Douglas-Home in 1963 and to Edward Heath in 1965. Hailsham became a life peer in 1970 and was Lord Chancellor from 1970 to 1974 and from 1979 to 1987.

# A Candidate who captured
# the Students' Hearts

Albert Luthuli (Glasgow University Archives)

*Albert Luthuli, campaigner against apartheid (1898-1967)*

*Elected 1962*

His election was exceptional because it was on a matter of true principle, not because he was a well-known politician or a colouful "character." Other people chosen on grounds of principle were Poincaré in 1914 and Dick Sheppard in 1937.

Luthuli suffered much for his fight against apartheid. He was born in Rhodesia (now Zimbabwe), was educated at a US mission school near Durban, and was a school teacher for 15 years. He was elected a tribal chief in Natal but was deposed by the Government for anti-apartheid activity. He was President-General of the African National Congress from 1952 to 1960, when he devoted himself to non-violent resistance. He was awarded the Nobel prize for peace in 1960.

Luthuli was elected when he was in jail and was never able to go to Glasgow to be installed and to give his Address because the South African Government forbade him to leave. He did however send this letter to the university:

> In the name of the lofty traditions of academic integrity and dedicated scholarship which are usually associated with the English university system, I salute the Principal, the learned members of the staff and each and every student of the University of Glasgow, of which it is my signal honour to have been chosen Rector. In any other milieu, there is no doubt that I would have spent my days in the academic field, in which I began my adult life as a teacher.
>
> I need hardly say how much I looked forward to attending personally in order to be invested in the distinguished office in which this humble being that I consider myself to be, finds itself. I regret, however, to state that this would be impossible owing to circumstances upon which I do not want to comment and which at the same time are completely beyond my control. It might, with some good fortune, fall to my lot, at some time in the future, to attain this consummation. But if this is not given to me in this life, I should like to say to every student, to the Principal and to the staff of the Glasgow University, that I shall endeavour, as in the past, never to act under any circumstances, no matter how trying, in any other way than that which will be worthy of you and your Institution.

He was backed by the Labour and Liberal clubs. Documents have survived that show the way in which his campaigners sought public support and financial help. These documents are probably typical of campaigns of the period but their survival is most unusual.

Letters were sent to trades councils and trade unions not only in Scotland but also in the rest of the country. One of the Luthuli committee was a student of Divinity; he arranged for letters to be sent to ministers.

The response was generally good. Some trades councils did not themselves contribute but held a whip-round at their meetings. Trade unions generally responded well. Contributions came from, for example, Mauchline (Ayrshire) local Labour party, Coatbridge trades council, Inverness and District Industrial Trades Council; and from the Amalgamated Society of Woodworkers, the Amalgamated Union of Foundry Workers, and the Society of Lithographic Artists, Designers, Engravers and Process Workers (one of the unions in the printing industry, always referred to as SLADE).

The response from public figures was generally very good but not always. Here is a selection of letters to show the spectrum. The actress Vanessa Redgrave sent money and wrote: "I am sorry it is not more." She also wrote:

> Please do ... let me know if there is anything else I can do. [And:] I suppose that a real figure of worth means somebody who is known to stand for certain qualities, who is known to have certain qualities of mind and spirit, that are not only admired by most people but are also very rare. At least, that is my idea of a figure of worth. ... I hope very much that your campaign succeeds.

Much less keen was Lord Reith, architect of the Reithian BBC, who replied through a secretary that he:

... fundamentally disagrees with the importation, into rectorial elections, of people who know little or nothing about the mis-en-scène.

He was to be Luthuli's successor and was a "working rector."

A popular television personality, Cliff Michelmore, wrote:

As one of my personal friends is a nominee for your rectorial, I think it would be very unwise of me to support one of his rivals. In any case I must admit that I am not very interested in who becomes Rector of Glasgow University.

Cheques came from political figures: Harold Wilson, Barbara Castle, Margaret Herbison, Eric Lubbock, and Anthony Wedgwood Benn (as he then was).

Luthuli was opposed by Robert McIntyre, president of the Scottish National Party (SNP); the Earl of Rosebery, racehorse breeder, politician, soldier, and landowner; and Edward Heath, Conservative statesman, former Minister of Labour, and future Prime Minister.

McIntyre was one of the most influential members of his party—for example, he helped to move the SNP's policy away from an extreme position to a more moderate one in 1948.

He improved its organisation during the 1930s and 1940s. He became the SNP's first Member of Parliament, winning Motherwell at a bye-election in 1945 although he lost the seat six months later. He fought many other parliamentary elections but without repeating that success.

His rectorial campaign newspaper, the *Fiery Cross*, declared:

We unashamedly affirm that we shall regard Dr McIntyre's victory as a blow struck for Home Rule ... Both in Westminster and in Glasgow the Tories have ruled too long for our good.

But there were other planks to the platform:

The issue in this election is perfectly simple. You have a choice of electing as rector a man who will play his full part in the University Court both as spokesman of the students and as a high Office Bearer of the University, or of making a gesture of support for a man who cannot play an active role in University Life.

Heath was then a rising man: he was negotiator for Britain with the Common Market. And he was one of R. A. Butler's intellectuals who held by the Conservative Party's traditional idea of "one nation." The Conservative Club said that Lord Hailsham, the previous Rector and a Conservative, had done a good job. Heath would follow his example, would negotiate with all comers on the students' behalf, and was young and energetic. He would be active, interested, and successful.

Lord Rosebery was perhaps the most colourful of the three. The future earl was returned to Parliament as a Liberal in 1906 at the age of 24, the youngest member of the House. His horses won many classic races, including the Derby twice. He became Secretary of State for Scotland in 1945, but that was in a caretaker government and his tenure lasted only two months. He went on to take an active part in Scottish affairs. Rosebery's father had been elected Rector in 1899.

The campaign newspaper, called the *Rosette*, said Rosebery would be a genuine Scottish Rector, use his extensive influence and his boundless energy to advance the Glasgow student cause through the whole of his three years in office, and always be available to represent the students. And he would attend all meetings of the university Court.

On the other hand the *Fiery Cross* said:

> Rosebery represents the Scottish aristocracy at its worst. He is by upbringing and background an Englishman[*], by ancestry Scottish. He and his kind have been selling Scotland down the river for 200 years. ...
>
> His sponsors ... are in this campaign for what they can get out of it, whether in the form of booze, food, fags, or best of all money. Their method of persuasion is not argument but bribery by means of lavish parties and sometimes simply with fat cheques. If Lord Rosebery wins this election, Glasgow students can hang their heads in shame. The rectorship should not be for sale.

A severe blow was dealt to the Rosebery campaign by the revelation that a wine and spirit merchant had sent an invoice to Rosebery's supporters for £117 13s 5d, a very large sum at that time. The drink supplied was six bottles of vodka, a dozen of martini, and quantities of whisky, gin, sherry, and cognac. There were also lemonade, tomato juice, and soda. No other such invoices appeared but there may have been some. The person who discovered the bill for drink was a Labour Club member, Donald Dewar, who was particularly proud of this coup.

The Conservative Club's campaign newspaper, the *Bandwagon*, said:

> There is a tradition in the University Rectorials that Campaign literature should be hard-hitting ... We prefer to remain aloof from the vulgar and despicable slanging that seems to be all the Rosebery campaign can manage. We are confident that their smear tactics will be scorned by all responsible students...

The *Bandwagon* however went on to speak of "sordid brigandry", an "aged dunce", "bribe-tainted", a "graft-spree", and "bloody liars".

Voting was Luthuli 1,291, McIntyre 844, Rosebery 832, Heath 733. Luthuli won all nations. The turnout was the highest for decades, at 61 per cent. Luthuli's candidature seemed to catch the spirit of the age. Even ultra-conformist law students in their three-piece suits sported pro-Luthuli badges in their offices.

---

[*] He was at Eton and Sandhurst.

# The Man who gave the BBC its Ethos

Lord Reith (Glasgow Herald)

*Lord Reith, one of the greatest public servants (1889-1971)*

*Elected 1965*

Reith created the ethos of the BBC: probity, balance, justice, public service, and education. He had an unflinching seriousness and strength of will yet suffered from agonising self-doubt, feelings of guilt, and desolation of spirit. His craggy, scarred face (from a war wound) masked his emotions. He was unusually tall. Churchill called him "Wuthering Heights."

The Reithian ideals have in the view of some observers been "dumbed down" in broadcasting—and indeed in newspapers. But the word Reithian has entered the language in Britain and his contribution to the cultural life of the country was enormous.

Reith was trained as an engineer in Glasgow and went into radio communication. He became the first general manager of the British Broadcasting Company in 1922 and went on to be Director General of the BBC from 1927 to 1938. He became a Member of Parliament in 1940 and was Minister for Works from 1940 to 1942. He held other posts in

Government and outside it—for example, on the Colonial Development Corporation.

Andrew Boyle wrote in his biography of Reith, entitled *Only the Wind will Listen*, about the day of the installation and Address:

On the way to the brilliantly lit Bute Hall elderly members of Glasgow University's academic court gathered their robes about them and lowered their heads against the stiff, cold wind. Only one man in the straggling procession seemed impervious to the darkening day and the first leaden touch of winter. Head slightly tilted, chin upthrust, as if to display like some old campaign ribbon the deep scar tissues that had disfigured his left cheek for half a century, John Reith strode forward with the rigid bearing of an antiquated guardsman. The bleak conditions suited him well, so that the swirl of dead leaves rustling and crackling underfoot, the plaintive cries of gulls wheeling towards the eternal throbbing sounds from the distant river, even the casual stares of the few bystanders, might have been theatrical props laid on for his special benefit...

Reith's genuine sense of homecoming complemented a natural sense of satisfaction. The honour of being installed at last as Lord Rector of this ancient university was all the more keenly felt because as a youth he had been denied the opportunity of studying at any higher seat of learning. Besides, he had come armed with something positive to say.

The incidental point that, in keeping with their rowdy tradition, most undergraduates probably regarded the ceremony as a ludicrous charade, and therefore as a fitting occasion for mischief, did not seriously occur to him. Nor did the unspoken apprehension of several members of the governing body, that Reith's indifference might in itself provoke a shambles, begin to touch the new Lord Rector-elect. His self-confidence was, as usual, supreme.

*The Times* had asked in a leading article:

Why should men of such eminence in different walks of life be prepared to risk the indignity which all too often seems to be the most notable badge of office? The memory of R.A. Butler assailed with flour and eggs during his installation address remains vividly in the mind.

His candidature was backed by the Scottish Nationalists, the Distributists, and a mixed bag of others such as the Dramatic Society, the Literary Society, and the Folk Song Club. His campaign was non-party and he was the only candidate on a "working rector" ticket.

Iain Macleod, nominated by the Conservatives, was a prominent politician and Cabinet member. He was a superb speaker. He was at one time strongly fancied as a future Prime Minister. One commentator wrote that it was hard to forecast who else might reach the prime ministership from the Tory party: "the future is too Macleody." A record by the Rolling Stones was a hit at the time, called "Get off of my cloud." The record was played at election meetings.

Macleod was appointed Secretary of State for the Colonies in 1959, charged with giving independence to colony after colony. That is his most enduring mark on history. He held other senior posts during the 1950s and 1960s and was Chancellor of the Exchequer in 1970 when he died suddenly.

Macleod's candidature was to prove notable in one way. He was the last of the line of politically-oriented people to be nominated: a line that began in 1820. He was the son of a Highland doctor. The Reith supporters asked:

> Which 'Scotsman' studied ENGLISH law at Cambridge? Who was rejected by the Scottish electors and then fled to a safe English seat?

That was an allusion to Macleod's standing for Parliament in 1945 in the Western Isles constituency, which was strongly Labour. He later became MP for Enfield.

The Liberal and Labour clubs put up Lord Caradon, who was formerly Sir Hugh Foot and was formerly the United Kingdom's permanent representative at the United Nations.

Reith said, in typical mood:

> I certainly said I thought he [Caradon] might be reluctant to stand against me; I would say so still; but I suppose he knows that I am a candidate and, therefore, I am wrong. I am surprised, though—knowing him—not surprised ... Macleod I have never met. I have always disliked him by sight and repute ... I never heard of Spike Milligan* but my secretary has just told me he is a comedian-actor, whatever that might be. This may surprise you, but I can be almost incredibly ignorant, particularly about people in whose activities I am not interested.

The voting was: Reith 1,857, Macleod 1,239, Caradon 750; the turnout was just over 50 per cent. Reith won all nations.

His address began dramatically: "Well, am I not far too old to be Lord Rector of this University?" He was 76. The students shouted: "Yes, yes, far too old." Reith waved his arms for silence—and got it.

Reith had a heart attack early in 1968, which in effect ended his attendance at meetings of the University Court.

The Rev George MacLeod, his successor as Rector, started an annual luncheon meeting for the Rectors and Rector's Assessors of the four ancient Scottish universities. The idea did not last for very long but the ones that were held were said to be interesting and enjoyable. MacLeod was the host of the first, in the House of Lords, to which Reith was invited as MacLeod's immediate predecessor. The Rector of Edinburgh University, Kenneth Allsop, was there. The Rev. Douglas Alexander, MacLeod's Assessor on the University Court, recalled later that Lord Reith, when introduced to Allsop, pretended not to know him although he was, through television, one of the most famous people in the country. Reith inquired: "What do you do, Mr Allsop?" Allsop was extraordinarily gracious in response, murmuring that he did a little television from time to time. Reith said: "Oh, I never watch any of that stuff."

---

* Spike Milligan had been a possible candidate.

# Left Wing Activist and Leading Clergyman

Lord MacLeod of Fuinary (Church of Scotland)

*The Rev George MacLeod, later Lord MacLeod of Fuinary*
*(1895-1991)*

*Elected 1968*

MacLeod was a leading churchman, writer, broadcaster, and left-wing activist. He founded the Iona Community, which restored the ancient church and other monastic buildings on the historic Isle of Iona and which was a strong force in the evangelical activities of the Church of Scotland.

He was Moderator of the General Assembly of the Church of Scotland in 1957-1958. MacLeod campaigned for decades to persuade the Church to condemn nuclear weapons and in 1986 succeeded.

His father, the first baronet, was a Unionist (Conservative) MP for one of the Glasgow constituencies. George MacLeod went to Winchester and Oxford University and served with distinction in the First World War. He did not to use the title from the baronetcy. He became a life peer in 1967.

MacLeod was the sixth member of his family to be Moderator of the General Assembly of the Church of Scotland. The Rev Douglas N. Alexander, who was a leading member of the Iona Community and was MacLeod's associate, as Rector's Assessor, on the University Court, has written:

> His ministry was tempestuous, controversial, and charismatic. Ecumenical before his time he was a preacher of brilliance yet best remembered for his public prayer of Celtic quietude. He could infuriate his friends and love his enemies and he often did.
>
> The Iona Community saw politics, peacemaking, and healing as all being part of the wholeness of the Gospel. These ideals reflected the conviction of their leader George MacLeod who was forever proclaiming Glory to God in the highest spelt High St.

When he was Moderator he supported a scheme for the introduction of bishops into the Kirk. The Anglican and the Presbyterian churches had been having talks on closer relations, talks which culminated in a report published in 1957. It said that the Church of Scotland ought to adopt a form of episcopacy in the interest of unity and that each presbytery should have a bishop from its membership. The reaction in Scotland as a whole was hostile and in the Scottish press was vitriolic. Opponents of the scheme were concerned about preserving the Kirk and its principles untouched and with keeping anglicising forces at bay. But MacLeod's thinking about episcopacy was by no means a major part of his ministry.

Standing against him were:

Lieutenant-Colonel Colin Mitchell, who was famous for exploits during the conflict in Aden in 1967. He also campaigned to save the Argyll and Sutherland Highlanders from amalgamation with other regiments. Mitchell was to be a Conservative MP, and in 1988 founded the Halo Trust, a charity for clearing land mines. In 2000 the Russians accused the Trust of spying against Russia and of helping rebels in Chechnya.

Daniel Cohn-Bendit, a leader of students in France, nicknamed Danny the Red; he was prominent in the unrest of 1968, the year of the election.

Winifred Ewing, who had sensationally won Hamilton for the Scottish National Party in the previous year. The SNP took 46 per cent of the vote in a constituency that had been one of Labour's safest. It was an earthquake in the political landscape. At the same time Plaid Cymru was winning a by-election and taking seats in local elections. It looked as if Scotland and Wales were losing the Labour faith. A veteran nationalist said: "A shiver ran along the Labour backbenches looking for a spine to run up."

The Conservatives were worried too. Edward Heath, the Conservative leader, made the Declaration of Perth in 1968 at the Scottish party conference, committing the Conservatives to a devolved Scottish Assembly. This contradicted a century of Conservative policy.

Lady Elliot of Harwood, widow of Walter Elliot and Scotland's first life peeress. She was nominated by the Tory Club but support for the Tories in Scotland was in decline and her association with Walter Elliot was not enough.

Voting was: MacLeod 1,293, Mitchell 861, Cohn-Bendit 836, Elliot 706, Ewing 554. MacLeod took all the nations.

The campaign was lively. MacLeod was nominated by the Labour and International clubs and ran as a "working rector" candidate. The Liberal Club called him 'Lord MacLeod of Funeral' and described him as:

> ... a swinging 73-year-old nominated as the representative of youth by a rabidly Presbyterian socialist clique ... Lord MacLeod is a prophet of doom, censorship, and sexlessness (for others.)

He spoke in his Address of religious matters. He attacked the universities for what he saw as their complicity in research for chemical and biological warfare and for making science a god. He said:

> We all know the key failure. It is lack of 'Universitas'. Lack of an all-embracing cult: a magnetic north star. Pluralism pulverizes. Theology, the Queen of Sciences to which all the others bowed (in the days, for instance, when the Rector had to be a Priest or Parson) has long ago been relegated to the cellar, a veritable Cinderella of the disciplines. That would not be so bad, save that all the sisters get uglier and uglier. And the ball becomes a cacophony.
>
> Man, destined to be higher than the angels, has descended lower than the beasts. And it is all because we haven't got a cult, a north star. We are fragmented ... There is only one hope for our society today, be it campus, or town council, or the courts at Westminster: to recover the realisation that Christ was a revolutionary; and to make Him our Way again, till we recover the Truth of things.

It was a most unusual Address and some of the staff and students had not bargained for such uncompromising and personal views. Science and knowledge were regarded as the ideal; religion was outmoded. Other people were offended by the radical politics.

# Communist Shop Steward and Folk-Hero wins the Day

Jimmy Reid (Glasgow University Archives)

*Jimmy Reid (1932- ), Communist shop steward who campaigned successfully to halt the closure of shipyards on Clydeside*

## Elected 1971

The choice of Jimmy Reid was to be the last time for decades that the honour of the Rectorship fell upon someone of serious significance in the wider world. A culture reared on television was to take over when his term came to an end.

Mr Reid had become a hero from his leadership and political skill in helping to save shipyards on the Clyde from closure.

Time overtook the shipbuilding industry in the 1950s and the West of Scotland's economy was badly affected. Inflation carried costs, especially wages, up and up. Strikes in the yards were as common as in the car factories. Foreign competition was savage. By 1962 most of the yards were losing money. The Labour Government, under strong pressure from the unions and fearing loss of support in its heartlands, agreed to finance a rescue. Upper Clyde Shipbuilders was formed in 1968, an amalgamation of five yards. Among them was John Brown which had built the great liners the *Queen Mary* and the *Queen Elizabeth*, but the market had collapsed for liners. By March 1970 the Government had advanced £20.2 millions in grants and loans. But the venture by June 1971 was in trouble and a liquidator for UCS was appointed. About 8,500 jobs were to go.

Jimmy Reid and James Airlie, both Communists, launched a "work-in." The men refused to take redundancy, occupied the yards, and worked on, being paid by the liquidator out of UCS's assets. Publicity was enormous. Many thousands of people went to a meeting at Glasgow Green, a very large open space in the east end of the city. Glasgow Green is a traditional place for political meetings. About 200,000 workers downed tools on 18 August 1971 and about 80,000 people matched for UCS. Support came from the people—old age pensioners, churches, Conservative women's groups.

The Government was by now a Conservative one but still did not want to let the yards disappear. It decided that only two yards were viable, Govan and Linthouse, and in September 1971 Govan Shipyards was formed from them. More Government money—£35 millions—was put up. Jimmy Reid had played a big part. A memorable television film shows him addressing the workers and exhorting them: "Nae bevvying."*

Arnold Kemp has written in *The Hollow Drum: Scotland since the War*:

> In the short term the successful resistance to the Government fed the nationalism that was to dominate Scottish politics and preoccupy Parliament between 1974 and 1979.

When the rectorial election came in October, Govan Shipyards had been saved only a month before. Mr Reid was a hero.

He had only two rivals:

Margaret Herbison was a Labour MP for West Lanark and a former schoolteacher. She had been chairman of the Labour Party, Minister of Pensions and National Insurance, and Minister of Social Security.

Teddy Taylor, Conservative MP, later Sir Teddy, had been an outstanding debater at the university union and became MP for Cathcart in Glasgow at the age of 27. He has been described as "one of the last exponents of the old urban Unionism [Conservatism] in Scotland" and a genuine populist. He was to become MP for English constituencies and was to campaign against closer links between Britain and Europe.

---

* "Bevvying" is from beverage. Drink was a permanent problem in Scottish industry.

Mr Reid took all nations. He had 1,458 votes; Taylor 891, and Herbison 810. Turnout was 39 per cent.

Mr Reid seems to have transcended party. Moreover, the Conservatives had not thriven in Scotland at the general election the year before, taking 38 per cent of the vote compared with Labour's 44.5 per cent.

A distinguished academic, Sydney Checkland, wrote in 1976:

> Jimmy Reid has been highly active politically through the UCS work-in and the Communist Party, and was chosen Rector of Glasgow University in 1971 when its students were in a mildly leftish phase. Highly articulate and deeply sincere, he has appealed for a new moralism and a rejection of the materialist society and the "rat race" it imposes. Though he can participate in the rude humour of the shipyards, he does not use it in his public appearances. Instead he is serious to the point of dedication, condemning the "uncaring society" and urging a form of socialism that would promote human brotherhood, but which is imprecise as to mechanics both economic and political. He is a moralist-populist, to whose idealism the academic young have responded.

Roger McGough, Merseyside poet, and Michael Parkinson, journalist, television personality, and future chat show host, were also nominated but their papers were ruled to be not in order and they were not allowed to stand.

Candidates had to give a signed declaration that they consented to being nominated. In both cases, University officials said, the rules had not been followed. Mr Parkinson and Mr McGough appealed to the University Court. The University officials told the Court that the nomination papers were accompanied by documents of consent—but described them as a letter "bearing to have been dictated" by Mr Parkinson but not signed by him, and a telegram "ostensibly" from Mr McGough.

The University Court held a special meeting and backers of each man appeared before it. Minutes of the meeting say that Mr Parkinson's backers produced:

> ... an undated letter of consent in the hand of Mr Parkinson, in an envelope addressed by the same hand, with an indistinct postmark, stated by Mr Simpson [his principal backer, Gordon W. Simpson] to have been posted in London at 4.30 p.m. on Saturday 9th October but delayed by the accident of a train derailment.

The deadline for nominations was Monday 11 at noon. Mr McGough's backers also put their views, on similar lines to the Mr Parkinson's. Both appeals were dismissed.

Mr Parkinson said afterwards that what happened was "absolutely diabolical." He was pleased at the choice of a militant shop steward, thought that Jimmy Reid was a "lovely fellow," and hoped Mr Reid would "give the University Court hell."

Mr Reid went on to become a broadcaster and a journalist with the *Daily Record*, the *Herald*, and other publications.

# End of the Tradition of Eminent Public Figures

Arthur Montford (SMG Newspapers, Ltd)

*Arthur Montford, sports reporter on Scottish Television*

*Elected 1974*

This was a significant choice. All the incumbents until this time had been persons of eminence in some distinguished field—politics, the Church, human rights, or public affairs. Mr Montford was well known but in a different field. He was the first of a line of Rectors to come from the world of television and other forms of public entertainment. Some of his success came from support by the group collectively called the "beer bar"—students who inhabited the Union bar and followed sport keenly.

An influence in his election was the relatively undistinguished nature of the opposition. Isobel Barnett (Lady Barnett) was famous for her appearances on the television quiz *What's My Line?* Lord George-Brown, Labour politician and former Foreign Secretary, was famous for becoming what journalists called "tired and emotional," or drunk. He had lost his

Commons seat in 1970. Janey Buchan was a journalist, scriptwriter, and Labour Party stalwart, later an MEP.

Although the field was very different from usual the turnout was nevertheless respectable: 40.36 per cent. Mr Montford carried all the nations. He received 1,461 votes; Lord George-Brown 731; Lady Barnett 716. Buchan and another, minor, candidate trailed.

Mr Montford was to be followed by a variety of people who were also not in the old tradition. Several were famous for their appearances on television; the students were from a background where television was of greater importance than ever before. This does not mean that someone famous from television cannot be a good holder of the office. Indeed the actor Richard Wilson (elected 1996) was hard-working, popular, and effective.

Mr Montford attended the University Court diligently—he was present at 23 out of 33 meetings. He was welcomed as a person of charm and benevolence. But a former President of the Students' Representative Council said that he was unused to committee work and unfamiliar with life at the University.

# The First Student to be Chosen— and probably the Last

John Bell (Wild Goose Resource Group)

*John Bell (1954- ), who was a student when he was elected. Later the Rev. Mr Bell*

## Elected 1977

Bell was the first person to be elected when a student and is almost certainly the last: the University shortly afterwards laid down that students were to be ineligible. It was the first election when the "single transferable vote" was used and the first after the abolition of the system of nations.

Mr Bell was on a "working rector" ticket.

Mr Bell had been President of the Students' Representative Council and his experience in that office was helpful to him during his term on the University Court.

This was at a difficult time for some students. More than 70 per cent lived at home within 30 miles of the university and commuted. But a higher proportion than before was beginning to come from outside that area. It was hard for them to find a place to live and the University did not have enough halls of residence. Some students were spending half their grants on rent and were taking weeks to find a place.

The University had empty houses and flats in, for example, Hillhead Street and Lilybank Gardens, close to the main buildings, but was unwilling to rent them to students. These properties were left at risk from vandalism and fire. Mr Bell, as president of the Student's Representative Council, drew attention to what was going on. He broke into some of the empty properties and chose one for a squat. He was arrested and charged but the court only admonished him. Other protests took place, such as an "occupation" of the Library to draw attention to the inconvenience of its hours of opening.

Mr Bell has said:

> As president of the Students' Representative Council, I campaigned against the renting to staff of houses in Professors' Square [next to the Gilbert Scott building]. The residents paid about £6 a week for a 14-roomed mansion and were sometimes letting the basement rooms to students for twice that amount."

He invented "Week Nothing", a programme for freshers to learn about the University and adjust to it. It was a successor to the "Freshers' Camps", which were held on the campus and at a Victorian mansion on Lochlomondside, named Auchendennan, which had been converted into a youth hostel.

Mr Bell, at the time of the election, had been away from the University for two years, working in the Netherlands for an English-speaking church. He returned to study for a degree in Divinity. He was therefore unknown to first and second-year students.

His backers said that the election was about:

> ... the safeguarding of students' personal and academic interests and their adequate representation.

The others nominated were:

Hortensia Allende, widow of the Chilean president Salvador Allende. A military junta, led by General Augusto Pinochet, overthrew him in 1973. Hortensia Allende was backed by the Labour Club, which said:

> A vote for Allende is a vote for world-wide recognition of civil liberties, religious freedom, and democratic rights.

Ian Archer, sports journalist, on a "working rector" ticket.

Sir Oswald Mosley (see also page 136.) His supporters said his opinions were not ultra right-wing. He was "directly in opposition to the National Front."

Canon Sydney MacEwan, who was a singer of Celtic ballads and made many recordings and broadcasts. He had a late vocation for the Roman Catholic priesthood. He gave his earnings to charity.

Norman St John Stevas MP, the Conservative front bench spokesman on education, science, and the arts. He was to become a Cabinet Minister, before being made Lord St John of Fawsley.

David Wilkie, Olympic gold medallist, nominated by members of the Athletic Club.

A very popular piece of music at the time of the election was *Tubular Bells* by Mike Oldfield. It was played constantly by Mr Bell's supporters. The number 59 bus which went along University Avenue, at the heart of the campus, had a huge advertisement for Bell's whisky.

In the first count of votes, Mosley, St John-Stevas, and Wilkie were eliminated early. The final count was Bell 2,135, MacEwan 993, and Archer 985. Another sports journalist, Arthur Montford, had been the previous Rector, so it was perhaps not surprising that Archer did comparatively well. Turnout was high at 42.92 per cent.

Mr Bell has said:

> One of the items on the agenda for my first meeting of the Court was the banning of students as candidates for the rectorship.* I was treated with polite suspicion because I was seen as possibly a difficult person. A professor who was among the people counting the votes was heard to say when the result came through: 'To hell with democracy.' But attitudes in the Court changed after my first year of office.
>
> I did not take the chair. It was better for me to sit as an ordinary member so that I could argue cases, which I could not have done from the chair.

Mr Bell has also said:

> I was frequently involved in advising and then representing students threatened with exclusion from the University. At that time few were aware that failure to gain passes in examinations because of prolonged absence through illness, bereavement, or marital difficulty did not spell the end of an academic career. There were compassionate grounds for allowing students to continue their courses, but the University was not famed for compassion. An amazing number of people fell through the net.

He was ordained as a Minister of the Church of Scotland during his Rectorship. He has worked for the Iona Community, has broadcast on radio and television, and has published 10 books of hymns and two of sermons.

---

* See page XXIII.

# Newscaster who fascinated his Viewers

Reginald Bosanquet (ITN)

*Reginald ("Reggie") Bosanquet, journalist and newscaster (1932-1984)*

*Elected 1980*

When he left Oxford University Bosanquet asked Independent Television News for a job, saying he wanted to be a star. He was told he could be a tea-boy at £10 a week. He soon became a sub-editor and in 1957 a reporter. He was diplomatic correspondent for four years. He was anchorman for the *Dateline* programme from 1959 for eight years. He was a newscaster from the start of the programme *News at Ten* in 1967: his style of newscasting was informal compared with the style at the BBC. Bosanquet once said that he "tried to think myself into people's drawing rooms, rather than addressing the nation."

Bosanquet was renowned for his lop-sided grin, slightly slurred speech, and unusual pronunciation of words such as "rahlway". His exuberant life was often reported in the newspapers. In later years his toupée was an object of fascination for viewers. The name is Huguenot, pronounced by the family to rhyme with "bet" but in his case everyone made it rhyme with "bay".

He stood for Rector at a time when the Union was in a time of trial. It desperately needed an extension to its building, which dated from 50 years before. The cost of an extension would have to come from public funds. That meant the Union would have to give up its cherished principles of being all-male, voluntary, and independent (see p. 173). The Union had been in tough negotiations with the Principal, Sir Alwyn Williams.

The President of the Union at this time was Charles Kennedy, later to become leader of the Liberal Democrat Party. I asked Mr Kennedy if it was true, as I had been assured, that he put up Bosanquet to annoy Sir Alwyn.

Mr Kennedy replied:

> The answer is both yes and no. We wanted a GUU[*]-backed candidate because we felt that the Principal was not terribly sympathetic to our cause, but equally Reggie was, at that point, at the peak of post 'News at Ten' fame and was an emphatically non-political candidate—and serious fun! For the record, I always did (and still do) enjoy cordial relations with Sir Alwyn.

Other contestants were:

Robin Cook, later to be an eminent figure in the Labour Party and Labour Government. At that time he was only an MP for an Edinburgh constituency. The *Glasgow University Guardian* described him as a Labour MP long associated with the issue of nuclear disarmament. He had been a Councillor on Edinburgh Corporation (1971-1974) and chairman of the Scottish Association of Labour Student Organisations.

Bill Aitken, a Conservative member of Glasgow District Council. He received 26 votes on the first count and was the first to be knocked out.

Jack House, a much-loved and brilliantly talented Glasgow journalist and erudite star of the radio programme Round Britain Quiz; he was also an authority on the Madeleine Smith poisoning case. He was the author of 60 books.

Anna Raeburn, journalist and agony aunt, who announced just before the poll that she no longer wanted the position.

Iain MacCormick, who had been Scottish Nationalist MP for Argyll from 1974 to 1979. He was backed by the Scottish Nationalist Association, although a former Scottish Nationalist MP, Margo MacDonald, was also standing.

Margo MacDonald, who had been Scottish Nationalist MP for Govan, Glasgow, in 1973-1974. She was to leave the party in 1982 over

---

[*] Glasgow University Union.

ideological differences. In the rectorial election she was backed by "a wide cross-section" of opinion. She promised to campaign on the role of women in the university, accommodation for students, the Government's education policy, and nuclear disarmament.

Raeburn and MacCormick each received only a handful of first votes and were soon to be knocked out, after Aitken. House ran a close second to the winner, with 1,278 to Bosanquet's 1,452. Turnout was 28.7 per cent.

Bosanquet had a poor record of attendance at the University Court —only 10 meetings out of 35—and when he did attend he was sometimes inebriated.

# Lord Provost who did much for the City

Michael Kelly (Glasgow University Photographic Unit)

*Michael Kelly (1940- ), who was Lord Provost of Glasgow*
*from 1980 to 1984*

## Elected 1984

Kelly was famous in the city; hardly a day passed without his name and photograph appearing in the newspapers. This was because he master-minded, as Lord Provost, a publicity campaign for the city with the slogan GLASGOW'S MILES BETTER, which was accompanied by the smiley face of "Mr Happy". The slogan and image together became familiar all over Britain.

The stereotype of Glasgow then was that it was dirty and poor; its hous-ing was dreadful; and it was full of football hooligans and louts. Dr Kelly brought journalists from London and showed them the city and its sur-roundings. The journalists learned that the reality was quite different. Dr Kelly took them, for example, to Loch Lomond; they had thought it was deep in the Highlands and were surprised to find that it was only 25 min-utes from Glasgow. Journalists began to write favourably about the city. It was a public relations turning-point. Dr Kelly was named Scot of the Year by the *Glasgow Herald* in 1983.

This publicity campaign was followed by Glasgow holding the Garden Festival of 1988. It became European City of Culture in 1990, beating Edinburgh, York, and Bath for the title by enthusiasm, lobbying and public relations.

Dr Kelly, when he stood for the Rectorship, promised to strive for more money for the University from the Government. Other matters of concern for him were sports facilities, accommodation, grants, and the cost of meals. He had taught economics at Aberdeen and Strathclyde Universities and knew how academics and university administrators thought.

Yasser Arafat, the Palestinian leader, was nominated by the Labour Club; this was at a time when Labour and left-wing groups nationally embraced the Palestinian and similar causes. Members of the Jewish community in Glasgow were upset by the choice of him as a candidate. They approached Dr Kelly to stand—someone with a good chance of beating Arafat. Dr Kelly, as a Labour Party member, was in two minds about what to do. He did not want to be seen as a representative of one group. He was then asked by the president of the University Union, Stephen Dunn, to stand. The Union's leading members thought that Arafat would not bring any direct benefit to the students. Dr Kelly agreed that his name could go forward. The Union did not campaign for him but many of its leading members backed him. He asked the Jewish community not to intervene and it did not.

Candidates for the post have to sign their nomination papers, stating that they were willing to stand. Arafat's papers raised some eyebrows. They were signed "Y. Arafat", which many people thought was an unusual signature for him. Why, for example, was it not in Arabic? Why was it not "Yasser Arafat"? Had he really signed?

Other candidates were:

Menzies (called "Ming") Campbell, ex-president of the University Union, former Olympic athlete, and ex-chairman of the Scottish Liberal Party. He was a competitor in the Olympic Games in Tokyo in 1964 but was not successful there. On his return the students in the beer bar of the Union, with Glasgow humour, sang: "Ming, Ming, you didnae win a thing ..." to the tune "The Lord of the Dance". He was to become a Liberal-Democrat MP in 1987.

Rikki Fulton, actor, writer and entertainer. He has worked in repertory, drama, and variety and on radio and television. He is one of the great pantomime dames. Mr Fulton has been described as the finest contemporary Scottish comic.

Jeffrey Archer, athlete in his youth, a former MP, a popular novelist, and a Tory party figure. He was later Lord Archer and was to be disgraced. Mr Archer moved into a hotel in Glasgow to take part in the election campaign and to show that he would, if elected, be available, but as a Tory he had no real chance. His entry in *Who's Who* still said, in the issue for the year 2000, that he was Honorary President of the Glasgow University Dialectic Society, a debating club.

Matthew Lygate was one of the most unusual candidates ever to be put forward. He had been chairman of the Worker's Party of Scotland and had run the party's bookshop. He had stood in a parliamentary by-election in the Gorbals in 1969. He and three other men were sentenced by the High Court in 1972 for robbing three banks in Glasgow of £13,000. Mr Lygate was sentenced to 24 years in prison.

Mr Lygate told the High Court:

I have associates in Glasgow and other parts of the world who are involved in guerrilla tactics on behalf of the working classes. I support action to liberate money from banks and furnish materials for us to move forward in the struggle.

It was said after the trial that he had had links with an extreme Irish republican group who robbed banks to raise money for the IRA.

He was described during the rectorial election as a Scottish Republican Socialist. "As an unemployed person," his backers told the student body, "he has none of the business or careerist involvement of the other candidates to prevent him from representing your views."

When the single polling station opened, Dr Kelly was standing outside and was shaking hands with everyone who went in. Jeffrey Archer turned up at lunchtime and Ming Campbell at teatime.

In the first rounds of the count, Matthew Lygate, Menzies Campbell, and Yasser Arafat were eliminated in that order. In the last round, Jeffrey Archer received 859 votes, Rikki Fulton 1,641, and Michael Kelly 2,590. Turnout was 43.66 per cent.

Dr Kelly attended 18 meetings of the Court out of a possible 29. He chaired his meetings.

Dr Kelly was to continue his career as a public relations consultant and broadcaster. He has held many public offices, including director of Celtic Football Club 1990-1994. He was Radio Scotland News Quiz Champion in 1986 and 1987, Radio Scotland Christmas Quiz Champion 1987, and is an Honorary Mayor of Tombstone, Arizona.

# Conservative Club says
# Rector should Resign

The enforced absence of the Rector symbolised by her Gown
(Glasgow University Photographic Unit)

*Winnie Mandela, charismatic and controversial South African
civil rights activist (1934-). She was the first woman but not the
first black to hold the position*

*Elected 1987*

Winnie Mandela became known as "the Mother of the Nation." She was
later perceived not only as a selfless campaigner for human rights but also
as profligate and as condoning violence.

She was a member of the Tembu royal house. She qualified as a social
worker. From the time she married Nelson Mandela in 1958 she campaigned against apartheid. The South African Government imprisoned him
from 1964 to 1990. During that time she was banned by the Government
(put under orders limiting where she could go and whom she could meet),
imprisoned (1969-1970), and sent into internal exile (1977-1985). Her term

of imprisonment included a long spell in solitary confinement. She campaigned all that time for her husband's release and for the rights of black people. Winnie Mandela became the representative of her husband and a symbol of heroism, dignity, and resistance.

Mrs Mandela's election looks superficially like that of Albert Luthuli in 1962 but the attitudes of students had changed in 25 years. The turnout in 1962 was 61 per cent and in 1987 was 17.69 per cent.

She was opposed by:

Esmond Wright, former lecturer in American history at the University; Emeritus Professor of American history at London University; and former Conservative MP for Pollok, Glasgow (he won because the Scottish Nationalist candidate split the anti-conservative vote.) He turned up during the campaign and handed out leaflets about himself.

Kenneth Dyer, teacher of mathematics at St Aloysius College, Glasgow; former senior vice-president of the Students' Representative Council, former member of the University Court (chosen by the SRC), and a "working rector" candidate.

Neil Henderson, graduate and former member of the staff of the University. "A familiar face around the campus." His supporters collected money in beer glasses outside the Queen Margaret Union.

Bishop Isaac Mokoena, an opponent of the apartheid regime. His supporters said he was not immune from:

> ... the brutal intimidation of Winnie Mandela's ANC—he features prominently on an ANC death list and his brother was murdered by this organisation's hitmen.

Mandela's campaign said that Mokoena was backed by groups sympathetic to the South African Government. This accusation was vigorously denied by Mokoena's campaigners.

Winnie Mandela received 1,350 votes and Esmond Wright 568 at the final count. The rest trailed. The South African Consul-General in Glasgow, Dr Sandy Shaw, said: "You cannot force my Government to talk with people of violence."

Mrs Mandela was not allowed to leave South Africa to be installed and deliver her Address to the students. She did however send a message which was read out by a South African black woman at a special ceremony. Her presence was symbolised by her gown of office, draped on a chair. The message said, in part:

> On very many occasions, honours have been bestowed on Nelson Mandela and myself in our representative capacity. Never before have I been elected to such a position. It is ironic that in our own tragic land I have never been allowed to stand for any position nor has any other person been allowed to do so freely. Only those who subscribe to and endorse a vicious system of discrimination may do so ... It is

particularly significant that unknown brothers, sisters, and friends so far away in Scotland care ... about us.

In the year after her election she was implicated in the kidnapping, beating, and murder of a fourteen-year-old black, Stompie Seipei, by her bodyguards. She was convicted of the kidnapping and sentenced to six years. The sentence was commuted to a fine of £9,000.

The Conservative Club called in 1989 for her resignation, saying:

Her connections with her own bodyguard, and in particular her failure to distance herself from their recent activities, show that she has shown scant regard for the rule of law and accordingly devalued the office of Lord Rector.

The president of the Students' Representative Council, Robert Pollock, said:

It is rather impetuous to call for Winnie Mandela's resignation when all the facts haven't emerged yet.

This is an issue of great magnitude and that's why we shouldn't make a hasty decision. This is a subject that can get the Tory Club of Glasgow University a nice wee bit of publicity and smear those naughty left-wingers up at the John McIntyre Building[*].

Nothing came of the Conservative Club's call for her resignation.

In 1992 she was accused of misappropriating funds and resigned from offices in the anti-apartheid movement. The Mandelas separated in 1992 and were divorced in 1996. Winnie Mandela continued to operate in the African National Congress as a militant figure. She was prominent in the proceedings of the Truth and Reconciliation Commission, set up after the fall of apartheid to investigate abuses of civil rights.

---

[*] the offices of the Students' Representative Council

# Rector walks out from Ceremony in Protest

Pat Kane with Principal and Clerk of Senate
(Glasgow University Photographic Unit)

*Pat Kane (1964-), rock musician and Scottish nationalist*

*Elected 1990*

Kane walked out of an honorary graduation ceremony in protest against the conferring of the degree of Doctor of Laws on George Younger, a leading Conservative, former Secretary of State for Defence, and former Secretary of State for Scotland. This action distressed many people.

Pat Kane, a graduate of the University, and his brother Gregory formed in Scotland the pop group Hue and Cry and from 1987 to 1989 achieved successes with singles and albums in the Top 10 and Top 20. This brought him widespread recognition within the student body.

His principal rival for the post was Tony Benn, the left-wing MP. Mr Benn visited the campus before the election and spoke in favour of himself. He said that the system of loans for students was part of a wider Tory campaign to pick off potential opponents. Students were one of the most important elements in a decent society and the Government was hoping to snuff them out. "Why should a London Tory Government decide how Scottish education is to be run?"

Mr Benn said Glasgow University should affiliate with the National Union of Students. A big debate was going on at that time about affiliation. The cost was said to be too much; and the NUS's attitude to abortion was contentious. A referendum was held at this time among the student body, with a big turn-out, and the result was a big majority against the NUS. Mr Benn's intervention was thought to have lost him votes.

The final voting was: Kane, 1,481; Benn, 845. The turnout was 16.56 per cent. Mr Kane in fact received votes from a fraction over 10 per cent of the electorate.

Mr Kane said after his installation and Address that he intended to spend a week overall each month working as Rector, with monthly surgeries. He was at 20 out of a possible 33 meetings of the University Court.

He was present, as Rector, at a ceremony in June 1992 when honorary degrees were being conferred in the Bute Hall, the main hall of the University. This was on Commemoration Day, an important event in the University's calendar. Among the recipients was George Younger, not only a distinguished politician but also a prominent businessman and a member of a great brewing family. He later became Lord Younger.

Mr Kane, wearing his robe of office, walked out, followed by about 20 students. Two young men on the balcony unfurled a banner with a St Andrew's cross and the phrase "Scotland United." This was the name of a group that wanted the Government to hold a referendum on Scotland's constitution. Mr Kane said that he took his action because Mr Younger was a high Tory, had brought the Trident nuclear missile system to Scotland when Secretary for Defence, and was part of a Tory Government that did much to destroy higher education and deny Scottish democracy.

> I am sure that the students of this University would agree with me to a man and a woman that we should not be legitimising Tories.

He also said:

> I couldn't sit as a Rector and represent the university as they were giving a degree to a Tory. It is a civil right to protest in this way. We did it in a very orderly fashion. There's no point in not using occasions like this to protest.

Mr Younger was afterwards asked about the demonstration by Pat Kane. He replied innocently: "Pat who?" When reminded who Pat Kane was he said:

> Oh, yes, I have met him before, in fact I did a debate with him at Oxford University. I think he is a Scottish Nationalist. He is a charming chap. It is a pity I did not meet him today ... I am used to protests and am delighted to take part in them.

The Principal, Sir William Fraser, said:

> I wish to make no comment other than that the Rector might have chosen an occasion other than Commemoration Day to draw attention to himself.

The incident happened when Sir William was giving an oration about Mr Younger:

> He gets credit from the Scots for very little and blame for practically everything. It is no wonder, then, that when he became the longest-serving Secretary of State for Scotland, his ministerial colleagues in the Scottish Office presented him with a specially made silver ornament in the form of a bed of nails ... He is remembered for his natural ability, his courtesy, his sense of proportion.

The *Sunday Mail* said that Mr Kane was a man of many parts—pop singer, self-appointed intellectual, Scottish Nationalist, "and also a man of no manners".

> When Pat grows up he'll learn an important part of life is being able to sit down with people of a different political persuasion. Democracy means you may not AGREE with their views—but you respect their right to hold them.

The *Herald* carried a letter from a reader:

> Interviewed on TV on the matter, Pat Kane's attitude of miscalling George Younger's political views did him no favours. Fortunately George Younger's good breeding was in evidence during his TV interview ... Let's hope that one day we will return to sanity and that the person appointed to the position of rector will be responsible, with a great respect for such a wonderful institution.

The *Scotsman* also had a letter from a reader:

> The unfurling of a banner and immediate interview, both for the benefit of the television cameras, show that his silly gesture was nothing more than a publicity stunt.

Almost immediately after the walk-out the University Court decided that it wanted the Rectors to lose their automatic right to chair the Court. The post, according to the Court, was effectively that of the chairman of a large company. Voting should be held to ensure that the right person was in the chair rather than someone who represented one "constituency." The Rector could better represent his or her own constituency when he or she was not expected to be neutral as the chairperson (see p. XXVI).

Mr Kane became a journalist and broadcaster.

# A Rector of the Television Age

Johnny Ball (Glasgow University Photographic Unit)

*Johnny Ball, entertainer and populariser*
*of science on television (1939-)*

*Elected 1993*

Students knew him well from his appearances on television programmes for children. He portrayed science as fun. He presented or performed in such shows as *Think of a Number* and *Playaway*. It has been said that through his skill and charm he led many a child on to the paths of knowledge and that he was a Rector of the television age. The *Sunday Times* said also that the result showed:

> ... a clear revulsion against the exploitation of the rectorship as a platform for gesture politics as typified by his predecessor in the office, Pat Kane.

Mr Ball had a Scottish grandmother—and not only Scottish but also from the Gorbals.

There were eight candidates. The others were: Russ T. Sharp ("Scottish Monster Raving Loony Alliance"); Helena Kennedy QC, chair of the reformist body Charter 88 and later to become Baroness Kennedy (Labour Club); Liz Lochhead, poet and playwright (Scottish Nationalist Club); Pamela St Clement, actress who appeared in the television soap *East Enders* (Gay and Lesbian Society); Mark Boyle, unemployed, a recent graduate who ran as the "man in the street" and "working rector" (Independent); Alex Duff, a teacher and formerly a prominent figure in the University Union (Glasgow University Union candidate); and Yusuf Abdullahi, one of the "Cardiff Three" (Socialist Worker Students' Society). Mark MacManus, who played the part of the television detective Taggart, withdrew the day before the vote because he was ill. His supporters said students who had wanted to vote for him should vote for Mr Ball.

The Cardiff Three were black men who were jailed for life for the murder of a prostitute, Lynette White, aged 20. She was hacked to death in 1988 at her flat in Butetown, a multi-cultural district of Cardiff. Two other men, also black, were acquitted.

Their trial was in 1990. A *Panorama* programme on BBC television in early 1992 investigated the police actions and the prosecution's case and concluded that the Cardiff Three were innocent. The Court of Appeal freed them in December 1992.

This rectorial election had the biggest field ever. In the previous contest, when Pat Kane won, only three people were running. Perhaps the size of the field and the fringe nature of some of the candidates reflected a change in attitude towards the rectorship.

Final count: Ball 1,806, Kennedy 843, Lochhead 841. Others received few votes. The number of votes cast was 3,494. The number eligible to vote was 19,874, including 3,193 from associated colleges.

The associated colleges included, for example, the Royal Scottish Academy of Music and Drama. Students at associated colleges who had matriculated at Glasgow University, to take degrees there, were entitled to vote but very few did. Omitting these students, the turnout was about 19 per cent.

Mr Ball's predecessor, Mr Kane, said in a broadcast the next year that the choice was fuelled by "the revenge of the anoraks." He also said that Mr Ball was "trivial man *extraordinaire*" and owed his election mainly to science students who were "fed up with an activist rector". Mr Ball said that Mr Kane's remarks, on a wider as well as a more personal basis, were outrageous.

> When I stood for election it was on the basis that I would be, or try to be, representative of all students, regardless of political orientation. I felt there was no place for party political activism in the role of Rector.

As Rector, Mr Ball gave much emphasis to the development of sports facilities and worked to promote the recruitment of students into science and engineering. He threw his weight behind the Faculty of Science's centenary celebrations in 1993. His efforts were recognised by the award of an honorary doctorate by the University.

# TV Actor, but not just another Media Personality

Richard Wilson (Glasgow University Photographic Unit)

*Richard Wilson, actor and theatre director (1936-)*

*Elected 1996*

Wilson has had a long career in television and films as actor and in the theatre as actor and director, but when elected was most famous for his part in the television comedy series *One Foot in the Grave*. He played a grumpy old man, Victor Meldrew, whose catchphrase, in a strong Scottish accent, was "I don't believe it."

Mr Wilson was born in Greenock, Renfrewshire, and trained as a lab technician at Stobhill Hospital, Glasgow. He recounted that on his daily journeys to and from work he passed the University and thought it was beyond the reach of the likes of him. He did his National Service with the Royal Army Medical Corps and went to live in London.

Mr Wilson had various jobs and at the age of 27 was accepted as a student by the Royal Academy of Dramatic Art. As soon as he left RADA he got a part in *Dr Finlay's Casebook*, an immensely popular television series based in a fictitious Scottish village. His career went from there.

Mr Wilson appeared in such notable television productions as *Tutti Frutti* (1987), *Only When I Laugh* (1979-1982), and *Crown Court* (1973-1984). Less well known to the public was his work in the theatre, as an actor (including Vladimir in *Waiting for Godot* and the name part in *Uncle Vanya*) and as a director (including *An Inspector Calls*). He appeared in films such as *Passage to India* and *Carry on Columbus*. He won Top TV Actor at the British Comedy Awards, 1991, and the Bafta Light Entertainment Award, 1991 and 1993. He was made an OBE in 1994.

Mr Wilson was nominated by members of the Labour Club. The other candidates were:

Johnny Ball, the retiring Rector. Never before had a retiring Rector stood and been defeated since Lord John Russell in 1847.

Dorothy-Grace Elder, a journalist on several Scottish papers and a television scriptwriter and producer. She was to be honoured as British Reporter of the year in the UK Press Awards, 1996-1997; and was to be elected to the Scottish Parliament, as a Scottish Nationalist, in 1999.

Muhammad A. S. Al-Mass'ari, nominated by the Liberal-Democrats. He was a Saudi Arabian dissident living in Britain and was threatened with deportation. His nomination was said unfairly by some people in the University to be a way of getting cheap publicity. The president of the Queen Margaret Union, Stephen Rixon, said: "He cannot hope to represent the interests or views of the majority of students."

Ian Hislop, editor of *Private Eye* and a performer on the television programme *Have I got News for You?*, was to run but withdrew. Jools Holland, pop musician, was nominated but his papers were handed in too late.

Voting: Al-Mass'ari was eliminated first, then Elder; at the last count Ball had 1,483 and Wilson 1,912. Turnout was 17.6 per cent.

Mr Wilson was a popular and admired Rector. Professor Rex Whitehead, the Clerk of Senate, gave the speech about him when he received the honorary degree of Doctor of the University. Professor Whitehead said that when Mr Wilson was elected the groan went up:

> Not another media personality ... But he chaired, most ably, almost every meeting of the University Court during his term of office. He opened everything that needed opening. He was to be found in the College Club or striding about the campus at the most unexpected times—here to promote this good cause, there to attend that function ... I never saw or heard him interviewed, on radio or TV, without his mentioning this university.

For every visit he wore a bright and different tie. He once conducted an auction to raise funds for a new medical building; six of his ties were for sale. He visited schools in poor districts to persuade the pupils that they could go to university. He was a great help to the Department of Theatre, Film, and Television Studies. Even after his term of office ended he would be around and brighten the place up.

Professor Whitehead referred in his speech at the honorary graduation to the feeling, prevalent in some academic circles in Scotland, that the Rector of the older Scottish universities should no longer be entitled to chair the University Court.

> These are confused times and there are those who would have us think of our students as customers with whom we should have contracts and service agreements. In such times the Rector is a glorious anomaly which explodes the business metaphor. What commercial organisation ... would allow the chairman of its board to be elected by the customers?

# Actor famous for Television 'Soap' Resigns from Rectorship Early

Ross Kemp (Glasgow University Photograhic Unit)

*Ross Kemp, actor (1964-)*

*Elected March, 1999. Resigned, November 2000.*

Mr Kemp was elected both as a celebrity—he appeared for 10 years in a television "soap"—and as a "working Rector". But he was soon perceived among the students as not being diligent enough in carrying out his duties. That was one reason why he resigned.

Mr Kemp was trained at the Royal Academy of Dramatic Art. He was a leading actor in the television soap *EastEnders* for 10 years and when elected was one of the most famous faces in the country. His fictional character was Grant Mitchell, an unsympathetic figure. A journalist wrote of Grant Mitchell:

> To some women he is nothing but a balding thug, but to others he is the epitome of the type of primitive masculinity that they find attractive in spite of themselves. He is the ultimate rough diamond, an emotional cripple who is just as likely to burst into tears as throw a left hook.

It would be a devastating blow to Mr Kemp's legions of fans "that he is leaving the BBC soap after signing a contract worth £1.2 million with ITV".

Mr Kemp was nominated by the Labour Club. He promised during his campaign that he would:

> ... work with University and local police to ensure student safety*, fight to ensure student issues are tackled by the new Scottish Parliament ... fight for more computers and core texts in the library, fight against Top-up fees, admin fees, and tuition fees increases, campaign with the SRC for a fair deal for students.

He would, said his campaign, be a hard-working Rector and a strong voice for students.

Shortly before the election was held, fire broke out in a basement flat in Glasgow occupied by students from Glasgow Caledonian University. James Fraser and Daniel Heron, both aged 20, were trapped and died. Windows in the basement had metal bars; there was only one smoke detector, which had been dismantled, and the fire escape was partially blocked by rubble. The Glasgow *Evening Times* campaigned against bad landlords (the *Evening Times* called them "slumlords") and the potential death-traps that students were forced to live in. The Scottish Executive later said it was to tighten the law on property with many tenants.

Mr Kemp, in the run-up to the election, endorsed the newspaper's campaign. After he was elected he said that students should be protected against "scum landlords" and said: "I want a blacklist [of them] at the University". He said in a message after his election: "Any problems and I assure you they will be SORTED".

The other candidates were:

Mrs Margaret Smith, "Jamie's Gran", whose cause was promoted by her grandson James Smith, a student of English literature. He claimed that her nurturing nature was an ideal qualification for the post and that his "supergran" would blow the opposition away. She would be a full-time Rector, he said, "not like these celebrity candidates". She would be more approachable than the stars. She had no party political allegiances.

A company in the fruit business gave her more than 1,000 Granny Smith apples, which she distributed to students. She also gave away pens, perhaps to balance business with pleasure.

Anthony Louden Connolly, who was present at debates in the Union over a period of 56 years. He was a kind of mascot for the debaters and was put forward half jokingly. He died soon after the election.

Will Pickering, an illustrator and a recent graduate, put forward by the Gaming Society. This society was not concerned with gambling but

---

* Women students had been attacked near the University.

with role play, fantasy games, myths, and mysticism. Mr Pickering also promised to be a dutiful Rector.

Ian Hamilton, put forward by the Student Nationalist Association. He was one of the Glasgow University students who took the Stone of Scone from Westminster Abbey at Christmas 1950. In the rectorial election that year he was a campaigner for the Scottish Nationalist candidate, John MacCormick, who won.

Mr Hamilton became a QC, Sheriff, and Rector of Aberdeen University. His supporters at the Glasgow University election produced leaflets showing him in leathers and astride a motorbike. One of his slogans was "Rebel with a cause". He was a figure, his supporters said, "universally respected in all areas of the media and politics".

But the chair of the Labour club, Mr Blair MacDougall, quoted Mr Hamilton's thoughts on the English "White settlers" or immigrants. Among the thoughts were: "Perhaps we should make English immigrants pass examinations on Scottish history and the Scottish Constitution". No English student, Mr McDougall said, could be expected to vote for Mr Hamilton.

John Sessions, entertainer, who was born in Ayrshire, was nominated but withdrew before the poll was held.

The poll. was, as usual, by "single transferable vote". (The electors list their preferences in order; the votes for the candidates in the last place are successively redistributed among the others until an overall winner emerges.) The voting was, in descending order, Kemp, Hamilton, Smith, Pickering, and Connolly. Turnout was 15 per cent.

Mr Kemp's performance when he was elected did not seem to match his promises. He was present at two Commemoration Days (when a great dinner is held, when honorary degrees are conferred, and when other events happen). But he did not attend as many meetings of the University Court as did nearly all his predecessors in the 1980s and 1990s—only six out of 11. He held only one "surgery". He failed to appear as Rector on some important occasions, and twice running missed the Freshers' Week, one of the big events on the students' calendar. He turned up 15 minutes late for the ceremony of his installation and Address.

The Students' Representative Council passed a motion of no confidence in him and he resigned just over half way through his term of office.

Mr Kemp wrote to the Students' Representative Council:

It is with great sadness and regret that I resign as Rector of Glasgow University in accordance with the wishes of the body of students whose opinion has always been my concern. Work pressures ... have overtaken me and made it impossible for me to fulfil my obligations in the way I would have liked, and that such a prestigious position deserves. I have fond memories of Glasgow and wish the students of the University the best of luck and success in all their future endeavours.

Ms Marilyn Croser, President of the Students' Representative Council, said: "Towards the end the Rector's absences had become a bit of a political issue, the student Nationalist Association against the Labour club". The Scottish Nationalists were the group who put forward Mr Kemp's principal opponent, Mr Hamilton.

The motion of no confidence at the meeting of the Students' Representative Council was moved by Kirsty MacDonald, a fourth-year student of English, who had been the campaign manager for Mr Hamilton. Ms MacDonald said that Mr Kemp had "betrayed and abused" the students.

Voting at the council meeting was 11 to 3 with 6 abstentions. Membership of the SRC was about 60. Attendance was poor for several reasons. The custom was for each Council to hold nine of its meetings during one academic session and the tenth and last in the early part of the next session, after the long summer break. Some members of the Council had left the University by that time. Interest in the Council's affairs was perhaps flagging: the great enemy, as always, was apathy. All that meant a low turn-out.

Ms Croser said:

> The students want to have their cake and eat it. They want both a celebrity and a working Rector. It is sad that he was forced to resign but in the end his resignation was a bit of a relief. It enabled us to draw a line under it all.

Mr Kemp had said, shortly before he resigned:

> The motion against me is by the Scottish Nationalist Party. I got this job under a Labour ticket, which is why the SNP are presenting the motion ... The position of Rector should not be chosen on a political basis but rather on the basis of what the Rector can do for the University.

Ms Sandra White, a Scottish Nationalist Member of the Scottish Parliament, replied that Mr Kemp was "trying to pass the blame on to others ". Mr Kemp's claim that his ousting was brought about by a group of nationalists on the student body was, Ms White said, completely and utterly false. She added: "The reality is that a wide range of students on the campus, supporters of various political parties and none, were unhappy with his performance".

Mr Kemp said that he had "done better than Winnie Mandela" {who was Rector from 1987 to 1990.) He said: "Do you know how many times she turned up? None". In fact the South African Government did not allow her to leave the country; and she was elected not as an active Rector but in a gesture of sympathy with the struggle against apartheid.

When Mr Kemp resigned, the *Herald* newspaper said:

> The students who voted in the rectorial election last year (or, more accurately, who did not vote last year) got the Rector they deserved. The turnout, only 15 per cent,

leaves students no grounds for complaint about Mr Kemp ... There will be renewed pressure to bar celebrities from standing, but it should be resisted. Richard Wilson at Glasgow University and Stephen Fry at Dundee, both celebrities, were effective rectors, the latter in particular working quietly yet assiduously to tackle student hardship. But if the rector's role is to be bolstered rather than undermined, many more students will have to take their voting obligations seriously.

After Mr Kemp's resignation, the Students' Representative Council issued a statement about the Rector's duties as the Students' Representative Council saw them. He or she was expected to attend (and chair, if he or she wished) meetings of the University Court and to liaise with the SRC over issues affecting students.

The Rector would also be invited to attend half a dozen annual events, such as Commemoration Day and the Chancellor's Dinner; and functions held by departments, groups, clubs, debating societies, and student Unions. The Rector, the SRC said, might "also wish to hold regular surgeries for students to come and discuss various matters, often relating to personal or academic issues". The SRC added: "In all aspects other than attending Court the Rector's participation in events is entirely voluntary and at his/her availability and choice".

# The Distributist Club:
# its Background and its Membership

The Distributist Club was (and indeed is) a force in student life, especially Union debates. Its principal beliefs were not clear to other students, nor even to its members. The outside world was baffled: a biographer of one eminent public figure (who became a Rector) wrote of "a group" at Glasgow University called the Distributists. One thing was however clear to all. If you were a Distrib you were a Roman Catholic and very likely of Irish descent. Debates were organised on a parliamentary system with political "parties"—the political clubs. The Distributist Club was a natural home for Roman Catholic students who wanted to take part in debates.

The Club's spokesmen and spokeswomen tended to say that their beliefs were based on the principle that each man should have three acres and a cow. On that slender phrase the "Distribs" managed to take part in Union debates on any political subject under the sun—from foreign policy to unemployment to the status of the pound to independence for British colonies. The phrase "three acres and a cow" was a short-hand way of expressing a political theory. Here is a better description of the movement than the catch-phrase.

Distributism was founded and promoted in the 1920s by G. K. Chesterton and Hilaire Belloc, both Roman Catholic writers. The movement had its roots in Pope Leo XIII's great encyclical *Rerum Novarum*, issued in 1891. The Pope offered an alternative to Socialism (or Communism) on the one hand and capitalism on the other. The Pope said that both systems deprived man of what man has by nature: "the right to possess property as his own." It was

> ... within man's right to possess things, not merely for temporary and momentary use, as other living things do, but to hold them in stable and permanent possession."

The old guilds of working men had been lost and had not been replaced.

> Hence it had come to pass that working men have been surrendered, isolated and helpless, to the hard-heartedness of employers and the greed of unchecked competition.

The encyclical demonstrated that the Protestant churches were not alone in wanting to change society.

Distributism said that ills of society could be cured by the sharing of wealth and the distribution of property. That idea was neither Capitalist nor Socialist. Chesterton put it well in a speech. The movement's supporters believed, he said, in the very simple social idea that a man felt happier, more dignified and more like the image of God, when the hat he is wearing:

... is his own hat; and not only his hat, but his house, the ground he trod on, and various other things. There might be people who preferred to have their hats leased out to them every week, or wear their neighbour's hats in rotation to express the idea of comradeship, or possibly to crowd under one very large hat to represent an even larger cosmic conception; but most of them felt that something was added to the dignity of men when they put on their own hats.

Or, indeed, owned three acres and a cow.

Belloc believed that:

... the Irish people [under legislation to reform the system of land ownership] have deliberately chosen to become peasant proprietors ... when they could have become permanent tenants under far easier terms.

Distributism attracted many adherents between the Wars, especially among young men who had been growing up during the First World War and had been too young to serve in it. And the 1920s was when Distributism took root at Glasgow University, first as a political concept. It later inspired the Distributist Club for some of the Roman Catholic students who were active in the "corporate life." The movement has survived at Glasgow University while it has vanished elsewhere.

Distributism's downfall began when Mussolini invaded Abyssinia in 1935. (The war is thought to have brought about the deaths of 500,000 people.) An outcry went up in Britain but Chesterton's newspaper, called *G.K.'s Weekly*, backed Mussolini wholeheartedly. Distributism was split and the movement never recovered. Chesterton was not responsible for the issue of the paper that endorsed Mussolini's war.

Glasgow was and is strongly Roman Catholic because of immigration. People arrived from Ireland in the 1810s and 1820s because the linen trade was in trouble. It has been suggested that in 1841 no fewer than one in three of Glasgow's population were of Irish descent. And Irish people came in great numbers during and immediately after the great famine of the 1840s. Nearly 43,000 Irish arrived in Glasgow between December 1847 and March 1848. The inflow reached a peak in 1891 when the country had 218,745 people who were born in Ireland.

Very large numbers went from Ireland to the United States, but they had to have some money to be able to do so. The Irish who arrived in

Glasgow and Liverpool had in most cases nothing. The *Glasgow Herald* said on 11 June 1847:

> The streets of Glasgow are at present literally swarming with vagrants from the sister kingdom, and the misery which many of these poor creatures endure can scarcely be less than what they have fled or been driven from at home. Most of them are absolutely without the means of procuring lodging of even the meanest description, and are obliged consequently to make their bed frequently with a stone for a pillow.

Many poor, starved and diseased creatures, wrote the *Edinburgh Medical Journal* at this period, were brought to the Glasgow Infirmary.

> In numerous instances it was destitution and starvation more than fever which was their chief affliction.

The immigrants met with hostility because they were willing to work for low wages. Glasgow already had plenty of problems: rivalry between Protestant groupings; shortage of jobs; shockingly bad housing.

But immigrants from Ireland were Protestants as well as Roman Catholics. They brought the religious tensions that were rife in their native land.

The Depression made worse the tensions in Scotland between Protestants and Roman Catholics: the Protestant foremen, charge-hands, and managers refused jobs to Roman Catholics. A person's name or place of education would reveal his or her religious affiliation. The Church of Scotland and the United Free Church led a public campaign to ban immigration from Ireland and said the "Scoto-Irish" were an inferior race. Even now the religious tension to some extent survives.

*Appendix B*

# How to Run a Campaign—and
# How Not to Do So

A list of candidates does not convey much about the run-up to an election and about the politicking that takes place when an election campaign is in progress. Candidates have first to be found. Reluctant candidates have to be persuaded to stand; if they persist in refusing, they have to be replaced. Some of the campaigns (but certainly not all) were fought not for political ends, nor for honouring both the university and a famous person, nor as a publicity stunt, but as vehicles for the energies and ambitions of the students running the campaigns.

A memorandum has survived about the candidature of Tom Johnston, distinguished Labour politician, in 1947. It was written by Kenneth Dallas of the Labour Club for his successors. I am grateful to Mr Dallas for preserving it and passing it on to me. It reveals the workings of one campaign. The memorandum reads in part:

> The Labour Club decided to approach Tom Johnston (Secretary of State for Scotland in the wartime coalition government) to ask him to stand. After some correspondence he accepted to stand although he had some misgivings about the time involved in the office of Rector, and he accepted no responsibility for raising funds.
>
> Contact was made with other political clubs. The Labour Club sought the support of the Liberal, Communist, Socialist* and Scottish Nationalist clubs for Johnston, The Liberals had first tried to get Lord Samuel to stand but failed.† Their club secretary said that their support for Johnston was reasonably sure but some of their members favoured Salvador de Madariaga.‡ The Communist and Socialist clubs promised support for Johnston. The Scottish Nationalists were also willing to support him but they were hankering after a candidate of their own, and they wrote to Johnston asking him to accept nomination from them. The Liberals finally withdrew altogether and decided to support no candidate.
>
> A campaign committee for Johnston was set up under the auspices of the Labour Club with a representative of the other clubs willing to co-operate. At the first meeting Communist, Socialist, and Scottish Nationalist representatives were present but a few days later the Scot. Nats. withdrew, having found a candidate of their own

---

* The Socialist Club was an old "popular front" body which had kept going during the war but declined after 1946 when the Labour Club became established.

† He was a philosopher and politician and had been Home Secretary.

‡ A Spanish writer, scholar, diplomat, and opponent of the Franco regime.

(O. H. Mavor, the playwright James Bridie). The Conservative candidate was Walter Elliot, MP since the previous year for the Scottish Universities.*

A fourth candidate emerged—David Niven who was currently involved in making a film about Bonnie Prince Charlie. Whatever the origins of his candidature it was clearly connected with getting publicity for the film. Some of his active supporters were Communists....

One (cheaply printed) handbill was produced to publicise Johnston's candidature. The aim was to have two or three speakers in the Men's Union and the QM Union but it proved difficult to get well-known speakers as Parliament reassembled in the last week of the campaign and one Johnston meeting had to be given up to accommodate Niven's candidature.

We wrote to prominent people asking for messages of support for Johnston. Not all replied but we got messages of support from Professors G. D. H. Cole and H. L. Laski, from Lord Lindsay of Birker (Master of Balliol College), Dr C. E. M. Joad, George Buchanan MP, John Wheatley MP, Arthur Greenwood MP, and George Mathers MP.

Naomi Mitchison, William Power, and Neil Gunn [all writers] were unwilling to support Johnston against Mavor. The press was informed of the messages received but only the *Daily Herald* made any use of them. We also had the support of an article by Dr William Boyd in the weekly *Forward*† which we managed to put up on a poster in the two unions.

Our publicity was limited by our own budget. Through inexperience of what was required for a Rectorial election our budget was not really ambitious enough and we made little attempt to raise funds with the result that we did not get across the case for Johnston to the large majority of students who did not attend meetings in the Union. The Conservatives made extensive use of posters, and whitewash and loudspeakers on the day before polling day, and they had good leaflets. Elliot's name was everywhere. What concerted action we did take to chalk and paint was left until the night before polling day, far too late to have any effect. The Johnston campaign cost less than £10. The Elliot expenses came to over £100 (paid, it was understood, by Conservative Central Office), Mavor's to about £30, while for Niven it was known that a cheque for £100 was received (presumably from the company producing the film), but there was not much visible evidence of how it was spent.

We were as weak on stunts as on publicity.....On polling day (Saturday, 25th October), we tried to redeem our poor showing up to then, we had a lorry and held a mock Rectorial installation in George Square. This earned a good photograph in the *Evening Citizen* but contributed nothing to the election result.

With hindsight, it was clear that our campaign was not positive enough in putting over a case for Johnston as Rector and a programme for him. Elliot's and Bridie's continuing close association with the University helped them while Johnston's reluctance to get involved in the campaign was a handicap to us. The vote for Johnston (448) was twice the combined membership of the Labour and Socialist clubs. It seemed doubtful if many Liberals voted for Johnston (most of them probably supported Bridie). A number of Communists supported Niven (perhaps more as a lark than for any political reasons) but they were numerically unimportant. The Distributists did not vote as a bloc; they would have supported us only if we had chosen a Catholic candidate.

---

* The voters in this constituency were the graduates. The university seats were abolished by the Labour Government of 1945-1951. The Conservative Party promised to restore them but never did.

† Johnston had edited *Forward*.

# *Ygorra*: Words and Music

No less an authority than Dr Robert Hutcheson (erstwhile Secretary of the University Court) reveals that several versions of the Glasgow University anthem have existed. The version given here is that remembered, and sung, by the author. No guarantees of proper tonality are made. What you see is what he sang.

Sa - la  Sa - va   Sa - la  Sa - va   Co - ra bel - la  co - ra bel - la   Ching ching ching - ho

Var - sit - y  yg - or - ra   var - sit - y  yg - or - ra   yg - or - ra   yg - or - ra   yg - or - ra.

# Sources

**Francis Jeffrey**

Cockburn, Lord, *The Life of Lord Jeffrey* (Edinburgh, 1852)

Cockburn, Lord, *Memorials of his time* (Edinburgh, 1856).

**Henry Brougham:**

Brougham, Lord, *The Life and Times of Henry Lord Brougham*, Written by Himself, Vol III (London, 1871)

Hibbert, Christopher, introduction to *Memoirs of the Public and Private Life of Queen Caroline*, By Joseph Nightingale (London 1978)

New, Chester, *The Life of Henry Brougham to 1830* (Oxford, 1961).

**Thomas Campbell:**

Beattie, William, *Life and Letters of Thomas Campbell* (London, 1849)

Redding, Cyrus, *Literary Reminiscences and Memoirs of Thomas Campbell* (London, 1860)

**Sir Robert Peel**

Cleland, James, *Description of the Banquet in honour of the Right Honble Sir Robert Peel, Bart. MP* (Glasgow, 1837)

Gash, Norman, *Sir Robert Peel: the Life of Sir Robert Peel after 1830* (London, 1972)

McRae, John, Speech to the Peel Club of Glasgow University, *Peel Club Papers* (Glasgow, 1836).

**Sir James Graham**

Erikson, Arvel B., *The Public Career of Sir James Graham* (Oxford, 1952)

McCullagh Torrens, Torrens, *The Life and Times of Sir James R. G. Graham* (London, 1863)

Parker, Charles Stuart, *The Life and Letters of Sir James Graham,* Vol I (London, 1907)

Ward, John T., *Sir James Graham* (London, 1987).

## Lord John Russell

Barker, Juliet, *Wordworth, a Life* (London, 2000)

Hill, Alan G (editor), *The Letters of William and Dorothy Wordworth, second edition,* Vol VI, part IV, 1840-1853 (from the first edition edited by the late Ernest de Selincourt), (Oxford, 1988)

Moorman, Mary, William Wordsworth, a Biography: the Later Years 1803-1850 (Oxford, 1965).

## Lord Macaulay

Beatty, Richmond Croom, *Lord Macaulay, Victorian Liberal* (London, 1971)

Macaulay, Lord, *Essays, and Lays of Ancient Rome* (London, 1888)

Trevelyan, Sir George Otto, *The Life and Letters of Lord Macaulay,* Vol II (London, 1923).

## Lord Eglinton

Anstruther, Ian, *The Knight and the Umbrella* (London, 1963.)

## Lord Elgin

Checkland, Sydney, *The Elgins, 1766-1917* (London, 1988)

Morison, J. L., *The Eighth Earl of Elgin* (London, 1928).

## Lord Palmerston

Ridley, Jasper, *Lord Palmerston* (London, 1970)

Woodham-Smith, Cecil, *Queen Victoria, her life and times* (London, 1972).

## Benjamin Disraeli

Allingham, H., and Radford, D., editors, *Lives and Letters of William Allingham* (London, 1985)

Blake, Robert (Lord Blake), *Disraeli* (London, 1966)

Buckle, George Earle, *The Life of Benjamin Disraeli,* Vol V (London, 1920)

Anonymous, Installation of Mr Disraeli, *Citizen* newspaper (Glasgow, 19 November 1873)

Smith, Paul, *Disraeli, a brief life* (Cambridge, 1999.)

### William Gladstone

Anonymous, *Glasgow University in the Seventies* (i.e. the 1870s) (Glasgow 1933)

Jenkins, Roy (Lord Jenkins of Hillhead), *Gladstone* (London, 1995)

Jenkins, Roy (Lord Jenkins of Hillhead), *Gladstone - a leader without equal, The Times,* 27 December 1999, page 15

Mann, Sir John, *Some Sidelights on the Rectorials of Gladstone (1879) and Bright (1883), College Courant* (Glasgow 1952)

Matthew, H. C. G., *Gladstone* (Oxford, 1995)

Morley, John, *The Life of William Ewart Gladstone,* Vol II, (London, 1903)

Nicol, J., *The Address of the Right Honourable William Ewart Gladstone when installed as honorary burgess of the city and Lord Rector of the University* (Glasgow 1902).

### John Bright

Mann, Sir John, *Some Sidelights on the Rectorials of Gladstone (1879) and Bright (1883), College Courant* (Glasgow, 1952)

Walling, R. A. J., *The Diaries of John Bright* (London, 1930)

Hilton, Tim, *John Ruskin, the later years* (New Haven and London, 2000)

### Henry Fawcett

Goldman, Lawrence, editor, *Henry Fawcett and British Liberalism* (Cambridge, 1989)

Holt, Winifred, *A Beacon for the Blind, being a Life of Henry Fawcett* (London, 1915).

### Arthur James Balfour

Alderson, Bernard, *Arthur James Balfour, the Man and his Work* (London, 1903)

Anonymous, leading article, *Glasgow Herald,* 14 March 1890

### Joseph Chamberlain

Creswicke, Louis, *The Life of the Right Honourable Joseph Chamberlain,* Vol. III (London, 1904)

Garvin, J. L., *The Life of Joseph Chamberlain,* Vol. Three (London, 1934)

Marsh, Peter T., *Joseph Chamberlain, Entrepreneur in Politics* (New Haven and London, 1994)

Petrie, Sir Charles, *The Chamberlain Tradition* (London, 1938)


**Lord Rosebery**

Anonymous, *Glasgow University in the Seventies* (Glasgow, 1933)

James, Robert Rhodes, *Rosebery, a life of Archibald Philip, fifth Earl of Rosebery* (London, 1963)

Raymond, E. T., *The Man of Promise; Lord Rosebery, a critical study* (London, 1923)


**Lord Curzon**

Gilmour, David, *Curzon* (London, 1994)

Mosley, Leonard, *Curzon. The End of an Epoch* (London, 1960)

Patterson, Jerry E., letter to the author, March 2000

Ronaldshay, Lord, *The Life of Lord Curzon* (London, 1928)

Rose, Kenneth, *Superior Person. A Portrait of Lord Curzon and his Circle in late Victorian England* (London, 1969).


**Augustine Birrell**

Anonymous, Glasgow University. Mr Birrell installed as Lord Rector. Address on the drama of life. Suffragist scenes, *Glasgow Herald,* 6 December, 1912, page 4

Anonymous, Glasgow students. Suffragist premises wrecked. Lively street scenes, *Glasgow Herald,* 6 December 1912, page 2.


**Raymond Poincaré**

Anonymous, A Memorable Day, *Glasgow Herald,* 14 November 1919, page 6

Anonymous, *The Chapel of the University of Glasgow,* pamphlet (Glasgow, n.d.)

Nayna, Estival, The Lord Rector, *Glasgow University Magazine,* 11 November 1914, page 26.


**Andrew Bonar Law**

Adams, R. J. Q., *Bonar Law* (London, 1999)

Blake, Robert (Lord Blake), *The Unknown Prime Minister* (London, 1955)

Clark, Ronald W., *The Life of Bertrand Russell* (London, 1975).

## Lord Birkenhead

Anonymous, article on League of Nations, *The Times,* 15 December 1923

Campbell, John, *F. E. Smith, First Earl of Birkenhead* (London, 1983)

Camp, William, *The Glittering Prizes* (London, 1960)

Taylor, H. A., *Smith of Birkenhead* (London, 1931)

MacAlister, Edith, *Sir Donald MacAlister of Tarbert* (London, 1935)

MacAlister, Sir Donald, letter to the editor, *Glasgow University Magazine* November 1931, page 76

## Austen Chamberlain

Anonymous, A Political Rectorial, and anonymous, "Austen, we love you so", *The Bulletin* (Glasgow), 3 November 1926

Anonymous, G. B. S. on the Glasgow Rectorial, *Daily Record* (Glasgow), 13 October 1925

Anonymous, Student's election, *Daily Record,* 16 October, 1925

Anonymous, Belloc ruse succeeds, *Daily Record,* 17 October 1925

Anonymous, An editor kidnapped, *Daily Record,* 21 October 1925

Anonymous, Kidnappers foiled, *Daily Record,* 23 October 1925

Anonymous, Big battle plans, *Daily Record,* 24 October 1925

Jenkins, Roy (Lord Jenkins of Hillhead), *The Chancellors* (London, 1998).

## Stanley Baldwin

Anonymous, articles in *Daily Record, Bulletin,* and *Glasgow Herald* (Glasgow, October 1928)

Young, Kenneth, *Stanley Baldwin* (London, 1976)

MacCormick, John M., *The Flag in the Wind* (London, 1955).

## Compton Mackenzie

Checkland, Sydney, *The Upas Tree, Glasgow 1875-1975 and later* (Glasgow, 1981)

Linklater, Andro, *Compton Mackenzie, a Life* (London, 1987)

MacCormick, John M., *The Flag in the Wind* (London, 1955)

Mackenzie, Compton, *My Life and Times, Octave Seven* (London, 1968)

Munro, Emeritus Professor J. Forbes, written communications to author, March 2000

## Sir Iain Colquhoun

Innes, Sir Thomas (of Learney), *Tartans of the Clans and Families of Scotland* (Edinburgh, 1971)

"W. R. C.", obituary in *College Courant,* Candlemas 1949, page 142 (Glasgow)

## Dick Sheppard

Roberts, R. Elli, *H. R. L. Sheppard, Life and Letters* (London, 1942)

Scott, Carolyn, *Dick Sheppard, a biography* (London, 1977).

## Archibald Sinclair

Anonymous articles in the *Glasgow Herald,* 3 October to 23 October 1938.

Archibald, Roy, letters to the author, 1999.

## Sir John Boyd Orr

Anonymous, obituary, *The Times,* 26 June 1971, page 14

Rae, James R., letter to the author, 16 January 1999

## Walter Elliot

Bridie, James (O. H. Mavor), Walter Elliot, *Scottish Daily Express,* 9 February 1947

Einstein, Albert, letter to J. F. Dick, Glasgow University Archives, 1 October 1947

Anonymous, Speaking of adventure, *The Bulletin,* Glasgow, 7 February 1948

Anonymous, Mr Elliot's call for courage, *Glasgow Herald,* 7 February 1948

Anonymous, obituary, *The Times,* January 8, 1958.

## John MacCormick

Checkland, Sydney, *The Upas Tree, Glasgow 1875-1975 and after* (Glasgow, 1981)

Anonymous, Students' torchlight procession, *Glasgow Herald,* 8 January 1951

Anonymous, Riotous scenes at "rectorial," *Glasgow Herald,* 9 January 1951

MacCormick, John M., *The Flag in the Wind* (London, 1955)

MacCormick, Neil, letters to the author, 1999 and 2000

Mackenzie, Compton, *My Life and Times, Octave Seven, 1931-1938* (London, 1968)

Munro, Emeritus Professor J. Forbes, written communications to the author, March 2000

## Tom Honeyman

Honeyman, Tom J., *Art and Audacity* (London, 1971)

Personal experience of the author.

## R.A. Butler

Alexander, Rev Douglas N., letter and verbal communications, December 1999 and January 2000

Anonymous editorial, *College Courant,* Vol 10, Whitsun, Glasgow 1958

Various authors, various articles, *Daily Record*, 22 February, 1958

Fee, W. Kenneth, conversations with the author, December 1999 and January 2000

Howard, Anthony, *RAB, The Life of R. A. Butler* (London, 1987)

Ramsay, Baroness (of Cartvale), conversations with the author, November and December 1999

Various authors, various articles, *Scottish Daily Express*, 22 February 1958

Anonymous, leading article, *The Times*, 22 February 1958

Personal experience of the author.

## Lord Hailsham

Lewis, Geoffrey, *Lord Hailsham, A Life* (London, 1997)

## Albert Luthuli

Archive relating to Luthuli's candidature, collected and preserved by Menzies Campbell (later MP), including letters written seeking money and the replies

Munro, Ken, conversations with the author. December 1999 and January 2000

Luthuli, Albert, Letter to the students and others, *Gilmorehill Guardian,* Glasgow, 25 October 1963

## Lord Reith

Alexander, Rev Douglas N., letters to and conversations with the author, December 1999 and January 2000

Boyle, Andrew, *Only the Wind Will Listen, Reith of the BBC* (London, 1972)

McIntyre, Ian, *The Expense of Glory, A Life of John Reith* (London, 1993)

Stewart, Andrew, obituary, *College Courant* (Glasgow, 1971) Martinmas edition, page 49.

### George MacLeod

Alexander, Rev Douglas N., letters to and conversations with the author, January and February 2000

Ferguson, Ronald, *George Macleod* (London, 1990).

### Jimmy Reid

Anonymous, I hope he gives them hell, *Glasgow University Guardian*, 29 October 1971, page 1

Checkland, Sydney, *The Upas Tree, Glasgow 1875-1975 and after*, (Glasgow, 1981)

Minutes of special meeting of the University Court, 20 October 1971

### John Bell

Bell, John, conversations with the author, June 2000.

Bell, John, letter to the author, 9 August 2000

### Reginald Bosanquet

Information from Independent Television News

Kennedy, Charles, letter to author, 15 March 2000

### Michael Kelly

Kelly, Michael, conversations with the author, June and July 2000

Anonymous, Four accused of £15,000 bank raid, *Daily Record*, 30 December 1971

Airs, Gordon, McWhinnie, Arnot, and Kerr, Jim, several articles under the general headline Downfall of Chairman Lygate, *Daily Record*, 21 March 1972.

### Winnie Mandela

Anonymous, several articles in *Glasgow University Guardian*, March 1987

Hunter, Roddy, Calls for resignation, *Glasgow University Guardian*, 9 March 1989, page 1

**Pat Kane**

Anonymous, George's tough degree, *Glasgow University Guardian*, 19 June 1992

Stewart, Graeme, Walkout met with degree of composure, *The Scotsman*, 18 June 1992

Easton, John, University ceremony goes on despite protest, *The Herald*, 18 June 1992

Briggs, Steve, University rectors rocked by moves to strip their powers, *Scotland on Sunday*, 28 June 1992

Anonymous, Kane is not so able, *Sunday Mail*, 28 June 1992

Crichton, Mrs A., Irresponsible action, *The Herald*, 25 June 1992

Moodie, Magnus K., Rude walk-out, *The Scotsman*, 24 June 1992

Simpson, James, conversation with the author, July 2000

**Johnny Ball**

Fraser, Nelson, Johnny comes home, *Glasgow University Guardian*, 10 March 1993

Linford, Paul, Butetown victim, *South Wales Echo*, 21 December 1993, page 11

Warner, Gerald, Winning without politics, *Sunday Times*, 7 March 1993

Woffenden, Mark, Johnny Ball under attack, *Glasgow University Guardian*, 19 May 1994, page one

Conversations of the author with Gavin Muir, Charles Dundas, and James Simpson, June and July 2000

Additional research by Derek Gibbons

**Richard Wilson**

Hattenstone, Simon, "I love dancing, I love music. I go to a lot of parties," *The Guardian*, 10 May 2000, tabloid section, page 12

McLeod, Malcolm, Vice-Principal, Glasgow University, conversation with the author, July 2000

Stevens, Tina, Last-minute drama of rectorial nominations, *Glasgow University Guardian*, 31 January 1996, page one

Whitehead, Professor Rex, speech on Commemoration Day, 16 June 1999

## Ross Kemp

Kemp, Ross, article in Students' Handbook for 1999-2000, page 13

Lawrence, Lucy, Grant throws a last punch as EastEnders' lovable thug, London *Evening Standard*, 24 March 1999, page 7

Various authors, various articles, Glasgow *Evening Times*, 6 April - 3 May, 1999

Various authors, various articles, Glasgow University *Guardian*

McKenna, Ron, End for killer slums, *Daily Record*, 1 October 1999

## Appendix A

Ffrench, Michael, *G. K. Chesterton* (London, 1986)

Wilson, A. N., *Hilaire Belloc* (London, 1984).

# General Bibliography

Anonymous: Many leaflets, posters, and other ephemera from election campaigns

Bridie, James (O. H. Mavor): *One Way of Living* (London, 1939)

Coutts, James: *History of the University of Glasgow* (Glasgow, 1909)

Devine, T. M.: *The Scottish Nation* (London, 1999)

Goring, Rosemary, editor: *Scottish Biographical Dictionary* (Edinburgh, 1992)

Greville, Charles: *The Greville Diaries,* edited by Philip Whitwell Wilson (London, 1927 )

Hay, John Barras: *Inaugural Addresses of Lord Rectors of the University of Glasgow* (Glasgow, 1839)

Hutcheson, Robert T.: *The University of Glasgow* 1920-1974, *the memoir of Robert T. Hutcheson* (Glasgow, 1997)

Kemp, Arnold: *The Hollow Drum, Scotland since the War* (Edinburgh, 1993)

Mackie, J. D.: *A History of Scotland* (London,1964)

*The University of Glasgow 1451 – 1951* (Glasgow, 1954)

Murray, David: *Memories of the Old College of Glasgow* (Glasgow, 1927)

Roy, Kenneth, editor: *Dictionary of Scottish Biography*, Vol I, 1970 - 1975 (Irvine, 1999)

Stewart, William: *University of Glasgow, Old and New* (Glasgow,1891)

*Who's Who* and *Who Was Who* (London, various dates)

Warner, Gerald: *Conquering by Degrees; a Centenary History of Glasgow University Union* (Glasgow, 1985)

Various Lord Rectors' Addresses, printed either especially or in newspapers; the *Glasgow University Magazine*; the *Gilmorehill Guardian* and its successor the *Glasgow University Guardian*. Minutes of the University Court and Senate.

# Picture Credits

Every effort has been made to establish the copyright holder for each picture; apology is made, and pardon sought for inadvertent unacknowledged use of copyright material. Many of the photographs are from the file of portraits of members of the Court of Glasgow University now stored in the University Archives.

Adam Smith: (p. IX): Hans Gasser, marble; Hunterian Museum.

Edmund Burke (p. X): John Jones, mezzotint (detail), 1790; Hunterian Art Gallery.

Kirkman Finlay (p. 1): Gilbert & Bell, engraving (detail); Scottish National Portrait Gallery.

Francis Jeffrey (p. 3): Samuel Freeman, stipple engraving (detail), 1812; Hunterian Art Gallery.

Sir James Mackintosh (p. 7): Sir Thomas Lawrence (detail), 1804; National Portrait Gallery.

Lord Brougham (p. 10): William Walker, mixed method engraving (detail), 1831; Hunterian Art Gallery.

Thomas Campbell (p. 14): steel engraving by W.H. Watt after Sir Thomas Lawrence, 1835 (detail); Hunterian Art Gallery

Lord Lansdowne (p.19): William Henry Eglinton after Sir Thomas Lawrence, mixed method engraving (detail); National Portrait Gallery.

Lord Cockburn (p. 21): Sir John Watson Gordon (detail); Scottish National Portrait Gallery.

Lord Stanley (p. 24): Frederick Richard Say (detail); National Portrait Gallery.

Sir Robert Peel (p. 26): Unknown artist (detail); Glasgow University Archives.

Sir James Graham (p. 31): Desmaisons, engraving; National Portrait Gallery.

Marquess of Breadalbane (p. 35): Hill and Adamson, photograph (ca. 1845); Glasgow University Library.

Fox Maule (p. 36): D.J. Pound, after a photograph by John Jabez Mayall, line and stipple engraving; National Portrait Gallery.

Lord Rutherfurd (p. 37): Sir John Watson Gordon (detail); Scottish National Portrait Gallery.

Lord John Russell (p. 38): James Faed, mixed method engraving (detail); Hunterian Art Gallery.

William Mure (p. 41): from the painting at Caldwell House; Glasgow University Archives.

Lord Macaulay (p. 42): Sir John Watson Gordon; Hunterian Art Gallery.

Sir Archibald Alison (p. 46): Maull and Polybank, photograph (detail); National Portrait Gallery.

Lord Eglinton (p. 48): Mezzotint by George Sanders after C. Smith (detail); Hunterian Art Gallery.

Duke of Argyll (p. 50): Stipple engraving by William Holl after George Richmond (detail); Hunterian Art Gallery.

Sir Edward Bulwer-Lytton (p. 51): Pellisier & Allen, photograph; Glasgow University Archives

Lord Elgin (p. 53): lithograph after a drawing by G. Richmond (detail); National Portrait Gallery).

Lord Palmerston (p. 56): lithograph; Glasgow University Archives.

Lord Glencorse (p. 59): photograph; Glasgow University Archives.

Lord Stanley (p. 61):, photograph; Glasgow University Archives.

Benjamin Disraeli (. 63): engraving; Glasgow University Archives.

W.E. Gladstone (p. 67): John King, etching (detail); Hunterian Art Gallery.

John Bright (p. 73): James H. Baker, mixed method engraving (detail); Hunterian Art Gallery.

Henry Fawcett (p. 77): engraving; Glasgow University Archives.

Edward Lushington (p. 80): photograph (detail); Glasgow University Archives.

Lord Lytton (p. 82): George Frederic Watts; National Portrait Gallery.

Arthur James Balfour (p. 84): photograph (detail); Glasgow University Archives.

Sir John Gorst (p. 87): caricature by Spy (Sir Leslie Ward), chromolithograph published in *Vanity Fair*, 1880 (detail); Hunterian Art Gallery.

Joseph Chamberlain (p. 89): photograph; Glasgow University Archives.

Lord Rosebery (p. 92): photograph; Glasgow University Archives.

George Wyndham (p. 97): photograph; Glasgow University Archives.

Herbert Asquith (p. 99): photograph (detail); Glasgow University Archives.

Lord Curzon (p. 103): photograph (detail); Glasgow University Archives.

Augustine Birrell (p. 110): photograph (detail); Glasgow University Archives.

Raymond Poincaré (p. 113): photograph (detail); Glasgow University Archives.

Andrew Bonar Law (p.116): photograph (detail); Glasgow University Archives.

Lord Birkenhead (p. 120): photograph; Glasgow University Archives.

Austen Chamberlain (p. 125): photograph, © Annan; Glasgow University Archives.

Stanley Baldwin (p. 129): photograph; Glasgow University Archives.

Compton Mackenzie, with the Duke and Duchess of York (p. 134): photograph (detail); Glasgow University Archives.

Sir Iain Colquhoun (p. 139): photograph; Glasgow University Archives.

Dick Sheppard (p. 143): photograph; Peace Pledge Union.

Sir Archibald Sinclair (p. 147): photograph; Glasgow University Archives.

Lord Boyd Orr (p. 151): photograph (detail); Glasgow University Archives.

Walter Elliot (p. 154): photograph (detail); Glasgow University Archives.

John MacCormick (p. 159): photograph; by permission of Professor Neil MacCormick.

Tom Honeyman (p. 165): photograph, © Stephens Orr; Glasgow University Archives.

R.A. Butler (p. 167): photograph; Glasgow University Archives.

Lord Hailsham (p. 175): E. Hamilton West, photograph, 2 April 1987: The *Guardian.*

Albert Luthuli (p. 179): photograph; Glasgow University Archives.

Lord Reith (p. 183): photograph, SMG Newspapers Ltd.

The Rev. George MacLeod (p. 186): Anne H. Maxwell, photograph, November 1985; © Church of Scotland, Department of Communication.

Jimmy Reid (p. 189): photograph; Glasgow University Archives.

Arthur Montford (p. 192): photograph; SMG Newspapers, Ltd.

John Bell (p. 194): photograph; reproduced by permission of the Wild Goose Resource Group.

Reginald Bosanquet (p. 197): photograph; ITN.

Michael Kelly (p. 200): photograph; Glasgow University Photographic Unit.

Winnnie Mandela (p. 203): photograph; Glasgow University Photographic Unit.

Pat Kane (p. 206): photograph; Glasgow University Photographic Unit.

Johnny Ball (p. 209): photograph; Glasgow University Photographic Unit.

Richard Wilson (p. 212): photograph; Glasgow University Photographic Unit.

Ross Kemp (p. 215): photograph; Glasgow University Photographic Unit.

# Index